African Immigrants
in the United States

African Immigrants in the United States

The Gendering Significance of Race through International Migration?

Mamadi Corra

LEXINGTON BOOKS
Lanham • Boulder • New York • London

Published by Lexington Books
An imprint of The Rowman & Littlefield Publishing Group, Inc.
4501 Forbes Boulevard, Suite 200, Lanham, Maryland 20706
www.rowman.com

6 Tinworth Street, London SE11 5AL, United Kingdom

Copyright © 2023 The Rowman & Littlefield Publishing Group, Inc.

All rights reserved. No part of this book may be reproduced in any form or by any electronic or mechanical means, including information storage and retrieval systems, without written permission from the publisher, except by a reviewer who may quote passages in a review.

British Library Cataloguing in Publication Information Available

Library of Congress Cataloging-in-Publication Data Available

ISBN 978-1-7936-4822-8 (cloth)
ISBN 978-1-7936-4823-5 (electronic)
ISBN 978-1-7936-4824-2 (pbk.)

This book is dedicated to my family of birth, from which I acquired the resilience, discipline, and dedication to undertake a task of this magnitude: my mothers, Aja Ceesay Conteh and Aja Kaddie Danso; my father, Alhaji Kuruba Corra; my brothers, the late Mohammed Corra, Alasana Corra, and the late Alfusaini Corra; and my sister, Mbagiba Corra. The fortitude I gained in growing up with you as a family in Gambia, West Africa, is what gave me the strength to immigrate to the United States even as a young high school student. It continues to be my enduring strength.

Contents

List of Figures and Tables	ix
Preface	xiii
Acknowledgments	xxvii
Chapter 1: Africans in the United States: An Increasingly Visible Immigrant Population	1
Chapter 2: Patterns of African Immigration to the United States and Sociodemographic Profile	15
Chapter 3: Immigration and the U.S. Experience: Theoretical Foundations	37
Chapter 4: An Intra-Group Comparison of African Immigrants in the United States: Gendered Variations?	55
Chapter 5: African Immigrants in the United States: The Gendering Significance of Race through International Migration?	95
Chapter 6: African Immigrants in the United States: A Comparison with Natives: A Comparison with Natives	123
Chapter 7: African Immigrants in the United States: Summary and Concluding Observations	147
Methodological Appendix	159
References	163
Index	177
About the Author	185

List of Figures and Tables

FIGURES

Figure 1.1 Total Number of Africans Who Have Obtained Permanent Residence Status by Year, 1820–2019.

Figure 2.1 Total Number of Africans and Caribbeans Who Have Obtained Permanent Residence Status by Decade, 1820–2019.

Figure 2.2 Africans and Caribbeans Who Have Obtained Permanent Residence Status, Percentage of Total by Decade, 1820–2019.

Figure 2.3 Percentages of the U.S. Foreign-Born Black Population that Are African and Caribbean Immigrants, 1980, 1990, 2000, 2010, and 2019.

Figure 2.4 Percentages of the U.S. Black Population that Are African and Caribbean Immigrants, 1980, 1990, 2000, 2010, and 2019.

TABLES

Table 2.1 Top Ten Sending African Countries to the United States by Year, 1980, 1990, 2000, 2010, and 2019.

Table 2.2 African Immigrants Admitted by Class of Admission, Fiscal Years 1996 to 2019.

Table 2.3 African Immigrants in the United States: A Demographic Profile.

Table 2.4 African Immigrants in the United States: A Socioeconomic Portrait of Immigrants 16–64 Years of Age.

Table 4.1 African Immigrants by Entry Status and Selected Sample of Countries of Birth, 1996, 1998–2019.

Table 4.2 African Immigrants in the United States: A Comparison of Immigrants on Four Economic Indicators by Year, 1980, 1990, 2000, 2010, and 2019.

Table 4.3 An Intra-Group Comparison of African Immigrants in the United States: Logistic Regression Estimates of Three Economic Indicators, Combined 1980, 1990, 2000, 2010, and 2019 Samples of the IPUMS.

Table 4.4 An Intra-Group Comparison of African Immigrants in the United States: General Linear Regression Estimates of Two Economic Indicators, Combined 1980, 1990, 2000, 2010, and 2019 Samples of the IPUMS.

Table 4.5 A Comparison of Top Sending Countries from Africa to the United States on Four Economic Indicators, Combined 1980, 1990, 2000, 2010, and 2019 Samples of the IPUMS.

Table 4.6 Logistic Regression Estimates of Three Economic Indicators for Top Ten Sending Countries from Africa to the United States, Combined 1980, 1990, 2000, 2010, and 2019 Samples of the IPUMS.

Table 4.7 General Linear Regression Estimates of Two Economic Indicators for Top Ten Sending Countries from Africa to the United States, Combined 1980, 1990, 2000, 2010, and 2019 Samples of the IPUMS.

Table 5.1 A Comparison of Immigrants 25 to 64 Years Old from Selected Countries and Regions of Origin on Educational Attainment, Combined 1980, 1990, 2000, 2010, and 2019 Samples of the IPUMS.

Table 5.2 Immigrants from Selected Countries and Regions of Origin: A Comparison on Four Economic Indicators, Combined 1980, 1990, 2000, 2010, and 2019 Samples of the IPUMS.

Table 5.3 Black and White African Immigrants Compared with Immigrants from Other Primary Sending Areas: Logistic Regression Estimates of Three Economic Indicators, Combined 1980, 1990, 2000, 2010, and 2019 Samples of the IPUMS.

Table 5.4 Black and White African Immigrants Compared with Immigrants from Other Primary Sending Areas: General Linear Regression Estimates of Two Economic Indicators, Combined 1980, 1990, 2000, 2010, and 2019 Samples of the IPUMS.

Table 6.1 Black and White African Immigrants Compared with Natives on Educational Attainment, Combined 1980, 1990, 2000, 2010, and 2019 Samples of the IPUMS.

Table 6.2 Black and White African Immigrants Compared with Natives on Four Economic Indicators, Combined 1980, 1990, 2000, 2010, and 2019 Samples of the IPUMS.

Table 6.3 Black and White African Immigrants Compared with Natives: Logistic Regression Estimates on Three Economic Indicators, Combined 1980, 1990, 2000, 2010, and 2019 Samples of the IPUMS.

Table 6.4 Black and White African Immigrants Compared with Natives: General Linear Regression Estimates on Two Economic Indicators, Combined 1980, 1990, 2000, 2010, and 2019 Samples of the IPUMS.

Preface

GENESIS OF THE BOOK

The genesis of this book lies in my own personal journey as an African immigrant to the United States. And although I would not have predicted it at the outset, the book's origins also rest on questions that have come to be uniquely intertwined with that journey: How have I become so fascinated with the question of race in U.S. society? What is it about race that motivated me to become a race scholar? And, relatedly, why and how does race so heavily influence the discussion on immigration in contemporary U.S. society?

I am a native of The Gambia, West Africa, who immigrated to the United States in 1987 to attend high school. As with many African countries, the indigenous population of Gambia is racially homogeneous—except for tourists and visitors, the racial composition of the native-born is exclusively "Black." To be sure, there exists the generic word "Tubaab" in the local languages that collectively refers to persons of European origins/westerners. But the closest to any meaningful discussion of race would have centered around our colonial and/or neocolonial history with Great Britain (and France when it comes to our immediate neighbor Senegal). It follows that one is seldom asked, if ever, his or her racial identity. Hence, prior to immigration to the United States, I had never filled out a form that asked me my racial identity. Nor do I recall having any substantive discussion with anyone about racial identity.

My first meaningful introduction to the complexity and multifaceted nature of race (and, apparently, immigration) in the United States occurred very soon after moving to the United States. To be sure, I had heard of the "N" word before my arrival. But I could have never imagined what I very soon came to understand the word to mean in the United States. Believe it or not, growing up as a kid in Gambia, I was of the impression that the word had a positive connotation.[1] I am the youngest sibling in my family and my sister, Sona Corra, was very fond of watching old American movies. She became taken by African American guys in these movies and thought they were the "coolest" looking. She picked up the "N" word as a characterization of these individuals, but her interpretation of it was that it meant a "cool Black American." And I remember distinctly that she would walk around imitating how these "cool Black N" guys walk with a swagger. As she walked around, she would say, "The Black N." So, from her, I also understood that the "Black N" meant a "cool looking Black American guy."[2]

Alas, my first lesson in race and immigration in the United States was to realize that I (and my sister) was dead wrong. The "N" word does not connote "a cool guy" in the United States. Rather, it is highly derogatory. And thank goodness I came to that knowledge early enough without calling anybody a "Black N." But this incident also made something clear to me that sociology later helped me conceptualize: race as a "social construct."

A second lesson in race (and, again, apparently immigration) also came not too long after my arrival to the United States. Less than a week after I landed in Atlanta on August 19, 1987, I started attending high school at the Georgia Academy for the Blind, a residential public school located in Macon Georgia. One evening I was sitting on the patio with a native Black friend and cottage mate, the late Menzel Brown. Out of nowhere, he said to me: "Hey Mamadi, if a White guy calls you a boy, call him a Cracker." I didn't know what "cracker" meant, but "boy" in my native country indicated camaraderie among youth. Young guys that are close friends call each other "boy" to denote friendship—"my good friend." Just like one might say "that's my bro." Youngsters that are close friends calling each other "boy" was (and remains) a common phenomenon in Gambia; and it carried (and continues to carry) no negative connotation there whatsoever. I, of course, soon came to learn what "boy" and "cracker" meant in American society. My good friend and fellow schoolmate was just socializing me into U.S. society, at least when it comes to race relations.

A third key (and eventually recurring) experience was also instrumental in directing my interest in the concept of race and, hence, my becoming a race and immigration scholar. It also happened early in my life in America: As I went about my business, I frequently found myself in one of two social situations that clearly made an impression on me. I kept finding myself in: (1) groups where everyone was native White and I was the only non-native Black person; or (2) where everyone was Black but I was the only non-native. What I came to quickly notice in each of these situations (and this continues even today) is that the conversation immediately changes when someone of a different race enters the setting—it suddenly becomes formal. Where people were talking freely, joking, and laughing, they immediately become guarded.

Consider, for example, a situation where I am sitting in an all-White group and having a conversation with everybody. The conversation is informal and generally unguarded. But as soon as a native Black American stops to say hello to me (or anyone else in the group), the conversation that until then was informal immediately becomes formal and, as long as that native Black person remains in that setting, the conversation remains formal. What was fascinating was that as soon as the said Black person leaves the setting, the conversation switches back to its previous state. And the same was true for social settings where everyone is Black but I am the only non-native and a native White person stops to speak to me (or anyone else in the group).[3] Moreover, fascinatingly enough, the people in these settings appear to have no idea that this was happening.[4]

Naturally, this intrigued me. Here is a group of people engaged in something that they were perhaps not even aware they were. It was like someone entering a room and finding a group of people watching a movie. The person switches the channel to a different movie and the people continue watching the new movie as if the channel hadn't changed. The person again later switches the movie back to the one the group was originally watching, and they simply pick up from where they were.

I was not yet then familiar with sociological concepts like "homophily," "status," "status characteristics," "dramaturgy," "code switching," "categoric knowing," and the "implicit association bias" (Lazarsfeld and Merton 1954; Berger, Cohen, and Zelditch 1972; Berger, Conner, and Fisek 1974; Ridgeway 2000, 2014; Ridgeway and Walker 1995; Myers and Twenge 2019; Parrillo 2019), nor was I familiar with the Du Bosian ([1903] 1994) concepts of the color line, veil, and double consciousness that he argued characterized the experience of being Black in America at the turn of the twentieth century.

Moreover, not yet known to me, of course, was that, almost a century prior, W. E. B. Du Bois ([1903] 1994) had also identified the nonrational, possibly unconscious, workings of the color line as such in his question, "How does it feel to be a problem?" ([1903] 1994, 3). Of this question, and how it came to define his own personal experience with race, Du Bois observed that:

> Between me and the other world there is ever an unasked question: unasked by some through feelings of delicacy; by others through the difficulty of rightly framing it. All, nevertheless, flutter round it. They approach me in a half–hesitant sort of way, eye me curiously or compassionately, and then, instead of saying directly, How does it feel to be a problem? they say, I know an excellent colored man in my town; or, I fought at Mechanicsville; or, Do not these Southern outrages make your blood boil? (p. 3)

Yet, of my own foregoing experiences, I kept saying to myself, "this is fascinating!" But the flip side to my experience in these situations is also that I, as a Black African immigrant, appeared to be curiously "an invisible man," putting it in the language of Black American novelist Ralph Ellison (1952). Here I was, clearly part of scenes that I also was seemingly not part of.

In August of 1989, I enrolled at Gardner-Webb College (now Gardner-Webb University) in Boiling Springs, North Carolina, as a freshman. My first college-level class was an introductory sociology course (sociology 101) taught by Professor Rudy Devon Boan. This was not only the first college-level course for me, it was also the first sociology course that I have ever taken. That course introduced me to a perspective, the "sociological perspective," which encouraged us to see the general in particular, i.e., to see the influence of general social patterns in the behavior of particular individuals (Berger 1963; Mills 1969).

Seeing individuality in social context as such (Macionis 2019; Mills 1969), or the "strange" in the "familiar," was indeed a new way of expressing social phenomena. For it was in that first sociology class that I immediately came to notice a phenomenon that continued in other classes and, hence, made a lasting impression on me.

The introductory sociology class was an early morning (9:00) course. On the first day, I got to class early, and simply took the first available seat at the front. The room began to quickly fill up with fellow students, and by the time class started, I noticed that students were seated in clusters clearly demarcated by race: sections of Black students seated around each other while White students were also seated in groups and a few, including myself, randomly seated. It was as if students were walking into the classroom, looking around, and eventually locating where they "belonged." Here, it is important to note, almost all of us were freshman, many probably being together for the first time.

I did not make much of this at first. But the cumulative observations of the phenomenon became inescapable. At 9:50 the course ended, and I headed to my next class, an English Composition course (English 101) taught by Professor Darlene Gravatt. There again, I noticed the same thing: Black students were seated in one group while White students were seated in another. And by the time lunch came around and I walked to the cafeteria at the Dover Campus Center (the "DCC," the then main student attraction on campus), I became cognizant of what eventually came to be an all-too recurring phenomenon. There as well, when I first walked in by myself, I took up the first open seat/table that I came across. Yet again, I came to notice that in the cafeteria, too, students sat in clusters of race. Being unfamiliar with this new culture I still didn't fully get it until much later, when it became unambiguously obvious to me that in fact during dinner an entire section of the cafeteria was noticeably the "Black student" section.

Professor Boan's sociology class, however, provided me with the initial conceptual framework for thinking about phenomena that, until then, remained undefined and perhaps elusive. It was in this class that I was introduced to key sociological concepts like stratification, categorical inequality, cast, status and ascription, and the social construction of reality. I took these concepts to heart, and eventually double-majored in sociology and business administration.

I continued with my undergraduate studies at Gardner-Webb, with similar experiences. But one Sunday morning in the early 1990s, an apparently notable incident occurred that, albeit fortuitously, must have been the initial impetus to the key question that I seek to examine in this book: How do African immigrants in the United States compare with other immigrant groups? Do African immigrants compare less favorably with immigrants from, say, Europe? More specifically, how do African immigrants in the United States compare in socioeconomic attainment with other immigrant groups?

That memorable Sunday morning, some roommates, who also happened to be Gambian immigrants attending Gardner-Webb, and I were following a discussion on one of the Sunday morning network stations that cover the previous week's news: "Meet the Press," "This Week with David Brinkley," Face the Nation," I can't remember. One of the guests that morning was syndicated conservative columnist Patrick J. Buchanan. Buchanan was making the argument that Western civilization is on the decline chiefly because of the uncontrolled flow, or "invasion," of non-European immigrants in the United States and Europe (Buchanan 2002).

The moderator of the Sunday morning show challenged Mr. Buchanan on his proposition on the decline of Western civilization due to uncontrolled immigration from non-European countries. In a style unique to Buchanan, he responded with a series of questions. Paraphrasing him here, he asked the moderator: "Now who do you think would do best in this country? Someone from Great Britain? Or a bunch of Zulus from Africa?" I vividly recall these series of questions throwing my friends/roommates and I into a prolonged and uncontrollable fit of laughter. "A bunch of Zulus from Africa," we kept saying.[5]

Returning for a moment to the state of my initial immigration to the United States, I was born with congenital glaucoma that affected my vision at birth. Thus, at the time of immigration, I had around 20/100 or 20/200 vision.[6] On Thursday March 28, 1991, I had an eye surgery at the Charlotte (North Carolina) Eye, Ear and Nose Associates that was aimed at correcting and/or containing the effect of the glaucoma. This was my second (sophomore) year at Gardner-Webb, and, to make a long story short, the surgery did not accomplish its intended goal. After a couple of days, on Saturday March 30, I lost the remainder of my vision and became totally blind.

I include this incident in the narrative here, because, intuitively, one might think that losing my sight might have dampened my ability to observe the workings of race thereafter. To the contrary, I believe it actually sharpened and enhanced it. Something akin to what African American novelist Ralph Ellison (1952) termed "the advantages of invisibility," I think my observational skills of the workings of race became heightened. On one hand, I became less distracted by visual cues that inhibit participatory observation due to racial status. And, on the other hand, I believe as a seemingly "invisible man," my being blind enhanced opportunities for such observations.

The PhD program in sociology at the University of South Carolina-Columbia was unique in its own ways, but the ubiquity of race was equally apparent. First, the program had fewer Black students (native-born or immigrant) than one would expect in a state with one of the highest percentages of Black residents. In fact, I cannot recall any time in my six years' program of study when we had more than three Black sociology graduate students, MA and PhD. And second, while discussions of race and race relations were noticeable components of almost all classes, race was not a distinct area of study. I recall that the only scholarly textbook focusing exclusively on race relations in America that was assigned as a required reading in any of my classes was William Julius Wilson's (1980, 1989) *Declining Significance of Race*.

Yet being part of the sociology department at the University of South Carolina was truly the first time that I got the chance to seriously begin to think about issues of race in America. I believe this was so because, first, located at the heart of the U.S. South, USC had one of the most racially and ethnically diverse undergraduate student population in the nation. And second, there I got the opportunity to teach some of those students in several classes, including the main undergraduate course on minority group relations. I taught these students as a PhD student for a little over two years (spring 2000 to summer 2002), and immediately after completing my program of study in 2002, for a year (2002–2003) as an instructor of sociology there. And third, sociology faculty at USC had a wide range of scholarly interests and expertise that included in-depth knowledge on race, ethnicity, and immigration. Direct and/or indirect discussions with professors like Jimy Sanders, David Willer, John Skvoretz, and Shelley Smith at USC began to sharpen my perspective on race and immigration. And so were discussions with other graduate students, sociology or not. Our department also had a "brown-bag" colloquium series to which leading scholars were invited to give lectures. In fact, one of those invited lecturers one year was noted race relations scholar William Julius Wilson. Thus, from the perspective of graduate students, these series gave us a chance to sharpen our thoughts on a variety of topics, including race and race relations. Because they were open for graduate student presentations as well, an opportunity I took advantage of liberally, the series became a helpful venue for critical dialogue and reflection for students and faculty alike.

In August of 2003, I took up a tenure-track position in sociology at East Carolina University, where I began to develop my own scholarly research and teaching program. In building that program, I began to hunt down and read sociological classics on race. I discovered, for example, that more than a century before, noted sociologist and civil rights activist W. E. B. Du Bois had proposed in his seminal work on race and race relations in America, *The Souls of Black Folk* (1903), that "the problem of the Twentieth Century is the problem of the color line—the relation of the darker to the lighter races of men in Asia and Africa, in America and the islands of the sea" ([1903] 1994, 9). The centennial edition of this classic work on race in America, with an introduction by noted historian David Levering Lewis, had then just been published (2003). In this work, Du Bois further illuminates that a key dimension of this color-line is the separation of the races, that is, the level of neighborhood segregation: "The physical proximity of homes and dwelling-places, the way in which neighborhoods group themselves, and the contiguity of neighborhoods" (p. 165).

At this point it became abundantly clear that seeking to understand the multifaceted nature of race in the United States would be a key component of my research and teaching agenda. And that attempting to understand the confluence of race and immigration would also be a key part of my research. W. E. B. Du Bois, for example, wrote of the "double consciousness" that he argued quintessentially characterized the experience of being Black in America at the turn of the twentieth century: "It is a peculiar sensation, this double-consciousness, this sense of always looking at one's self through the eyes of others, of measuring one's soul by the tape of a world that looks on in amused contempt and pity. One ever feels his two-ness—an American, a Negro; two souls, two thoughts, two unreconciled strivings; two warring ideals in one dark body, whose dogged strength alone keeps it from being torn asunder" (p. 3). Reflecting upon some of the experiences noted above, I began to wonder, as a Black African immigrant in the United States, might some of these be reflective of a similar phenomenon, albeit in a limited and/ or different sense? That is, a man with a "triple heritage," as noted Kenyan political scientist Ali Mazrui (1987) might put it. That is to say, being in a state of "triple consciousness," in the Du Bosian language.

In any case, pursuing such research gave me a glance at the depth, complexity, and pervasiveness of race in the United States, including:

1. The finding that race is correlated and intertwined with virtually every measurable macro-level variable in the United States, including

education; occupation; earnings; wealth; employment/unemployment; morbidity and mortality; poverty; victimization rates; arrest rates; incarceration rates; etc. (see Corra 2009; Hurst et al. 2019).

Here again, another personal experience is most illustrative. In 2018, I was awarded a Science and Technology Policy Fellowship by the American Association for the Advancement of Science. As the 2018–2019 Judicial Branch Fellow, I moved to Washington DC and took up my fellowship-in-residence at the Federal Judicial Center (FJC) in September of 2018. Established by Congress in 1967 (28 U.S.C. §§ 620–629), the Federal Judicial Center is the research and education wing of the judicial branch of the U.S. government, and is located right across from Union Station, the main metro station in DC.

Prior to living in DC, I thought I truly understood inequality and how it was intertwined with race. But it turned out that I did indeed need real-life instruction. It is said that experience is the best teacher, and the real-life experience of living in a large metropolitan area like DC was indeed a real memorable instruction in social inequality and its confluence with race. First, I noticed that, with the exception of two or three people, the entire security staff at the Federal Judicial Center (then, about 54 in total) was Black. Second, I lived and worked blocks away from the Capitol, the US Supreme Court, and Union Station. In these corridors of power and influence, I observed the mega rich and the absolutely poor and homeless walk side-by-side with one another, while also living in totally, and completely, different lives. I remember walking to Union Station and trying to carefully navigate with my cane, less I would walk on a sleeping homeless person. Third, toward the end of my fellowship, the entire security staff were given notice that they were being terminated. Apparently, these individuals were all working as contractors with an outside company, and a change in management of that company resulted in the decision to terminate all and start anew. I remember one of these individuals telling me that he "had never been unemployed" in his adult life.

2. Directly from my own research, I learned that race is also distinctly correlated and intertwined with every measurable micro-level variable/process in the United States, including attitudes toward the police use of force (Carter and Corra 2016; Carter, Corra and Jenks 2016; Carter, Corra and Okorie 2018); beliefs about racial inequality (Carter and Corra 2012; Carter, Corra, and Carter 2011; Carter, Corra, Carter, and McCrosky 2014; Miller, Corra, and Smith 2019); attitudes toward the role of women in society (Carter, Carter and Corra 2016); the racial academic gap (Corra, Carter, and Carter 2011; Corra and Lovaglia 2012); trust in the institutions of science and medicine (Corra and Carter 2008); marital

happiness (Corra et al. 2009); and racial status and power exercise (Corra 2014, 2020). In the words of early race scholar E. C. Hughes (1945), race is a "master status characteristic."

My interest in research on immigration came later, but it also discovered race and ethnicity to be key variables.[7] But, yet again, events in the news continued to amplify that interest. Consider recent controversy surrounding the famous poem, "The New Colossus," a sonnet by American poet Emma Lazarus (1883). In 1903, the poem was engraved on a bronze plaque and mounted inside the lower level of the pedestal of the Statue of Liberty. It reads:

The New Colossus

Not like the brazen giant of Greek fame,
With conquering limbs astride from land to land;
Here at our sea-washed, sunset gates shall stand
A mighty woman with a torch, whose flame
Is the imprisoned lightning, and her name
Mother of Exiles. From her beacon-hand
Glows world-wide welcome; her mild eyes command
The air-bridged harbor that twin cities frame.
"Keep ancient lands, your storied pomp!" cries she
With silent lips. "Give me your tired, your poor,
Your huddled masses yearning to breathe free,
The wretched refuse of your teeming shore.
Send these, the homeless, tempest-tossed to me,
I lift my lamp beside the golden door!

The poem is said to express a view of the United States as a land of immigrants, welcoming all who seek freedom and liberty. And, in many ways, the United States is indeed a land of immigration—if you look far enough, just about all of us have origins outside of this land we call the United States. Yet, more than a hundred years after Lazarus's famous description of the United States as a land open to immigration "of all kinds," the issue of immigration remains one of the most contentious in U.S. society.

For example, while appearing on NPR's "Morning Edition" on Tuesday morning, August 13, 2019, Ken Cuccinelli, then acting director of U.S. Citizenship and Immigration Services, offered a recent interpretation. Host Rachel Martin asked Cuccinelli if those lines still mattered in the wake of the Trump administration's announcement of a new rule that would substantially curb legal immigration.: "Would you also agree that Emma Lazarus's words, etched on the Statue of Liberty, 'Give me your tired, your poor,' are also part of the American ethos?" Martin asked. "They certainly are," Cuccinelli said.

"Give me your tired and your poor who can stand on their own two feet, and who will not become a public charge."[8]

Cuccinelli's comments, of course, were given against the backdrop of that of his own boss, Donald J. Trump, then president of the United States. Echoing those of conservative commentator Patrick Buchanan over two decades prior, on January 12, 2018, Trump was reported to have asked in a meeting with lawmakers in the White House: "Why are we having all these people from shithole countries come here?" ("Trump Derides Protections for Immigrants from 'Shithole' Countries," *Washington Post*, January 12, 2018). Instead, the president is further reported to assert that the United States should bring more people from countries like Norway, a notably predominantly White population.

Suffice it to say that so it was that I became fascinated with the concepts of race and immigration in America and continue to be so. Content that is reported in this book is a product of that fascination and resulting scholarly interest. The book addresses a question that I believe is an important one, for both theoretical and practical reasons: Exactly how are patterns of socioeconomic attainment for African immigrants different from those of other immigrant groups? That is to say, do U.S. African immigrants exhibit socioeconomic attainment profiles that markedly differ from those of other immigrant groups?

BRIEF SUMMARY OF CHAPTERS

The first chapter of the book, "Africans in the United States: An Increasingly Visible Immigrant Population," introduces the text and key related issues in the study of African immigrants in the United States. That chapter notes that, while voluntary immigration from Africa to the United States, at least in large numbers, is a very recent phenomenon, these "new" immigrants are nevertheless adding to the increasing diversity and racial/ethnic transformation that U.S. society is currently experiencing (Anderson 2015; Anderson and López 2018). For example, figures reviewed in that chapter show that, today, African immigrants constitute a growing and increasingly visible component of the U.S. and foreign-born Black populations.

The second chapter of the book, "Patterns of African Immigration to the United States and Sociodemographic Profiles," takes a closer look at recent trends in African immigration to the United States, as well as sociodemographic qualities associated with these immigrants. One notable finding reported in that chapter is a clear pattern of the changing racial and gender composition of the U.S. African immigrant population. That is to say, until very recently, voluntary immigration from Africa to the United States has been disproportionately those who identified themselves as White. More recent immigration from Africa, by contrast, has increasingly included Black Africans (see Borch and Corra 2010; Elo et al. 2015 for similar patterns). A similar trend is shown for the gender composition of the African immigrant population in the United States, which is shown to have shifted from a predominantly male population to one that has reached gender parity.

The third chapter, "Immigration and the U.S. Experience: Theoretical Foundations," examines scholarly explanations of immigrant adaptation in the United States. As noted in that chapter, recent theoretical approaches to the study of immigration suggest that the multicolored nature of U.S. society along ethnoracial lines means that immigrants experience a segmented form of assimilation (Portes and Böröcz 1989; Portes and Rumbaut 2001, 2006). What theoretical insights can be gained by investigating this group of immigrants who are mostly Black and poor?

Notably, examining the place of African immigrants in the U.S. context is complicated by the fact that these immigrants come from countries and regions that are culturally, linguistically, politically, and/or economically distinct. This makes lumping African immigrants into one homogeneous group for theoretical and/or empirical analyses problematic. It is in this light that Model (2008,12) suggests that: "One way to circumvent these difficulties is to undertake an intra-African comparison" (see also Kim and Kemegue 2007). The fourth chapter of the book, "An Intra-Group Comparison of African Immigrants in the United States: Gendered Variations?" directly examines this issue by analyzing disparities in socioeconomic attainment between African immigrant groups. What qualities, if any, differentiate these groups from one another? Highlighted in that chapter is the growing diversity in recent flows of African immigrants to the United States.

Moreover, contemporary debates on the incorporation of African immigrants in the United States center around their relative attainment prospects. And, for both theoretical and practical reasons, that issue is an important one. Exactly how do African immigrants in the United States compare in socioeconomic status with other immigrant groups? Examining this question is the focus of chapter 5, "African Immigrants in the United States: The Gendering Significance of Race through International Migration?" That chapter provides the main comparison between African immigrants and other immigrant groups (e.g., those from Asia, Europe, and North and Central America), and shows that, like all immigrant groups, African immigrants exhibit varying levels of socioeconomic status that compare favorably and unfavorably with differing groups and with differing measures. Nevertheless, the measures for African immigrants, relative to other immigrant groups, are shown to vary by gender and sending area. Moreover, the results also show race to be a salient and consistent predictor of labor market disparities.

The sixth chapter, "African Immigrants in the United States: A Comparison with Natives," provides analyses analogous to the ones in chapter 5, with the distinction being that the comparison here is with natives. Looking forward to chapter 1 of this book, nativity (i.e., native versus foreign-born/immigrant) comes to the forefront of immigration theory and research when the key question is how immigrants compare with their native counterparts in terms of socioeconomic attainment.[9] And early migration theory and research (Chiswick 1978; Carliner 1980; DeFreitas 1980) portrayed a rather linear picture of U.S. immigration and successful immigrant adaptation. After a relatively short adaptation period, immigrants are said to "catch up" with and/or "overtake" comparable natives in socioeconomic attainment. Yet, again looking forward to the discussion in chapter 3 of this book, analyses reported by Borjas (1985, 1987, 1991, 1994, 1995) suggest waning immigrant quality among recent immigrants, a phenomenon he attributed to changes in the mix of sending countries (see a fuller discussion in chapter 3 of this book). More specifically, Borjas reported finding no declines in immigrant quality among immigrants from Europe and Canada to the United States. He then predicted that, after a decade or so in the United States, the earnings of immigrants from Europe and Canada would overtake those of their native White counterparts, while the earnings of immigrants from the rest of the world, including Africa, would never surpass those of their native counterparts. Data reported in chapter 6 of this book, however, suggest that African immigrants do indeed compare favorably with many native groups, with no notable detected uniquely "African" pattern(s). That chapter, however, nevertheless shows the continued salience of race that is mediated by gender.

The final chapter, "African Immigrants in the United States: Summary and Concluding Observations," provides a synopsis of key findings and conclusions drawn from them. It summarizes some of the major results of the empirical examinations in the first six chapters and speculates on what can be made of them.

NOTES

1. Here, as a native-born American colleague of mine correctly reminds me, context is important. "Americans of African descent have used the 'N' word among themselves for generations. And many continue to do so, and the word populates the contemporary world of rap and hip-hop. Those who use the word in those genres—and elsewhere—will often explain the importance of context in understanding their use of the word. The word is used as either a negative or positive descriptor." It follows that "linguistic" and "social context" are important to a proper (i.e., correct) interpretation of usage of the word.

2. Here, I should note that my knowledge of the word was exclusively restricted to this narrow, but apparently false, understanding. In fact, I doubt I would have ever made much of it except for the fact that I immigrated to the United States, and came to find out what the word actually means here.

3. The experience discussed here, as a colleague reminds me, illustrates several phenomena, including the now well-known distinction between being "on stage" or "front stage" and being "backstage," famously used by ethnomethodologist Erving Goffman (1956) to illustrate his idea of dramaturgy (Henry Walker, personal communication). A second phenomenon is that of "code switching." Linguists use this term to describe speakers shifting from one language to another language or language variant (e.g., a dialect) (Henry Walker, personal communication). Proper socialization in the etiquette of race relations in the United States, for example, makes "race talk" become second nature (i.e., habitual). Hence, a group of Black males may engage in "Black talk" (i.e., speaking in Black English vernacular or BEV). If an "outsider" (e.g., a White male) entered the setting, the Black males would instantaneously begin speaking in more conventional English. Here, the shift in speech is what is labeled "code switching." The group, of course, does have the power to admit outsiders backstage, in which case code switching need not occur. Finally, actors may use insider language to conceal information from outsiders.

4. This is also true when a woman suddenly enters an all-male group or a male enters an all-female group, a phenomenon Kanter (1977) associated with "tokenism."

5. Incidentally, this is not a new view. The 1922 immigration act intended to encourage Anglo-Saxons to immigrate to the United States while discouraging people from the Mediterranean Basin, Asia, South America, and Africa to immigrate.

6. Visual acuity scores like 20/100 are descriptive of sharpness of vision and are representative of distance (sharpness/clarity of vision at a distance) based on a standardized measure. Normal visual acuity is 20/20. This means the person can clearly and accurately see at 20 feet any object that is in fact 20 feet away. Someone with a visual acuity score of 20/100 would have to be 20 feet close to an object that one with normal acuity (20/20) would clearly and accurately see 100 feet away.

7. See, for example, Model 1991, 1995, 2008; Dodoo 1991a-d, 1997; Butcher 1994; Kalmijn 1996; Model and Ladipo 1996; Bashi and McDaniel 1997; Alba and Nee 1997; Reitz and Sklar 1997; Zhou 1997; Dodoo and Takyi 2002; Corra and Kimuna 2009; Borch and Corra 2010; Corra and Borch 2014; Thomas 2014; Kusow, Kimuna and Corra 2016; Kusow, Ajrouch and Corra 2018.

8. Here, as a colleague recently reminded me, it is important to note that these ideas have been engrained in U.S. immigration policy for the better part of 150 years. Enforcement has simply been relaxed and the "guidance," which is decided administratively, has varied over the years.

9. See, for example, Chiswick 1978, 1979; Sowell 1978; Borjas 1995; Kalmijn 1996; Waters 1999; Shaw-Taylor and Tuch 2007; Model 2008, 2018; Corra and Kimuna 2009; Mason 2010; Jasso 2011; Corra and Borch 2014; Hamilton 2020.

Acknowledgments

As with all works of this kind, this book benefited immensely from the works of scholars that preceded me in investigating topics examined in this manuscript. Too numerous to enumerate here, the bibliography provides a list of the many authors and investigators, whose works provided crucial insights. For both this manuscript and my overall work on African/Black immigrants in the United States, however, the work of Suzanne Model, Professor Emerita of Sociology, University of Massachusetts, Amherst, and Research Associate, Center for Research on International Migration, University of California at Irvine, is foundational. Professor Model's early work on "the black experience" provided an initial roadmap for my own work on African immigrants in the United States, beginning in the mid-2000s. It continues to illuminate that work.

More specific to the current manuscript, in 2008, Professor Model published her pathbreaking book, "West Indian Immigrants: A Black Success Story?" While focusing on immigrants from the West Indies, this book also examines, in passing, the relative standing of African immigrants in the United States. In a concluding remark on the book's findings, professor Model observed that: "research on black immigrants from sub-Saharan Africa would constitute a useful supplement to the present undertaking." (2008: 11). Further noting possible complexities in investigating this group of immigrants (African immigrants) with diverse political, economic, and colonial backgrounds, however, Dr. Model suggested that: "One way to circumvent these difficulties is to undertake an intra-Africa comparison" (2008:12). Suffice it to say that this manuscript is, in part, a respond to this call.

Moreover, ongoing personal communications between Professor Model and I continue to be equally instrumental sources of intellectual and scholarly undertakings. Prior to being aware of my working on this book, the good professor mentioned in several of our communications that I should not hesitate to send her manuscripts that I am working on for her review, comments, and suggestions. Little did she know that I planned on sending her an entire book-length manuscript to review and offer comments. Suffice it to say she agreed promptly when I asked her to review this manuscript, and her comments on a previous draft undoubtedly improved this final version immensely!

More generally, I first met Professor Model at the 2007 American Sociological Association annual meetings in New York, where I presented a paper at a session on international migration. Professor Model attended this session and, at its conclusion, worked up to me and told me that my presentation was especially good. Suffice it to say that this casual encounter became a pivotal one in the direction of my work on African immigrants in the United States: here is an established authority on a topic, whose work I recently read and used to form my own arguments, telling me as a beginning assistant professor that my work was of importance. During this encounter, Professor Model gave me her card and suggested that I establish contact with her. In short, personal communications since then continue to illuminate my work. Thank you, professor, for all the help and encouragement in the past years!

One also seldom works on works of this type, without ongoing dialog with, and assistance of, immediate colleagues. Here, I especially acknowledge the contributions of my colleagues Dr. Arunas Juska, Dr. Susan Pearce, and Dr. Henry Walker. Professor Juska helped in a variety of areas, including helping in the construction of the many graphs included in this manuscript. Dr. Pearce helped immensely by simply being a springboard for all types of questions that came up during the development of the manuscript. And, as always, enduring conversations with Professor Henry Walker have always been helpful. Finally, ECU Assistive Technology Specialist, Brian Stanford, offered a myriad of technical support during the course of the work, while Airene Costelo provided formatting assistance with text and tables. Thank you all for being excellent colleagues. Moreover, I could not have finished this manuscript without the assistance of the many ECU graduate students that helped in the construction of tables and graphs, among other useful tasks. These students include, in alphabetical order, Jasmin Harris, Gabrielle Horne, Sabrina Huapaya, Nykaysia King, Hanna Norman, and Myrtie Reilly. A special thanks, however, goes to ECU graduate sociology student Hannah Norman, who created final versions of the tables and graphs reported in this manuscript. I can't thank you much, Hannah, for your most valuable contributions! My thanks also to my acquisition editor at Lexington Books, Courtney Morales, for always being there to answer my many questions and for helping shepherd this manuscript to its completion. Finally, the work reported here was supported by a 2020 ECU Faculty Senate Research and Creative Activity Award (RCAA), a 2014–2015 award from the ECU Division of Research and Graduate Studies Research and Creative Activities Reassignment Grants Program, and support of the ECU Thomas Harriot College of Arts and Sciences and the ECU Department of Sociology.

Chapter 1

Africans in the United States

An Increasingly Visible Immigrant Population

Voluntary immigration from Africa to the United States, at least in large numbers, is a very recent phenomenon (Kent 2007; Thomas 2011; Capps, McCabe, and Fix 2012; Anderson and López 2018; Tamir 2022; Tamir and Anderson 2022). Nearly 80 percent of African immigrants in the United States arrived after 1990 and more than 40 percent of this pool arrived in just the six years from 2000–2005 (Kent 2007; Elo et al. 2015; Tamir 2022; Tamir and Anderson 2022). According to Elo and associates (2015): "For the first time in America's history, among all foreign-born migrants, those born in Africa are growing at the fastest rate . . . a rate of growth more than twice that for migrants from Asia, the next-fastest growing source" (p. 1514).

Today, African immigrants constitute a growing and increasingly visible component of the U.S. and foreign-born Black populations (Shaw-Taylor and Tuch 2007; Logan and Deane 2003; Capps, McCabe, and Fix 2012; Thomas 2014; Elo et al. 2015; Hamilton 2020; Tamir 2022; Tamir and Anderson 2022).[1] Kent (2007) reports that, before 1980, Africans accounted for just 10 percent of the U.S. Black foreign-born population. In the first six years of the 2000s, however, Africans accounted for the majority of immigrating Blacks to the United States. Kent (2007) reports that, in 2005, for example, nearly one-third of the 2.8 million foreign-born Blacks were born in Africa, and that more Africans immigrated to the United States between 2000 and 2005 than in the previous decade. A more recent Pew Research Center analysis (Anderson and López 2018) revealed that, between 2000 and 2013, the number of Black African immigrants living in the United States rose by about 137 percent, from 574,000 to 1.4 million, and that Africans made up 36 percent of the total foreign-born Black population in 2013, up from about 24 percent in 2000 and just 7 percent in 1980. The title of a Pew Research Center analysis released just this year (January 2022), "The Caribbean is the largest origin source of Black immigrants, but fastest growth is among African immigrants," is instructive. That analysis revealed that Black immigrants from Africa have been the primary driver for much of the overall recent growth in the Black immigrant population (Tamir and Anderson 2022). According to Tamir and Anderson (2022), between 2000 and 2019, the Black African immigrant population grew 246 percent, from roughly 600,000 to two million. They further report that such immigrants now make up 42 percent of the overall foreign-born Black population, almost double of this percentage in 2000 when that share was about 23 percent.

Data presented in Figure 1.1 is illustrative of these patterns and trends. From the U.S. Department of Homeland Security's *Yearbook of Immigration Statistics* (2019), that figure represents a cumulative graph depicting data on the total number of Africans who have obtained legal permanent residence (LPR) status in the United States, by decade, beginning with the 1820s to the 2010s. Accordingly, for each decade on the x axis of that graph, the y axis conveys the total number of Africa-born persons who have ever received LPR status.

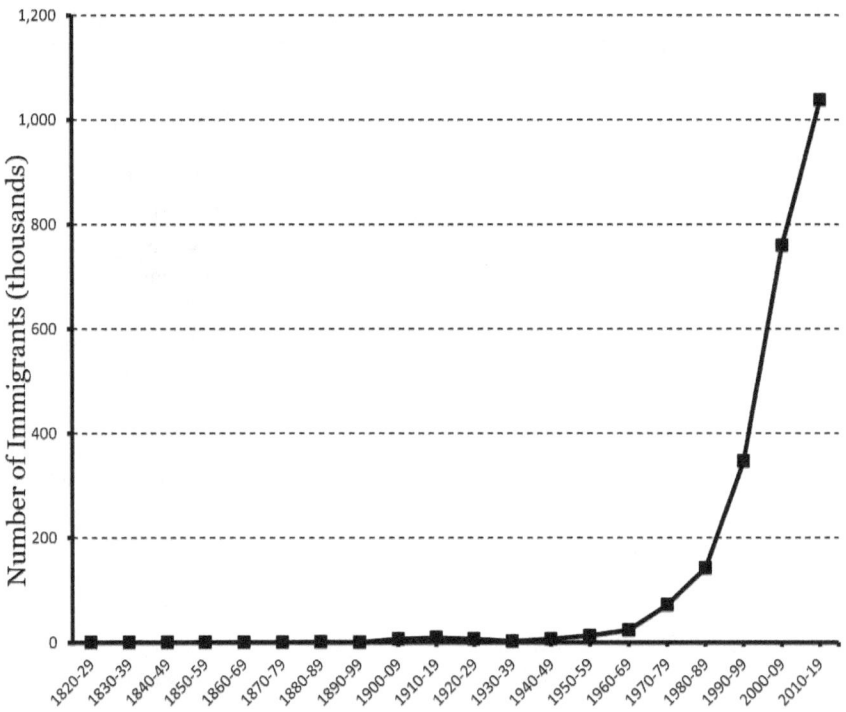

Figure 1.1. Total Number of Africans Who Have Obtained Permanent Residence Status by Year, 1820–2019. Source: U.S. Department of Homeland Security, *Yearbook of*

Immigration Statistics indicators of immigration flows, these figures have some limitations. First, as official enumerations of legal permanent residence status, they are not inclusive of illegal/undocumented immigrants. Moreover, the reported year of admission is the year in which the individual immigrant is officially granted legal permanent residency. Increasingly, this is not the year in which the immigrant initially arrived (Model 2008). For example, some "aliens already living in the United States, including certain undocumented immigrants, temporary workers, foreign students, and refugees, file an application for adjustment of status (to legal permanent residence) with I.N.S." (U.S. Immigration and Naturalization Service 1999, 14). Another drawback is that the figures also do not report the racial status of immigrants (Model 2008).

As can be seen in Figure 1.1, however, African immigration to the United States was relatively lowl until the decade of the 1900s, when it first reached and went into the thousands. It continued to grow for the next few decades but began to truly take off in the 1960s and 1970s, and noticeably starts to accelerate thereafter. And especially notable is that the decades of the 2000s and 2010s witnessed a particularly pronounced expression of this trend.

2019.

Some scholars have observed that these trends suggest that, collectively, immigration from Africa in the past two decades has been the largest flow of Africans to the United States since the trans-Atlantic slave trade (Anderson and López 2018; Konadu-Agyemang and Takyi 2006; Roberts 2005). According to data presented by Kent (2007), for example, the annual number of African arrivals in the United States was close to 60,000 between 2000 and 2005. By contrast, an estimated 460 African immigrants arrived from Africa to the United States annually between the years 1861 and 1961 (Konadu-Agyemang and Takyi 2006).

These "new African Americans" (Millman 1997, 172) or "new Americans" (Barone 2001) are adding to the increasing diversity and racial/ethnic transformation that U.S. society is currently experiencing (Fears 2002; Shaw-Taylor and Tuch 2007; Anderson 2015; Tamir 2022). For example, scholars and commentators alike have observed that the new flow of African immigration to the United States is further contributing to the remaking of the U.S. Black population in fundamentally different ways (Shaw-Taylor and Tuch 2007; Kunkle 2015; Hamilton 2019, 2020). In terms of numbers, a recent Pew Research Center report (Anderson 2015) indicates that a record 3.8 million foreign-born Blacks were then living in the United States. Moreover, the share of foreign-born Blacks, largely from Africa and the Caribbean, grew from 3.1 percent of the Black population in 1980 to 8.7 percent in 2013 (Anderson 2015; Kunkle 2015). In addition, the 2015 Pew Research Center report (Anderson 2015) projects that, by 2060, 16.5 percent of the U.S. Black population will be foreign-born.

An important question that immediately comes to mind, however, is how are these immigrants adapting into the social and economic fabric of their new country? For African immigrants, the answer to this question is compounded by the fact that they are both immigrants and, for many, Black[2]—two socially significant variables shown to influence immigrant adaptation in the United States.[3] Punctuating this compounding, on January 12, 2018, Donald Trump, the then president of the United States, was reported to have asked in a meeting with lawmakers in the White House: "Why are we having all these people from shithole countries come here?"[4] ("Trump Derides Protections for Immigrants from 'Shithole' Countries," *Washington Post*, January 12, 2018). Instead, the president was further reported to have asserted that the United States should bring more people from countries like Norway, a notably predominantly White population.

Yet, for both theoretical and practical reasons, the question is an important one. Exactly how are patterns of incorporation of African immigrants different from those of other immigrant groups? Are African immigrants less able to successfully incorporate into U.S. society than immigrants from, say, Europe or Asia? And if so, what specific variables act as impediments? Or if not, what qualities enhance the status of African immigrants in the United States? And finally, what theoretical insights can be gained by investigating this group of immigrants who are mostly Black and poor?

Notably, African immigrants are themselves a very diverse group, coming from countries and regions that are culturally, linguistically, politically, and/or economically distinct. One key variable, for example, is that recent waves of immigrants from Africa increasingly include people of Arab ethnic origins that come mainly from North and East Africa. As an example, it is estimated that, between 1990 and 2000, Arab immigration from Egypt increased by 82 percent (De la Cruz and Brittingham 2003). According to Thomas (2014): "Arab immigrants are particularly overlooked in the scholarly discourse on African immigration to the United States or the African diaspora in general. As a result, little is known concerning whether there are variations in incorporation processes of Africans of Arab and non-Arab ethnic origins" (p. 2). Do Arab-origins African immigrants exhibit greater or lesser measures of socioeconomic attainment than non-Arab-origins African immigrants? Moreover, according to the U.S. Census, 80 percent of Arab immigrants identify themselves as "White" (De la Cruz and Brittingham 2003). What effect does this have on trajectories of incorporation of Arab immigrants in the United States? How about Black African immigrants that are also of Arab origins? Do these immigrants exhibit greater or lesser socioeconomic outcomes than their White counterparts? What about the female counterparts of all these groups? Do they exhibit greater or lesser socioeconomic profiles than their male counterparts? Thomas's work (2014) found variations, suggesting the need for a more comprehensive analysis of the socioeconomic trajectories of the various racial, ethnic, and linguistic backgrounds of U.S. African immigrants.

Addressing these and related issues are the objectives of this book. I seek to investigate the foregoing and related questions using three sets of quantitative data: (1) waves of the Decennial U.S. Censuses, as represented in the Integrated Public Use Microdata Series/Samples (IPUMS)[5]; (2) the Census Bureau's American Community Surveys (ACS), also taken from the IPUMS; and (3) figures on the number of immigrants admitted by sending country and class of admission from the Department of Homeland Security's *Yearbook of Immigration Statistics*.[6] Taken together, these three sources provide nationally representative cross-sectional and temporal data that are used to examine several of some of the following issues:

- The relative socioeconomic profiles of African immigrants by region of origin (East, North, etc.).[7]
- The relative socioeconomic profiles of "Black" and "White" U.S. African immigrants.
- The relative socioeconomic profiles of Arab- and non-Arab-origins African immigrants.
- How female African immigrants compare in socioeconomic attainment with their male counterparts.
- How African immigrants compare in socioeconomic attainment with other immigrant groups.
- How overall patterns of attainment for African immigrants compare with those of other immigrant groups.[8]
- How African immigrants compare in socioeconomic attainment with the various U.S. native groups.
- Long-term trends that can be inferred from the past several decades of U.S. African immigration.
- Theoretical insights that can be inferred from these.

The section to immediately follow provides a brief review of previous sociological research on immigrant adaptation in the United States, focusing on African/Black (relative to White African) immigrants. As part of this discussion, I identify key variables shown to influence immigrant incorporation into U.S. society, and how such variables might influence the incorporation of African immigrants into U.S. society. I end the chapter with an outline of key objectives of the book, as well as its general outline.

SOCIOLOGICAL RESEARCH ON IMMIGRANT ADAPTATION: SOME KEY VARIABLES

Nativity

Current sociological literature suggests at least three key variables that can influence immigrant adaptation in contemporary U.S. society. Nativity (i.e., native versus foreign-born/immigrant) comes to the forefront when the key question is how immigrants compare with their native counterparts in terms of socioeconomic attainment;[9] or how well particular immigrant groups are doing/being incorporated into U.S. society (Portes and Rumbaut 2001, 2006; Borch and Corra 2010). Early migration theory and research (Chiswick 1978; Carliner 1980; DeFreitas 1980) portrayed a rather linear picture of U.S. immigration and successful immigrant adaptation. After a relatively short adjustment period, immigrants are said to "catch up" and/or "overtake" comparable natives in socioeconomic attainment. Chiswick (1979) estimated the "overtaking" point for immigrants at 10–15 years after immigration.

Recent theoretical approaches to the study of immigration, however, suggest that the multi-colored nature of U.S. society along ethnoracial lines means that immigrants experience a segmented form of assimilation. Some recent approaches to the study of migration, for example, emphasize the "context of reception" to the host society and the modes of incorporation of different groups into its labor market (Portes and Böröcz 1989; Portes and Rumbaut 2001, 2006). By "context of reception" it is meant (1) differential (positive, negative, or neutral) state policies directed toward specific immigrant groups; (2) favorable or unfavorable/less favorable public opinion toward immigrating groups (e.g., public reactions to the increased presence of African or Black immigrants in the United States); and (3) the presence or absence of an ethnic community in the host country/destination that helps in the adaptation process. Accordingly, the context within which different immigrant groups find themselves provides the condition that either enhances or impedes labor market incorporation. Post-migration outcomes, therefore, are said to be shaped by the interaction of the numerous elements that constitute an immigrant group's "context of reception."

The U.S. labor market, for example, may be more or less receptive to African immigrants (or some African immigrant groups) than other immigrant groups. There is, for example, some evidence that African immigrants believe they encounter substantial discrimination in the U.S. labor market (Scroggins 1989; Portes and Zhou 1993; Takougang 1995; Apraku 1996; Arthur 2000; Kposowa 2002). Over half a century ago, Du Bois (1962) observed that the primary bases of prejudice toward Africans are degrading assumptions and stereotypes held by people of European descent. More recent scholars argue that the ubiquity of negative portrayals of Africa in academic, political, media, and other such entities may also serve to undermine the valuation of Africans in the United States (Hawk 1992; Zaffiro 1992; Mpanya 1995; Dodoo 1997). While the extent of such discrimination is yet to be fully known, "it is not inconceivable that Africans may be received differently, and perhaps less favorably, than . . . [other immigrant groups]" (Dodoo 1997, 530).

An area's "context of reception" for differing groups, for example, can be measured by controlling for region (Portes and Bach 1985; Borch and Corra 2010). As argued by Borch and Corra (2010), regional employment rates for Black and White immigrants (especially for those with similar human capital), for example, imply more or less favorable "receptions" in those areas. The context of reception hypothesis suggests that Black immigrants (relative to White immigrants) will be accorded less favorable reception in the United States, and more in some U.S. regions than others; and Borch and Corra argue that employment rates, controlling for other factors, should show this.

As a way to illustrate this idea, for example, Borch and Corra (2010) computed the ratio of the 2000 unemployment rates for Whites and Blacks across all nine U.S. Census regions. They found the following rank ordering (higher numbers indicate greater disparity in unemployment rates): Mountain (1.34), Pacific (1.55), New England (1.99), South Atlantic (2.19), Middle Atlantic (2.35), West South Central (2.39), East South Central (2.67), East North Central (2.71), and West North Central (3.14). From these values, Borch and Corra deduced that the "context of reception" argument would suggest that immigrants should earn the highest wages in the Mountain and Pacific regions and lowest in the West North Central region.

Racial Status

The significance of race for socioeconomic attainment in the United States is, of course, a classic issue in stratification research (Wilson 1980, 1989; Farley 1984; Burstein 1985; Tomaskovic-Devey 1993; Cancio, Evans, and Maume 1996; Borch and Corra 2010; Thomas 2014). In terms of migration, race comes to the forefront when the question focuses specifically on how racial status influences immigrant adaptation (Borch and Corra 2010; Thomas 2014). Yet, compared to Hispanic and Asian immigrants, Black immigrants in the United States have been considerably less researched and, until very recently, Black African immigrants remained a relatively understudied group. With a few exceptions, early studies defined Black immigrants as one homogeneous group (Chiswick 1979; Dodoo 1991a-c), mainly focused on Caribbean immigrants (Butcher 1994; Kalmijn 1996; Model 1991, 1995, 2008), or examined small samples of highly skilled workers (Apraku 1991).

With respect to Black immigrants, Thomas Sowell's (1978) work provided an early point of reference. Sowell had then observed that Caribbean-born Blacks who migrated to the United States were much more successful in occupational attainment and in earnings than were native-born Blacks. He went on to argue that "color alone, or racism alone, is clearly not a sufficient explanation of the disparities within the black population or between the black and white populations" (1978, 41–48). He concluded that: "The West Indian success pattern undermines the explanatory power of current white discrimination as a cause of current black poverty" (1978, 49).

Shortly after the publication of his essay, however, a growing literature began to develop that challenged Sowell's findings (for more recent analyses, see Ifatunji 2016, 2017, 2018; Model 2018; Hamilton 2020). Aggregate national statistics suggest that Caribbean-born Blacks tend to work more hours, hold more prestigious jobs, and earn more than native-born Blacks, but once controls are introduced for educational attainment and for local labor market conditions, the Caribbean advantage diminishes, often to the point of statistical insignificance (Model 1991, 1995, 2008; Butcher 1994; Kalmijn 1996; Model and Ladipo 1996).[10] The work of Model (2008) and Hamilton (2020) are two of the most comprehensive analyses on Black immigrants in the United States to date. Both provide convincing evidence that any difference in attainment between native-born Blacks and Black immigrants is primarily due to selectivity of migration. Unlike the native-born, immigrants are not from a sample of randomly selected individuals from their countries of origins. Rather, they are a highly selected group that, as economist Kristin Butcher (1994) suggests, are appropriately comparable to native-born "internal movers" (frequently operationalized as the native-born living in states different from their state of birth—see Hamilton 2020) rather than the overall native-born Black population. Such movers are found to exhibit similar socioeconomic trajectories with immigrants (Butcher 1994; Model 2008; Hamilton 2020).

Next to Caribbean immigrants, African immigrants constitute the largest flow of Black immigrants to the United States (Reid 1986; Takougang 1995; Djamba 1999; U.S. Immigration and Naturalization Service 1998; Snyder 2002; Zeleza 2002; Elo et al. 2015; Hamilton 2019, 2020; Tamir 2022; Tamir and Anderson 2022). And importantly: "The condition of Africans in the diaspora proffers insight into not just their adaptation to their new countries, but also the nature of racial stratification at their destinations" (Dodoo and Takyi 2002, 913).

Not surprisingly, some recent evidence does indeed show that Black immigrants from Africa to the United States fare worse in socioeconomic attainment than their White African counterparts (Dodoo and Takyi 2002; Borch and Corra 2010; Thomas 2014; Hamilton 2020). In exploring racial differences in earnings between Black and White African immigrants in the United States, Dodoo and Takyi (2002), for example, report "sizeable differences among immigrants who have relatively similar human capital" (p. 913). They find that "Whites have annual earnings 80% higher than their Black counterparts, and the gap in hourly wage is almost 48%" (p. 913). Notably, Dodoo and Takyi (2002) report that "more than half (53%) of the race difference in wages remains unexplained by earnings-related attributes such as education, occupation, and hours worked" (p. 913). Borch and Corra's (2010) more recent analysis of three decades of census data (from 1980, 1990, and 2000) also found race effects, with the gap in earnings between Black and White male immigrants shown to have especially widened over time. Hamilton's (2019) recent trajectory models of socioeconomic attainment show no Black immigrant group reaching convergence with those of non-Hispanic native-born Whites.

Gender and Status Attainment

The enduring influence of gender in status attainment in the United States is also well-documented in the sociological literature.[11] And recent migration data indicate that women constitute more than 50 percent of international migration to the developed world, and in many cases outnumber male migrants (Djamba and Bean 1999; Batalova 2020). According to the U.S. Census Bureau (2010), nearly 40 million, or 13 percent of the total U.S. population, is foreign-born. Of this total, about 20.4 million, or approximately 51 percent, are female. For the African foreign-born, about 761,677, or 47 percent, are female (Corra and Borch 2014). These figures suggest that the increasing presence of female immigrants (especially Black/African female immigrants) may indeed be changing the size, demographic composition, and dynamics of the U.S. labor market. This begs the question: Are the socioeconomic trajectories of male and female immigrants from Africa markedly different from one another? And if so, are these patterns like those previously shown for male and female natives? How about those shown for other immigrant groups? How have these patterns changed in the past several decades? And what do answers to these questions suggest about the state of theoretical understandings of the salience of gender for status attainment in contemporary America? As Corra and Kimuna recently observed: "The experience of Black female immigrants to the United States has been ignored in discussions of economic outcomes, mainly because they have been traditionally viewed as 'dependents,' moving as wives, mothers or daughters of male migrants" (2009, 1032).

Intersectionality

Importantly, intersectionality theory and research also suggest that social categories like nativity, race, and gender interact in unique ways that produce outcomes markedly different from these variables acting independently (Collins 2000; Dugger 1988; Kane 1992; Zinn and Dill 1996). The concurrent and multiple interactions of such variables are said to produce systems of inequality that reflect "intersections" of these variables (Crenshaw 1991; Collins 2000a and b; Brown and Misra 2003; Cho, Crenshaw, and McCall 2013; McCall 2001, 2005a, 2005b). It is in this context that Dugger (1988, 425) makes the poignant observation that: "For Black women, racism and sexism should be viewed as combining in such a way that they create a distinct social location rather than an additive form of 'double disadvantage.'" Intersectionality, as such, is "the view that women [(native or foreign-born)]experience oppression in varying configurations and in varying degrees of intensity" (Ritzer 2007, 204).

Dodoo (1997), for example, raises an important empirical question in these contexts. Is the Black African female encumbered by three strikes: immigrant status, gender, and race interacting to place her at the bottom of the American stratification hierarchy? What combinations (if any) of nativity, race, and gender influence the socioeconomic trajectories of African immigrants in the United States? For example, Borch and Corra (2010) found a race-gender interaction effect, showing that the U.S. labor market favors White male immigrants, Black male and White female immigrants, and Black women, in that order. But because, until very recently, relatively few studies have investigated African immigrants in the United States, findings of such interaction effects have been limited.

SUMMARY

To summarize, this introductory chapter has noted that voluntary immigration from Africa to the United States, at least in large numbers, is a very recent phenomenon (see Figure 1.1). The chapter also noted that these "new" immigrants are adding to the increasing diversity and racial/ethnic transformation that U.S. society is currently experiencing (Fears 2002; Anderson 2015; Tamir 2022). Moreover, it is also suggested that the presence of these immigrants in such large numbers begs the question: How are these immigrants adapting into the social and economic fabric of their new country? Do African immigrants exhibit trajectories of incorporation that are markedly different from those of other immigrant groups? More directly, are African immigrants less able to incorporate into U.S. society than other immigrant groups?

The review above suggests that, for African immigrants, answers to the foregoing questions may be influenced by at least three key variables: nativity (i.e., native-born versus immigrant); race (i.e., Black vs. White); and sex/gender (i.e., male vs. female). The review also suggested that the various intersections of these can also affect incorporation. Finally, it has also been noted that African immigrants are themselves a very diverse group, coming from countries and regions that are culturally, linguistically, politically, and/or economically distinct. Recent waves of immigrants from Africa increasingly include people of Arab ethnic origins that come mainly from North and East Africa. Accounts of the African immigrant experience in the United States, it is suggested, must incorporate ethnic differences among African groups.

OBJECTIVES OF THE BOOK

Following from the foregoing, the objectives of this book are threefold. First, I seek to provide a detailed demographic portrait of African immigrants in the United States. What key qualities differentiate these immigrants from one another? What do these attributes suggest about differences in socioeconomic attainment among African immigrants? Second, I seek to examine how African immigrants compare in socioeconomic attainment with other immigrant groups. Do African immigrants exhibit socioeconomic profiles that are markedly different from those of other immigrant groups? Third, I seek to provide a comprehensive comparison of the socioeconomic profiles of African immigrants with the various U.S. native groups (e.g., native-born Asians, Blacks, Hispanics, and Whites). The next chapter of the book (chapter 2) takes a closer look at the growth of African immigration to the United States. That chapter indicates a trend of substantial numerical increases from increasingly diverse origins, but that is nevertheless shown to sizably flow from a limited number of countries. The third chapter, "Immigration and the U.S. Experience: Theoretical Foundations," provides the main theoretical underpinnings for the empirical chapters of the book to follow (chapters 4–6): It examines theoretical explanations of immigrant adaptation in the United States. As noted above, examining the place of African immigrants in the U.S. context is additionally complicated by the fact that these immigrants come from countries and regions that are culturally, linguistically, politically, and/or economically distinct. This makes lumping African immigrants into one homogeneous group for theoretical and/or empirical analyses problematic. It is in this light that Model (2008, 12) suggests that: "One way to circumvent these difficulties is to undertake an intra-African comparison" (see also Kim and Kemegue 2007). Chapter 4 of the book addresses this issue directly by providing an African immigrant intra-group comparison. What key qualities differentiate African immigrants from one another? What do these attributes suggest about differences in socioeconomic attainment among African immigrants? Chapter 5 of the book provides the main comparison between African immigrants and other immigrant groups (e.g., those from Asia, Europe, and North and Central America). How do these groups compare in socioeconomic status with African immigrants? How do they compare in patterns of immigration? The sixth chapter provides analyses similar to the ones in chapter 5, with the distinction being that the comparison is with the various native groups. Finally, the concluding chapter (chapter 7) provides a synopsis of key findings and conclusions that can be drawn from them.

NOTES

1. A 2012 American Immigration Council report indicated that, as of 2010, African immigrants comprised 4 percent of the foreign-born population of the United States. And that, between 2000 and 2010, the proportion of the U.S. foreign-born population that is African doubled in size—from 881,300 in 2000 to 1.6 million in 2010.

2. Census data indicates that as of 2010, 74.3 percent of African immigrants were Black, while 20 percent were White, and 2.7 percent were Asian.

3. See, for example, Model 1991, 1995, 2008; Scroggins 1989; Dodoo 1991a-d, 1997; Butcher 1994; Kalmijn 1996; Dodoo and Takyi 2002; Corra and Kimuna 2009; Borch and Corra 2010; Corra and Borch 2014; Hamilton 2014, 2019, 2020; Elo et al. 2015; Kusow, Kimuna, and Corra 2016; Kusow, Ajrouch, and Corra 2018; Tesfai 2017a and b, 2019; Nawyn and Park 2019.

4. The sentiment here is not new, nor is it unique to Trump. It was famously expressed by longtime conservative columnist Patrick J. Buchanan, who was twice a candidate for the Republican presidential nomination and the presidential nominee of the Reform Party in 2000: "I think God made all people good, but if we had to take a million immigrants in, say Zulus, next year, or Englishmen, and put them in Virginia, what group would be easier to assimilate and would cause less problems for the people of Virginia?" (ABC-TV's "This Week With David Brinkley," 12/8/91).

5. Funded by the National Science Foundation, the University of Minnesota, and the National Institutes of Health, the Integrated Public Use Microdata Series (IPUMS) are nationally representative samples of U.S. Census data specifically compiled and made available for social and economic research. Compiled and put together by the Minnesota Population Center, the series contains microdata samples (5%, 1%, etc.) of Decennial U.S. Census as far back as 1850 and up to the 2010 Decennial Census. It also currently has samples of the American Community Survey (ACS) from 2000 all the way to 2020. Conducted annually by the U.S. Census Bureau, the ACS is an annual statistical survey of a small (nationally representative) percentage of the population. For a complete description of the IPUMS dataset (including sample and variable descriptions, data compilation, and storage), see the IPUMS website at http://www.ipums.org.

6. Here I note that these datasets are not all equally amenable to testing the many hypotheses on immigrant incorporation that can be investigated. Decennial Census data, for example, does not delineate immigrants into admission categories like the *Yearbook of Immigration Statistics*. Similarly, the *Yearbook* does not report data on the race of individuals. Hence, each of the datasets are tailored to addressing a specific set of questions, allowing for the more comprehensive sets of analyses taken up here.

7. Here and in all parts of this book, socioeconomic status is operationalized to broadly refer to measures like education, occupation, labor market earnings, and related measures.

8. The broader concept of assimilation, of course, has both objective and subjective dimensions. Here and in all parts of this manuscript, reference of this concept is delimited to objective measures—strictly operationalized quantitatively. Thus, the measures employed do not really touch the harder-to-measure subjective aspects of assimilation. I am indebted to a reviewer of a grant proposal on this topic who brought this important distinction to my attention. That reviewer rightly noted that "phrased more accurately, the study is really an investigation of only one very important aspect of assimilation."

9. See, for example, Glazer and Moynihan 1963; Sowell 1978, 1981; Chiswick 1979; Lewis 1983; Foner 1985; Butcher 1994; Hossfeld 1994; Waters 1994a and b; Dodoo 1997; Portes and Rumbaut 2001, 2006; Corra and Kimuna 2009; Corra and Borch 2014.

10. Nevertheless, an important and lasting contribution of Sowell's (1978) essay is that it emphasized another dimension to the study of race and ethnicity in the United States that, until then, remained relatively under-studied: Black immigrants as a natural comparison group to native-born Blacks.

11. See, for example, Oaxaca 1973; Beck, Horan and Tolbert 1980; Hodson and Kaufman 1982; Coverman 1986; Reskin 1988; Williams 1992; Tomaskovic-Devey 1993; Budig and England 2001; Kaufman 2002; Cohen and Huffman 2003; Mishel, Bernstein, and Allegretto 2007; England 2010.

Chapter 2

Patterns of African Immigration to the United States and Sociodemographic Profile

The previous chapter of this book noted a dramatic increase in African immigration to the United States in the past three decades. This chapter extends that discussion by taking a closer look at patterns and trends associated with this increase. It also explores implications that can be drawn from these. Exactly what has been the trend of African immigration to the United States? How has this trend changed in the last few decades? And how does this compare with the flow of other comparable immigrant groups? As to African immigration to the United States, what regions/countries have been the main sources of immigrants? And how have such sources changed (or not) over the last few decades? And exactly who are these immigrants? What qualities distinguish them from one another? What do these qualities suggest about the changing racial and ethnic composition of the United States?

Data presented in Figures 2.1-2.4 are illustrative of some of the issues taken up in this chapter. From the U.S. Department of Homeland Security's *Yearbook of Immigration Statistics* (2019), Figure 2.1 depicts data on the total number of Africans who have obtained legal permanent residence (LPR) status in the United States, by decade, beginning with the 1820s to the 2010s. By contrast, Figure 2.2 displays the information presented in Figure 2.1, but in the form of percentages. Accordingly, data reported in the two figures are cumulative, such that for each decade on the x axis, the y axis conveys the total number/percentage of Africa-born persons who have ever received LPR status, out of the total in the time period represented. For the purpose of comparison, both figures (2.1 and 2.2) also display the same information on Caribbean immigrants, a group that has historically provided large flows of immigrants (especially Black immigrants) to the United States. Finally, representative of samples from waves of the 1980, 1990, and 2000 Decennial U.S.

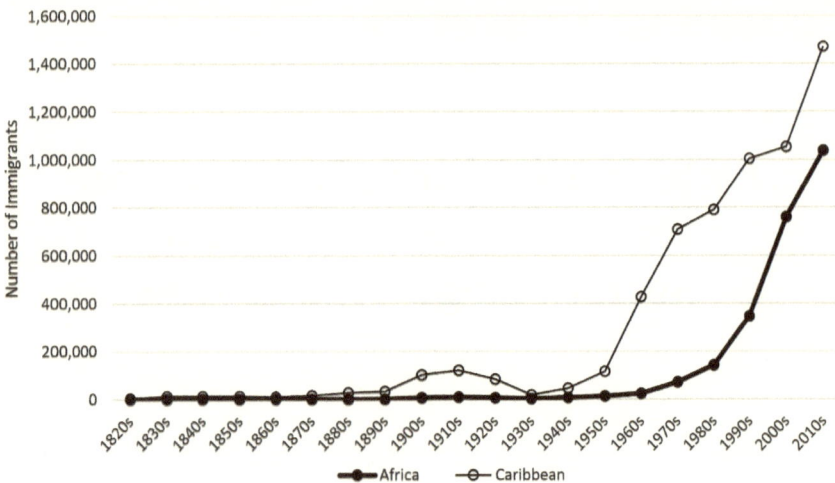

Figure 2.1. Total Number of Africans and Caribbeans Who Have Obtained Lawful Permanent Residence Status by Decade, 1820–2019. Source: U.S. Department of Homeland Security, *Yearbook of Immigration Statistics*, 2019.

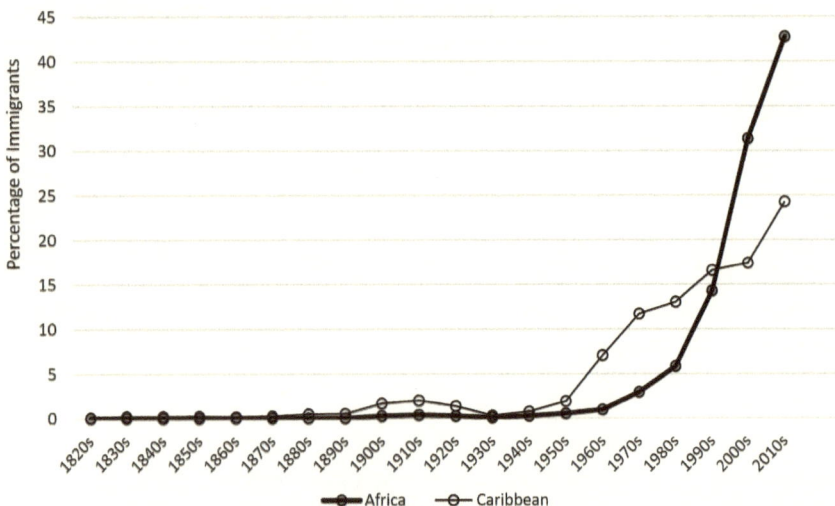

Figure 2.2. Africans and Caribbeans Who Have Obtained Lawful Permanent Residence Status, Percentage of Total by Decade, 1820–2019. Source: U.S. Department of Homeland Security, *Yearbook of Immigration Statistics*, 2019.

Censuses and the 2010 and 2019 American Community Surveys (ACS), as represented in the Integrated Public Use Microdata Series (IPUMS) (Ruggles et al. 2020),[1] Figure 2.3 displays percentages of the foreign-born Black population of the United States that are African and Caribbean immigrants,

Patterns of African Immigration to the United States 17

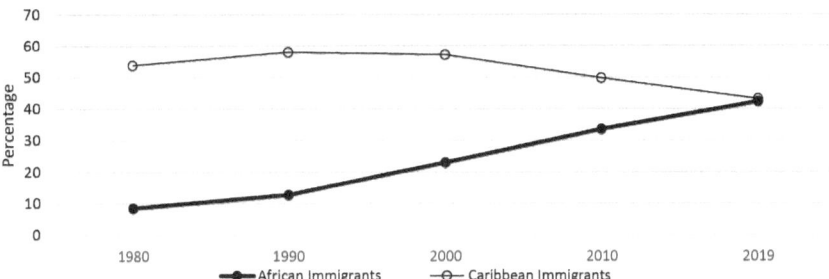

Figure 2.3. Percentages of the U.S. Foreign-Born Black Population that Are African and Caribbean Immigrants, 1980, 1990, 2000, 2010, and 2019. Source: 1980, 1990, and 2000 5% Integrated Public Use Microdata Series/Samples (IPUMS); 2010 and 2019 American Community Surveys (ACS), as represented in the IPUMS. Data limited to persons 16 years and older.

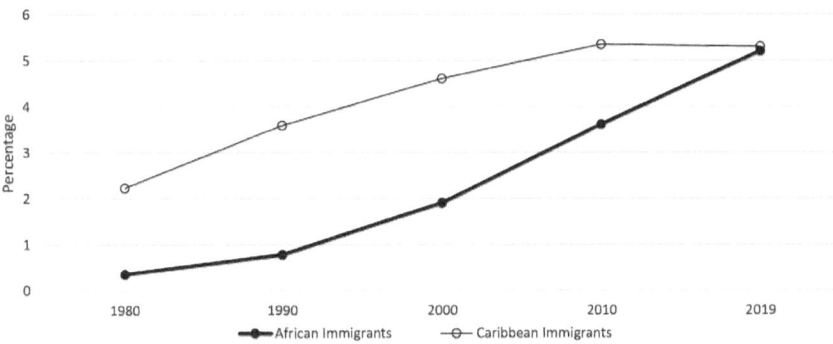

Figure 2.4. Percentages of the U.S. Black Population that Are African and Caribbean Immigrants, 1980, 1990, 2000, 2010, and 2019. Source: 1980, 1990, and 2000 5% Integrated Public Use Microdata Series/Samples (IPUMS); 2010 and 2019 American Community Surveys (ACS), as represented in the IPUMS. Data limited to persons 16 years and older.

respectively, for the time periods 1980, 1990, 2000, 2010, and 2019.[2] Whereas Figure 2.4 presents percentages of the U.S. Black population that are African and Caribbean immigrants, respectively, for the same five time periods.

Before proceeding with the discussion of the data presented in these figures, however, a cautionary note discussed in the previous chapter is worth repeating here. As indicators of immigration flows, the values presented in Figure 2.1 must be interpreted with certain caveats in mind. First, as official enumerations of legal permanent residence status, they are not inclusive of illegal/undocumented immigrants. And, importantly, the reported year of admission is the year in which the individual immigrant is officially granted legal permanent residency. As noted in the previous chapter, increasingly, this is not the year in which the immigrant initially arrived (Model 2008).

For example, some "aliens already living in the United States, including certain undocumented immigrants, temporary workers, foreign students, and refugees, file an application for adjustment of status (to legal permanent residence) with I.N.S." (U.S. Immigration and Naturalization Service 1999, 14). Nevertheless, the figures provide a good approximation of patterns of African immigration flows to the United States.

THE CHANGING COMPOSITION OF IMMIGRANTS AND THE FOREIGN-BORN AND U.S. BLACK POPULATIONS

Looking at Figure 2.2, for example, we see that, of the total number of Africans that were granted legal permanent residency in the United States between the 1820s and 2010s, the percentage of immigrants did not reach the 1 percent mark until the decade of the 1960s. By contrast, the percent of Caribbean immigrants granted legal permanent residency in that time period reached the 1 percent mark as early as the 1900s. This pattern remained until the 1990s, when the percent of African immigrants (about 15%) caught up with that of Caribbean immigrants (about 17%). Notably, by the 2000s, the percent of Africans that were granted permanent residency status more than doubled to about 33 percent of the total number of African immigrants, while that of Caribbean immigrants barely increased by 1 percent (from about 16.95% of the total number of immigrants from the Caribbean in the 1990s to 17.78% in the 2000s). Similarly, about 40 percent of Africans granted legal permanent residency in the United States between 1820 and 2019 acquired this status between 2010 and 2019, whereas only about 22 percent of Caribbean immigrants did so during the same period. Taken together, close to 90 percent (about 88%) of African immigrants granted legal permanent residency in the United States between the 1820s and 2010s acquired that status between the decades of the 1990s, 2000s, and 2010s. By contrast, only 57 percent of Caribbean immigrants in the United States were granted U.S. permanent residency during the same time period.

Looking at the foreign-born Black population, data presented in Figure 2.3 depicts similar patterns. In 1980, African immigrants constituted about 8 percent (8.42%) of the U.S. foreign-born Black population. By 1990, that percentage had grown to about 13 percent (12.63%), and almost tripled by 2000 to 23 percent (22.98%). It goes up again appreciably by 2010 to about 34 percent (33.5%) and, by 2019, noticeably so to about 42 percent (41.72%).

By contrast, in 1980, Caribbean immigrants constituted a little over half of the U.S. foreign-born Black population (53.8%). By 1990, that percentage had increased markedly to about 58 percent (57.98%), but virtually stayed the same by 2000 (about 57%). By 2010, however, we see a sizeable decline in the percentage of the Caribbean immigrant proportion of the U.S. foreign-born Black population to about 50 percent (49.67%) and, by 2019, noticeably so—down to about 43 percent (42.68%).

Moreover, data presented in Figure 2.4 is similarly illustrative. Looking at the percentage of the U.S. Black population that is African immigrant, we see that this percentage was under 1 percent in both 1980 and 1990 (about 0.35% and 0.78%, respectively). By 2000, however, that percentage reached approximately 2 percent (1.86%), but almost doubled by 2010 to about 4 percent (about 3.61%). It reached 5 percent by 2019 (about 5.1%).

In contrast, the percentage of the U.S. Black population that is Caribbean immigrant between 1980 and 2019 started above the 2 percent mark at the outset (about 2.23%) in 1980. Unlike the African percentage of the U.S. Black population, however, the Caribbean percentage continued to increase but at a steady rate. By 1990, for example, the Caribbean immigrant proportion of the U.S. Black population grows to about 4 percent (about 3.59%), only increases by about 1 percent by 2000 (about 4.61%), slightly increases to about 5 percent (approximately 5.35%) by 2010, and remains about the same by 2019 (about 5.2%).

Taken together, the data presented in Figures 2.1-2.4 suggest at least three key discernible patterns in the flow (and presence) of African immigrants to the United States. First, we see an appreciable increase in the total number of African immigrants to the United States in recent years (Figures 2.1 and 2.2), noticeably in the 1990s and accelerating in the 2000s and 2010s.[3] Several factors are cited in the literature for this dramatic increase, including changes in U.S. immigration policy and economic and political instability in many African countries (Jasso 2011; Kollehlon and Eule 2003; Thomas 2011; Logan and Thomas 2012). The Immigration Act of 1990, for example, introduced a Diversity Visa Lottery Program designed to increase the number of immigrants from countries underrepresented in the United States. This program, however, required attainment of certain basic skills of immigrants premigration. And since many recent immigrants from Africa acquired legal permanent residence status under this program (see below), it has led to the increase of the number of African immigrants admitted on the basis of job skills, thus providing new avenues for highly skilled/educated African immigrants to enter the United States (Lobo 2001; McCabe 2011; Thomas 2011; Hamilton 2020). Second, and relatedly, the percentage of the U.S. foreign-born Black population that is of African origins has also increased dramatically (Figure 2.3). And third, African immigrants now constitute a growing and increasingly visible component of the overall U.S. Black population (Figure 2.4). Discussed throughout this book, these patterns and trends clearly have important implications for understanding the changing racial and ethnic composition of the United States (Shaw-Taylor and Tuch 2007; Tamir 2022).

A TREND OF SIZEABLE NUMERICAL INCREASES: CONCENTRATED PRESENCE AND DIVERSITY

The data presented in Table 2.1 suggest that the information discussed so far on the recent flow of African immigrants to the United States needs some qualifications. That table presents the top ten countries of immigrants from Africa in the United States for the years 1980, 1990, 2000, 2010, and 2019, at least in terms of proportionate representation in census data. It also shows the percent of immigrants from the top sending ten countries by year, as a percentage of the total from Africa. Table 2.1 Top Ten Sending African Countries to the United States by Year, 1980, 1990, 2000, 2010, and 2019.

As can be seen in Table 2.1, the patterns and trends noted above are closely illustrative of ten sending African countries in any given year. For example, for the five time periods represented in Table 2.1 (1980, 1990, 2000, 2010, and 2019), Egypt alone accounted for about 22 percent, 19 percent, 13 percent, 9 percent, and 9 percent, respectively, of the total number of African immigrants in the United States. Although these percentages illustrate a decreasing pattern, the trend shown means that Egypt alone accounted for as high as two out of every five African immigrants in the United States for the first two of the five time periods, and at least one out of every ten in the most recent decades. Similarly, Nigeria alone accounted for more than one out of every ten African immigrants in the United States: about 14.10, 14.30, 15.50, 14.10, and 16.13 percent, respectively, for the five time periods. Moreover, with only a few exceptions, Nigeria, along with Ethiopia, Egypt, South Africa, Ghana, and Morocco, has consistently been among the top ten countries of African immigrants in the United States.

Notably, Table 2.1 shows that, in almost all of the five time periods examined here, immigrants from ten sending countries have collectively constituted about seven out of ten African immigrants in the United States. Looking at the bottom row of Table 2.1, for example, we see that ten countries represented about 71 percent, 76 percent, 71 percent, 69 percent, and 70 percent, respectively, of the total number of African immigrants in the United States in 1980, 1990, 2000, 2010, and 2019, respectively, at least as revealed by census data. Notable is the fact that this percentage has virtually remained constant throughout the five time periods examined.

Table 2.1 Top Ten Sending African Countries to the United States by Year, 1980, 1990, 2000, 2010, and 2019.

Rank	Country of Origin	1980 (Percent of Total)	Rank	Country of Origin	1990 (Percent of Total)	Rank	Country of Origin	2000 (Percent of Total)
1	Egypt/United Arab Rep.	21.73	1	Egypt/United Arab Rep.	19.05	1	Nigeria	15.45
2	Nigeria	14.09	2	Nigeria	14.26	2	Egypt/United Arab Rep.	12.93
3	South Africa (Union of)	7.29	3	South Africa (Union of)	9.70	3	Ethiopia	8.13
4	Morocco	7.02	4	Ethiopia	9.53	4	South Africa (Union of)	7.88
5	Ethiopia	4.53	5	Morocco	6.23	5	Ghana	7.56
6	Ghana	4.42	6	Ghana	5.17	6	Morocco	4.87
7	Libya	4.29	7	Kenya	4.23	7	Kenya	4.74
8	Kenya	3.61	8	Liberia	2.90	8	Liberia	4.29
9	Algeria	2.11	9	Uganda	2.32	9	Somalia	2.95
10	Liberia	1.85	10	Libya	2.26	10	Sierra Leone	2.42
Total		70.94			75.65			71.23
N		8,559			14,232			32,665

Table 2.1 Top Ten Sending Countries by Year, 1980, 1990, 2000, 2010, and 2019

Rank	Country of Origin	2010 (Percent of Total)	Rank	Country of Origin	2019 (Percent of Total)
1	Nigeria	14.06	1	Nigeria	16.13
2	Ethiopia	10.14	2	Ethiopia	10.49
3	Egypt/United Arab Rep.	9.22	3	Egypt/United Arab Rep.	9.36
4	Ghana	8.28	4	Ghana	7.84
5	South Africa (Union of)	6.65	5	South Africa (Union of)	6.73
6	Kenya	5.23	6	Kenya	6.05
7	Morocco	4.79	7	Morocco	4.50
8	Somalia	4.01	8	Liberia	3.19
9	Liberia	3.96	9	Cameroon	2.98
10	Cameroon	2.68	10	Somalia	2.78
Total		69.03			70.06
N		10,961			14,418

Source: Author's calculations based on samples of the 1980, 1990, and 2000 Decennial U.S. Censuses and the 2010 and 2019 American Community Surveys (ACS), as represented in the Integrated Public Use Microdata Series (IPUMS) (Ruggles et al. 2020). Data limited to persons 16 to 64 years old.

In short, for the five time periods displayed in Table 2.1, from 69 to 76 percent of immigrants from Africa in the United States are representative of ten sending countries. Here, I term this "concentrated presence" of African immigrants in the United States: a sizeable increase in the flow of immigrants from a limited number of African countries.

Yet, a second emerging trend is also clearly noticeable. The percentage of African immigrants representative of a limited number of countries has been on the decline. Top ten sending countries have been changing over the years, with some countries reaching that threshold (and some dropping below) as time progressed. Egypt, for example, has consistently provided a sizeable proportion of African immigrants to the United States over the years. Yet, for the five time periods represented in Table 2.1 (1980, 1990, 2000, 2010, and 2019), we have seen a progressive decline of this proportion, about 22 percent, 19 percent, 13 percent, 9 percent, and 9 percent, respectively. By contrast, Somalia and Sierra Leone did not reach the threshold of being one of the top ten countries representative of African immigrants in the United States until 2000. Similarly, Cameroon did not reach this threshold until 2010, but it remained as one of the top ten countries represented in the U.S. African immigrant population in 2019. This is an indication of "diversity" in the representation of African immigrants in the United States in recent years.

Several "push" and "pull" factors are cited for this shift in source countries, including changing political and economic circumstances in different African countries, as well as shifting U.S. immigration policy (Konadu-Agyemang and Takyi 2006; Tamir and Anderson 2022). In a 2022 Pew Research Center report, for example, Tamir and Anderson note that immigration from Somalia to the United States has been on the rise, resulting in a 205 percent increase in the Somali-born population in the United States since 2000. Looking forward to immigration data from the U.S. Department of Homeland Security reviewed in chapter 4 of this book, the country of Somalia also has one of the highest percentages of immigrants granted permanent residency status as refugees and asylees.

Taken together, the data presented thus far suggests that the number of African immigrants to the United States has indeed increased appreciably in recent years. However, information presented in Table 2.1 indicates that the pattern of dramatically increasing immigration has occurred appreciably for immigrants from a limited number of long-term sending countries, although immigration from other African countries has also increased noticeably. Finally, these patterns and trends have, for the most part, persisted throughout the time period examined. By identifying key characteristics of this immigrant population, the section to immediately follow explores what the foregoing patterns and trends might suggest about the demographic (e.g., racial, ethnic, and gender) composition of the U.S. African immigrant population.

U.S. AFRICAN IMMIGRANTS: VARIATIONS IN LEGAL ENTRY STATUS

The foregoing analyses lead to several questions that are examined in this section. Exactly who are these immigrants? What are some of their distinguishing characteristics? Table 2.2 gives an initial answer to these questions.

From the U.S. Department of Homeland Security's *Yearbook of Immigration Statistics*, Table 2.2 displays the number of African immigrants admitted to the United States by class of admission for the fiscal years 1996–2019. It also

Table 2.2 African Immigrants Admitted by Class of Admission, Fiscal Years 1996 to 2019.

Entry Status	Number of Immigrants	Percent of Total
Immediate Relatives of U.S. Citizens	801,876	39.21
Family-Sponsored Preferences	160,888	7.87
Employment-Based Preferences	124,967	6.11
Diversity	427,920	20.92
Refugees and Asylees	520,527	25.45
Other	9,021	0.44
Total	2,045,199	100.00

Source: U.S. Department of Homeland Security, *Yearbook of Immigration Statistics*, 1996–2019.

gives percentages of those totals by class of admission. The table gives totals on five main admission categories, as classified by the U.S. Immigration and Nationality Act (INA): "Family-sponsored preferences," "Employment-based preferences," "Immediate relatives of U.S. citizens," "Refugees and asylees," and "Diversity." The U.S. Immigration and Nationality Act provides several broad classes of admission for foreign nationals to gain LPR status in the United States. Those classified as immediate relatives of U.S. citizens include spouses, children, and parents of U.S. citizens age 21 and older. Those admitted based on family-based preferences include relatives/family members not included in the immediate relative class of admission, for example, married, or unmarried adult sons/daughters of U.S. citizens, brothers/sisters of such citizens, and so forth. Specific subcategories in the family-based preferences include "Family First Preference" (unmarried sons/daughters, over the age of 21, of U.S. citizens), "Family Second Preference" (spouses and unmarried children of permanent residents), "Family Third Preference" (married sons/daughters of U.S. citizens), and "Family Fourth Preference" (brothers and sisters of U.S. citizens). Admissions based on employment are given to those seeking to provide needed skills in the U.S. workforce or invest in new U.S. jobs, along with their dependents. Refuge is granted to two sets of immigrants who have been persecuted or have a "well-founded" fear of persecution, refugees and asylees. Refugees are those admitted outside the United States with their immediate relatives, while asylum is given to those seeking refuge, but are already inside the United States, and their immediate relatives. Finally, those gaining LPR based on the diversity program come from countries with relatively low levels of immigration to the United States.

As shown in Table 2.2, of the 2,045,199 Africans granted legal permanent residency between the years 1996–2019, 801,876 (about 39.32%) were admitted as "Immediate relatives of U.S. citizens," 160,888 (about 7.87%) were based on "Family-sponsored preferences," and 520,527 (about 25.50%) were admitted as refugees and asylees. Collectively, these three categories of admissions constituted about 73 percent (72.53%) of Africans granted legal permanent residency in the United States during that time period. By contrast, 427,920 (about 20.92%) African immigrants were admitted based on the Department of States' "Diversity lottery program," and 124,967 (about 6.11%) were admitted based on employment-based preferences.[4] The latter two (diversity and employment), largely skilled-based immigration categories (McCabe 2011; Capps, McCabe and Fix 2012; Logan and Thomas 2012; Thomas 2011; Elo et al. 2015; Hamilton 2020), constituted about 27 percent (27.03%) of African immigrants granted legal permanent residency between the years 1996–2019.

These figures suggest several questions that are examined in later chapters, including: Are African immigrants more or less likely than other immigrant groups to be admitted as political or family-based immigrants? Alternatively, are African immigrants more or less likely than other immigrant groups to be admitted based on employment and skills-based preferences? What about African immigrants themselves, are some groups more or less likely to be admitted into the United States based on one entry status or the other? What socioeconomic inferences can be drawn from these?

These questions are important for both theoretical and practical reasons. For example, migration theory and research suggest that how well immigrants do may be uniquely tied to whether they are "economic" or "political" migrants (see chapter 3 of this book). At least since Everett Lee's "A Theory of Migration" (1966), researchers have hypothesized that "politically motivated emigrants" are less positively selected (pushed) than "economically motivated emigrants" (pulled) (Borjas 1994; Chiswick 1978, 1999; Jasso and Rosenzweig 1990a&b; Tesfai 2019). If many African immigrants have political rather than economic motives to relocate (Gordon 1998), then one hypothesis is that these immigrants will be less selective than other immigrant groups. Alternatively, if some groups of African immigrants are more likely than others to be political rather than economic immigrants (Gordon 1998), then another hypothesis is that the former is predicted to be less selective than the latter.[5] More specifically, the type of visa an immigrant holds is hypothesized to influence immigrant incorporation (Jasso 2004; Jasso, Rosenzweig and Smith 2000).

SHIFTS IN THE RACIAL, GENDER, AND LINGUISTIC COMPOSITION OF IMMIGRANTS

Table 2.3 continues this probe by displaying key sociodemographic characteristics for African immigrants in the United States. From samples of waives of the 1980, 1990 and 2000 Decennial U.S. Censuses and the 2010 and 2019 American Community Surveys (ACS), as represented in the Integrated Public Use Microdata Series (Ruggles et al. 2020), that table displays key demographic characteristics of the African immigrant population in the United States.

Looking at the data presented in Table 2.3, we see that one clear pattern is the changing racial and ethnic composition of the African immigrant population in the United States. Here, and consistent with previous studies (Kollehlon and Eule 2003; Elo et al. 2015; Borch and Corra 2010), we see that the pattern has been a growing proportion of self-identified "Black" African immigrants, on one hand, and a decreasing proportion of self-identified "White" immigrants, on the other hand. In 1980, for example, about 33 percent of African immigrants in the United States self-identified

Table 2.3 African Immigrants in the United States: A Demographic Profile.

Attribute	1980	1990	2000	2010	2019
Period of Immigration					
Pre-1965	27.43	10.34	3.45	1.84	1.11
1965–1974	32.25	20.47	8.71	4.32	1.93
1975–1984	40.32	42.04	21.53	11.62	6.19
1985–1994	0	27.15	32.21	17.95	11.65
1995–2004	0	0	34.11	41.49	28.31
2005–2019	0	0	0	22.78	50.81
Mean Years in U.S.	13.34	12.80	12.60	14.84	16.19
Race (%)					
Black	32.98	44.04	56.09	69.2	71.98
White	58.14	47.78	27.27	25.01	23.94
Other[a]	8.88	8.19	16.64	5.79	4.79
Sex (%)					
Male	59.63	59.18	55.28	52.8	51.82
Female	40.37	40.82	44.72	47.2	48.18
Linguistic heritage					
Arab (Official) (%)[b]	38.52	31.13	22.88	19.61	20.14
English (Official) (%)[c]	40.24	46.95	48.14	47.30	50.52
Region of Origin (%)					
Central	2.48	3.06	3.35	4.48	8.46
East	16.91	22.92	20.25	25.83	26.18
North	39.09	31.34	20.89	19.12	18.43
Southern	8.93	10.1	7.88	6.65	6.73
West	25.45	26.91	30.94	34.57	35.23
Marital Status (%)					
Married	59.63	60.39	57.65	58.89	58.3
Not Married	40.37	39.61	42.35	41.11	41.7
U.S. Region of Residence (%)					
Northeast	30.52	30	28.69	25.48	23.52
Midwest	17.12	11.01	13.24	14.86	15.36
West	24.19	25.32	20.76	19.01	19.42
South	28.18	33.67	37.3	40.64	41.7
Mean Age[d]	32.74	35.1	36.96	39.6	42.12
N	8,559	14,232	32,665	10,961	14,41

a. A catchall category that includes individuals reporting various race combinations like two major races, three or more races, etc.

b. Includes immigrants from countries with Arab listed as an official language by the U.S. Central Intelligence Agency's *World FactBook* (https://www.cia.gov/the-world-factbook). They include Algeria, Chad, Comoros, Egypt, Eritrea, Libya, Mauritania, Morocco, Somalia, Sudan, Tunisia, and Western Sahara.

c. Includes immigrants from countries with English listed as an official language by the U.S. Central Intelligence Agency's *World FactBook* (https://www.cia.gov/the-world-factbook). They include Gambia, Ghana, Liberia, Nigeria, Sierra Leone, Kenya, Malawi, Mauritius, Tanzania, Uganda, Zambia, Zimbabwe, Cameroon, Botswana, Lesotho, Namibia, South Africa (Union of), and Swaziland.

d. Data limited to persons 16 to 64 years old.

Source: Author's calculations based on samples of the 1980, 1990, and 2000 Decennial U.S. Censuses and the 2010 and 2019 American Community Surveys (ACS), as represented in the Integrated Public Use Microdata Series (IPUMS) (Ruggles et al. 2020).

as Black. That percentage increased to about 44 percent by 1990, 57 percent by 2000, 69 percent by 2010, and finally 72 percent in 2019. By contrast, the percent of African immigrants identifying as White begins at a relatively high point—at about 58 percent. That percentage declines appreciably to 48 percent by 1990, declines again dramatically to 27 percent by 2000, to 25 percent by 2010, and ends up down to about 24 percent by 2019. In other words, until very recently, voluntary immigration from Africa to the United States has been disproportionately those who identified themselves as White. More recent immigration from Africa, by contrast, has increasingly included Black Africans (Borch and Corra 2010; Elo et al. 2015; Tamir and Anderson 2022).

And, as noted in chapter 1 of this book, an important question that the foregoing trends suggest is how these "new" African immigrants are adapting into the social and economic fabric of their newly adopted country? What theoretical insights can be gained by investigating this group of immigrants who are mostly Black and poor?

Looking back at the information presented in Table 2.3, we see a similar pattern with the gender composition of the African immigrant population in the United States. That composition begins in 1980 with males constituting about 60 percent of the African immigrant population. By the end of the time period examined in Table 2.3 (2019), however, the proportion of male African immigrants declines to about only half. In other words, in 1980, three out of every five African immigrants in the United States were male. By 2019, that number declined to one out of every two—exactly half of the total African immigrant population.

Moreover, the information presented in Table 2.3 on the linguistic heritage measures suggests a continual decline in the proportionate representation of African immigrants from countries officially designated as Arab speaking, on one hand, and a continual increase in the proportionate representation of immigrants from countries officially designated as English-speaking, on the other hand. In 1980, for example, the proportion of African immigrants from officially Arab-speaking countries was about 39 percent. By 2019, this percentage had declined almost by half to about 20. By contrast, the proportion of African immigrants from English-speaking countries was 40 percent in 1980. Unlike the proportion of immigrants from Arab-speaking countries, however, the percentage of immigrants from English-speaking countries continued to grow throughout the years, reaching about 52 percent by 2019.

And what might we make of the foregoing pattern of linguistic heritage, at least when it comes to immigrants from Arab-speaking countries? The previous chapter of this book (chapter 1), for example, cited recent scholarship that notes that recent waves of immigrants from Africa increasingly include people of Arab ethnic origins. By one estimate cited in that chapter, between 1990 and 2000, Arab immigration from Egypt increased by 82 percent (De la Cruz and Brittingham 2003).

A simple explanation is that the patterns displayed in Table 2.3 are more nuanced than the percentages represented therein might suggest. For example, a review of the IPUMS samples (not reported here) shows the total number of immigrants from most Arab-speaking countries to more than double between 1980 and 2000. That review also revealed those numbers to decline sharply in 2010, some almost by more than half, but then begin to go back up by 2019.

More generally, the values displayed in Table 2.3 are proportionate representations. A closer look at census data (not reported here) does indeed indicate that the presence of immigrants from most African countries have been on the rise, including those from many Arab-speaking countries. A notable point being that the recent growth has been greater from some regions and countries than others, and thus the changing proportionate patterns represented in Table 2.3. In other words, immigration from most African countries has been on the rise, but the recent dramatic increase is more pronounced among immigrants from Sub-Saharan Africa, and greater in some years/decades than others.

Returning to Table 2.3 again, regional differences in representation are also evident, with African immigrants from Northern and Southern Africa decreasing proportionately, while immigrants from the other three regions increasing or holding steady. Immigrants from Central Africa, for example, represented about 3 percent of the total number of African immigrants in the United States in 1980. By 2019, however, the percentage of immigrants from this region had increased to about 9 percent, a growth representing a threefold increase. By contrast, the percent of immigrants from North Africa was as high as 39 percent in 1980. By 2019, however, that percentage had dropped dramatically to about 18 percent, a more than one-half decline.

As to the overall African immigrant population in the United States, additional patterns can also be noted. Most U.S. African immigrants are married, with virtually 60 percent reporting being married throughout the years. African immigrants also increasingly reside in the southern region of the country, and decreasingly reside in other regions. And while they are a relatively young population, the mean age is shown to be increasing over time (mean age ranging from a low of 33 years in 1980 to 42.12 in 2019). Moreover, amplifying the point made in the previous chapter, that voluntary immigration from Africa is a very recent phenomenon, the mean years in the United States measure ranges between about thirteen to sixteen years.

SHIFTING SOCIOECONOMIC PROFILES

To end the analyses of this chapter, Table 2.4 displays some key socioeconomic measures for African immigrants. Here again, we see some clearly identifiable patterns. For example, the percent of African immigrants that are naturalized citizens has been on the rise. In 1980, that percentage stood at about 33 percent (32.45%). It reached nearly 55 percent (54.74%) by 2019. By contrast, the percentage of African immigrants that reported proficiency in English has declined over time, at least in some measures, while remaining high in others. In 1980 and 1990, about 4 percent of African immigrants reported speaking English "poorly." By 2000, this percentage had grown to 6 percent and remained so through 2019. By contrast, in 1980, less than 1 percent (about 0.69%) of African immigrants reported speaking English "only." By 2010, this percentage had grown to above 1 percent (1.35%). Those reporting speaking English very well, however, grew slightly between 1980 and 1990 (from about 46% to about 50%), and remained steady thereafter. These changes in English language proficiency are likely reflective of the increasing diversity in the racial and ethnic composition of contemporary African immigration to the United States.

The educational attainment measures reported in Table 2.4 are especially noteworthy. In 1980, for example, the percent of African immigrants with only (no more than) a bachelor's degree/four years of college education stood at 13.38 percent. By 1990, this percentage had almost doubled to about 24.49 percent, and remained about the same through 2000 and 2010 (23.45% and 23.92%, respectively). By 2019, the percentage of African immigrants with a bachelor's degree/four years of college education had risen to about 25 percent (25.02%). Here, I note in passing, that the percent of African immigrants with a bachelor's degree/four years of college education was greater than the overall percentage of the U.S. population with such degrees, consistently exceeded those of all but Asian Americans, and noticeably so.[6] These are impressive numbers, but especially so if you add the percentage of immigrants with degrees/years of education beyond a bachelor's degree. Taking the latter into account puts the percentage of African immigrants with a college degree to more than 30 percent in 1980, and 40 percent or above in all other years (for similar patterns, see Corra and Borch 2014).

The reported employment-related measures are similarly notable. The percent employed, for example, begins at a relatively high point in 1980—at about 61 percent (60.45%). This is three out of every five individuals. By 1990, this percentage had gone up to about 72 percent, and, by 2019, it stood at about 76 percent. Compare this with the reported unemployment rate that mostly stood around 5 percent, with the single exception of 2010, when the

Table 2.4 African Immigrants in the United States: A Socioeconomic Portrait of Immigrants 16–64 Years of Age.

Measure	1980	1990	2000	2010	2019
Human Capital					
Citizenship (%)					
Born Abroad to U.S. Parents	8.55	8.75	5.27	4.88	5.93
Naturalized	32.45	33.2	35.51	46.61	55.94
Not a Citizen	59	58.05	59.22	48.51	38.13
English (Percent)					
None	0.69	0.51	0.79	1.35	0.88
Only	30.63	30.66	24.95	23.88	27.16
Very Well	45.94	49.93	51.68	49.29	48.97
Good	18.86	15.25	17.03	19.08	17.75
Poorly	3.88	3.65	5.56	6.4	5.24
School (%)					
Not in school	65.19	72.47	76.84	76.7	79.42
In school	34.81	27.53	23.16	23.3	20.58
Education (%)					
<HS	13.98	11.3	13.71	12.26	11.28
HS/GED	16.82	15.5	18.08	18.39	17.41
Some College	34.01	29.05	28.25	29.44	27.35
Bachelor's[a]	13.38	24.49	23.45	23.92	25.02
MA, Prof., & Doctorate[b]	21.81	19.66	16.51	15.99	18.19
Foreign Degree	73.14	59.17	64.88	65.77	64.25
U.S. Degree	26.86	40.83	35.12	34.23	35.75
Mean Yrs Ed.	14.5	15.87	15.72	15.67	15.75
Work					
Employment (%)					
Employed	60.45	72.34	69.02	70.02	74.52
Unemployed	4.50	5.00	4.56	9.17	3.97
Not in Labor Force	35.05	22.66	26.41	20.81	21.51
Class of Worker (%)					
N/A	20.5	13.09	13.75	14.71	14.69
Self-Employed	6.33	9.3	7.96	8.54	7.79
Wage-Worker	73.16	77.61	78.29	76.75	77.78
Mean Hours Worked per week	25.92	31.81	31.58	29.9	30.76
Annual Hours Worked	1103.23	1424.94	1432.61	N.A.	1459.47
Yrs of Work Exp.[c]	12.24	13.24	15.24	17.93	19.05
Economic Measures					
Annual Income[d]	$39,718.26	$49,726.72	$52,898.38	$51,283.85	$55,581.49
Hourly Earnings[e]	$26.63	$27.86	$30.08	N.A.	$35.43

Ownership of Dwelling (Percent)					
N/A	4.65	2.62	2.32	2.51	5.44
Bought (loan)	40.04	44.12	41.11	47.99	46.57
Rented	55.31	53.26	56.57	49.5	47.99
N	8,559	14,232	32,665	10,961	14418

Source: Author's calculations based on samples of the 1980, 1990, and 2000 Decennial Censuses, and the 2010 and 2019 American Community Surveys (ACS), as represented in the Integrated Public Use Microdata Series (IPUMS) (Ruggles et al. 2020). Data limited to persons 16 to 64 years old.

a. Data for 1980 represent those reporting four years of post-secondary schooling; 1990, 2000, 2010, and 2019 represent those having earned a bachelor's degree.

b. Data for 1980 represent those reporting five-plus years of post-secondary schooling; 1990, 2000, 2010, and 2019 include those reporting having earned a master's degree, professional degree beyond a bachelor's degree, and a doctoral degree.

c. Calculated from the product of (age minus number of years of schooling) minus 6.

d. Based on pre-tax earnings from wages and salary in the year preceding the census, computed in constant 2019 dollars.

e. To obtain hourly earnings, annual earnings are divided by the product of weeks worked per year and hours worked per week. All earnings measures are computed in constant 2019 dollars, and are limited to persons earning at least $500 annually.

reported unemployment rate was about 9 percent (9.17%), possibly reflective of the economic downturn caused by the 2008 recession. Less than 10 percent reported being self-employed. Not surprisingly, the average years of work experience has also been on the rise. In 1980, this value was about 12.24. It goes up to 13.24 in 1990, and continues to rise through 2000, 2010, and 2019—about 15.24, 17.93, and 19.2 in 2000, 2010, and 2019, respectively. Finally, virtually all African immigrants reported working for wages (well over two-thirds for all years), and this seems to have been on the rise. The usual hours worked per week also seems to have been on the rise, although no data was available for two of the time periods.

With respect to measures of earnings, these also seem to be on the rise. Adjusted for inflation, the calculated average annual earnings for African immigrants were $39,718.26 in 1980. This average rose to $49,726.72 by 1990, and again rose to about $52,898.38 by 2000. It declined slightly by 2010 to $51,283.85 but went up again by 2019 to $55,581.49.

SUMMARY

To summarize, at this point the discussion has shown a dramatic increase in the flow of African immigrants to the United States in the past couple of decades. Consequently, African immigrants now constitute a growing and increasingly sizeable component of the foreign-born and U.S. Black populations. The recent dramatic increase in the flow of African immigrants to the United States, however, is notably shown to have been appreciably from a limited number of sending countries already with sizeable flows of immigrants to the United States. Nevertheless, the "concentration" of the flow of African immigrants from a limited number of countries has been on the decline in recent years, with African immigrants coming from a more diverse set of countries. And as to the immigrants themselves, the largest have been admitted under the status of family reunification, and as refugees and asylees. An increasing number are being admitted under the diversity classification as immigrants from countries with relatively low levels of immigration to the United States, while a smaller but growing number/proportion have been admitted under employment preferences.

Key demographic trends shown include the changing racial, linguistic, and gender composition of the African immigrant population in the United States. Over time, more and more African immigrants have reported being Black, and more and more come from English-speaking countries. By contrast, the gender composition of the African immigrant population in the United States continued to approach parity, and by 2019, had in fact reach such parity—half are male, and half are female. Finally, African immigrants exhibit demonstrably favorable socioeconomic measures, including high educational attainment, high employment, and an increasing percentage becoming naturalized citizens.

Assuming that the sociodemographic and socioeconomic measures discussed are good indicators of potential incorporation into the U.S. labor market, then, to be sure, African immigrants exhibit qualities favorable for such incorporation. Yet, the main hypothesis implicit in much of the discussion of this chapter is that as the relative size of a given minority group grows, so would discrimination against members of that group. To that end, I end this chapter with a perceptive observation in the sociological literature: "One of the most frequent 'common sense' generalizations made in the field of minority-group relations concerns the relationship between discrimination and the relative size of the minority" (Blalock 1967, 143). Might we expect discrimination against African immigrants to also be on the rise as the size of these immigrants continues to grow? Might that influence their attainment prospects?

The chapter to immediately follow continues our probe by providing theoretical foundations for the empirical chapters (4–6) to follow. Exactly what does theory from the social sciences offer, which can help us better understand the migration experiences of African immigrants in the United States? What theoretical insights can be gained by investigating this group of immigrants who are mostly Black and poor?

NOTES

1. Funded by the National Science Foundation, the University of Minnesota, and the National Institutes of Health, the Integrated Public Use Microdata Series (IPUMS) are nationally representative samples of U.S. Census data specifically compiled and made available for social and economic research. Compiled and put together by the Minnesota Population Center, the series contains microdata samples (5%, 1%, etc.) of Decennial U.S. Census as far back as 1850 and up to the 2010 Decennial Census. It also currently has samples of the American Community Survey from 2000 all the way to 2020. Conducted annually by the U.S. Census Bureau, the ACS is an annual statistical survey of a small (nationally representative) percentage of the population. For a complete description of the IPUMS dataset (including sample and variable descriptions, data compilation, and storage), see the IPUMS website at http://www.ipums.org.

2. The U.S. Census Bureau defines the foreign-born as individuals who had no U.S. citizenship at birth. African and Caribbean immigrants included those who recorded their birthplace in any of the African or Caribbean countries in the census documents. Of these, those who self-identified as "Black" are included in the Black foreign-born.

3. It is important to note here that, because they exclude undocumented immigrants, the data presented in these graphs do not completely reflect immigration patterns from Africa. By one estimate, for example, there were 619,000 unauthorized Black immigrants living in the United States in 2015, that accounted for 15 percent of foreign-born Blacks (Anderson and López 2018). This compares with 24 percent of the overall immigrant population that is unauthorized (Anderson and López 2018). Census data used later in this and other chapters partially captures the undocumented population. The data presented in Figures 2.1 and 2.2, however, do reflect "legal" or "documented" immigration patterns and trends, and thus provide useful estimations of immigration flows from Africa.

4. Compare these figures with those for some of the other major sending regions of immigrants to the United States. Of the 397,187 immigrants from Asia granted legal permanent residency in 2018, 83,115 (about 20.93%) were based on family-sponsored preferences, 139,024 (about 35%) were immediate relatives of U.S. citizens, and 64,547 (16.25%) were admitted as refugees and asylees. Taken together, these three categories of admissions constituted about 72.18 percent of Asians granted permanent legal residency in 2018. Employment-based Asian immigrants accounted for about 21.10 percent (83,802) admissions in 2018, whereas 14,714 (3.71%) were based on the Department of States' Diversity Lottery Program. Among the 78,869 South American immigrants granted permanent legal status in 2018, about 18.16 percent (14,326 cases) were admitted under family-sponsored preferences, 61.501 percent (48,511 cases) were immediate relatives of U.S. citizens, and 3.84 percent (3,028) were admitted as refugees and asylees. These three categories of admissions constituted about 83.501 percent of South American immigrants granted permanent legal status. About 13.18 percent (10,385 cases) of South Americans in 2018 were employment-based admissions, while about 1.50 percent (1,207 cases) were diversity-based admissions. Contrast these with the numbers and percentages for Europe and North America. For

the 80,024 European admissions in 2018, about 6,065 (7.60%) were based on family-sponsored preferences, 35,746 (about 44.67%) were admitted as immediate relatives of U.S. citizens, and 6,335 (about 7.92) were admitted as refugees and asylees. These three categories of admissions constituted about 60.19 percent of European immigrants granted permanent legal status in 2018. About 20,689 (25.85%) admissions from Europe in 2018 were employment-based, whereas 10,985 (about 13.73%) were diversity-based. For the 418,991 admissions from North America in 2018, 99,744 (23.81%) were family-sponsored preferences, 207,224 (about 49.46%) were admitted as immediate relatives of U.S. citizens, and 77,701 (18.55%) were admitted as refugees and asylees. Collectively, these three categories of admissions constituted 91.82 percent of admittees from North America. Employment-based admissions from North America in 2018 accounted for about 3.9 percent (16,254 cases), while 380 (0.1%) were diversity admittees.

5. Another distinction between political and economic migrants is Portes and Rumbaut's expectation that political migrants (such as refugees) get various kinds of assistance from the government that economically motivated migrants do not get (Model, personal communication). One of the characteristics of "contexts of reception," that expectation may or may not be applicable to African immigrants. Arguably, this expectation might apply primarily to Cubans. The forthcoming book, *Seeking Refuge, Finding Inequality: Refugees Navigating Their Way*, by Blair Sackett and Annette Lareau (Sackett and Lareau forthcoming; also see Sackett and Lareau 2022), is an ethnographic study that documents the impediments that refugees to the United States from the Democratic Republic of Congo encountered, trying to secure the benefits to which they were entitled.

6. Compare these with the calculated percentages of the overall U.S. population that reported earning just a bachelor's degree/four years of college education (not reported in Table 2.4): 8.06 percent in 1980, 12.33 percent in 1990, 14.1 percent in 2000, 17.46 percent in 2010, and 23.27 percent in 2018. And the calculated percentages for the different racial and ethnic groups suggest similar patterns. The percentages of Whites with a bachelor's degree/four years of college education only, for example, were 8.53 percent, 13.23 percent, 15.35 percent, 18.49 percent, and 17.93 percent for 1980, 1990, 2000, 2010, and 2018, respectively. And that for Blacks with a bachelor's degree/four years of college education was 3.96 percent in 1980, 6.58 percent in 1990, 8.22 percent in 2000, 10.64 in 2010, and 15.61 percent in 2018, respectively. The percentages for Native Americans/Alaska Natives were 3.07, 4.76, 5.89, 7.32 and 10.19 in 1980, 1990, 2000, 2010, and 2018, respectively. For Hispanics, the reported percentages are 4.04, 6.6, 7.64, 11.35, and 16.78 for 1980, 1990, 2000, 2010, and 2018, respectively. By contrast, 13.83 percent, 21.91 percent, 26.6 percent, 29.47 percent, and 33.55 percent of Asians reported earning a bachelor's degree/four years of college education in 1980, 1990, 2000, 2010, and 2018.

Chapter 3

Immigration and the U.S. Experience

Theoretical Foundations

As noted in the introductory chapter of this book (chapter 1), nativity (i.e., native versus foreign-born/immigrant) comes to the forefront of immigration theory and research when the key question is how immigrants compare with their native counterparts in terms of socioeconomic attainment,[1] or how well particular immigrant groups are doing/being incorporated into U.S. society.[2] The residual effect of group membership (once relevant human capital variables are controlled) has generally been attributed to one of three phenomena: premigration cultural legacies of countries of origin, the selectivity of migration, or differential treatment in the host country (hereafter, demand-side/discrimination). As discussed in the three sections to immediately follow, each of these explanations has some relevance in understanding the immigration experiences of African immigrants in the United States.

THE CULTURAL ARGUMENT

Proponents of the cultural perspective pose that immigrating groups differ markedly in their value-orientations. Some cultures nurture individualism, industriousness, commercialism, and the like, while others foster collectivism, familism, and so forth. These differing cultural value-orientations are said to manifest themselves into differing attitudes toward family, education, work, and relocation itself (Greeley 1976; Sowell 1994).

Thus, differing premigration cultural value-orientations among groups as such are proposed to be crucial determinants of postmigration group outcomes. In a capitalist, competitive-based economy like the United States, individuals from groups with premigration cultural values that emphasize commercially useful traits, the argument goes, succeed more than those that do not. Hence, group postmigration outcomes are said to be attributable to premigration cultural legacies.

Early proponents of this perspective, comparing Black immigrants in the United States and their native-born counterparts, for example, have used the "cultural superiority" or "cultural inferiority" hypothesis to explain differences in socioeconomic attainment (Glazer and Moynihan 1963; Sowell 1975, 1978, 1981, 1983). And, until very recently, researchers defined Black immigrants as one homogeneous group (Chiswick 1979; Dodoo 1991a-c), mainly focused on Caribbean immigrants (Butcher 1994; Kalmijn 1996; Model 1991, 1995, 2008, 2018; Ifatunji 2016, 2017, 2018), or examined small samples of highly skilled workers (Apraku 1991). Because immigrants from the Caribbean provided the largest flow of Black immigrants to the United States for much of the better part of the twentieth century (Reid 1939; Model 2008), the "immigrant cultural superiority" hypothesis was not, surprisingly, framed in the context of comparisons between Caribbean immigrants and native-born Blacks.

As Model (2008) recently noted, the immigrant cultural superiority hypothesis comes in two different versions, one primarily historical and the other contemporary. Accordingly, unexplained residual differences in socioeconomic attainment between Caribbean immigrants and native-born Blacks have been attributed to cultural factors, both historical and contemporary, which are said to favor immigrant success (Glazer and Moynihan 1963; Sowell 1978, 1981; Lewis 1983). The reverse is a purported "cultural inferiority" hypothesis, said to impede the attainment of native-born Blacks.

The Historical Perspective

In the mid-1970s and early 1980s, Thomas Sowell, an early proponent of the cultural perspective, published a series of essays (1975, 1978, 1981, 1983) in which he observed that Caribbean-born Blacks who migrated to the United States were much more successful in occupational attainment and in earnings than were native-born Blacks. He then went on to offer a culturally based interpretation that drew heavily on differences originating in differing systems of slavery. More specifically, Sowell (1975, 1978, 1981, 1983) attributed a Caribbean advantage in socioeconomic attainment to differences between the American and Caribbean systems of slavery, which he argued produced disparate value systems and divergent orientations and resulting life outcomes.

Two key variables are said to be historically determinative: the provision ground economy/system that is said to have characterized the Caribbean system of slavery and the racial demographic composition of the Caribbean, relative to the United States. Because of the monoculture of the islands and their large enslaved population, the former describes the policy of allowing for subsistence agriculture among the enslaved that left the production and marketing of food for both Blacks and Whites to the responsibility of Blacks, enslaved or free (Model 2008). The demographic argument simply rests upon the idea that Blacks in the Caribbean constituted a high proportion of the population of the Caribbean, such that many inevitably had to be granted a wider range of opportunities for occupational advancement.

According to Sowell, the enslaved in the Caribbean did not experience strong economic competition from a large White lower class as did their counterparts in the American South. Accordingly, enslaved Caribbeans had early socialization into a "spirit of capitalism" that allowed for a greater opportunity for economic initiative than the enslaved in the American South (1978, 46). By contrast, generations of dependency under the system of slavery in the United States "depressed initiative, so slaves developed foot-dragging, work-evading patterns that were to remain as a cultural legacy long after slavery itself had disappeared. Duplicity and theft were also pervasive patterns among antebellum slaves and these too remained long after slavery ended" (Sowell 1981, 187).

Importantly, Sowell went on to argue that "color alone, or racism alone, is [therefore] clearly not a sufficient explanation of the disparities within the black population or between the black and white populations" (1978, 41–48). He concluded: "The West Indian success pattern undermines the explanatory power of current white discrimination as a cause of current black poverty" (1978, 49).

As noted in chapter 1 of this book, shortly after these series of pronouncements, however, a growing literature began to develop that challenged Sowell's findings. Aggregate national statistics suggest that Caribbean-born Blacks tend to work more hours, hold more prestigious jobs, and earn more than native-born Blacks, but once controls are introduced for educational attainment and for local labor market conditions, the Caribbean advantage diminishes, often to the point of statistical insignificance (Model 1991, 1995, 2008; Butcher 1994; Kalmijn 1996; Model and Ladipo 1996).

More recently, Model (2008) has offered several substantive challenges to the historical perspective as such (also see James 2002). As she put it, a key problem with this interpretation is "its failure to specify the mechanisms through which values are transmitted over a 150-year period" (p. 51). According to Model: "While transmission is not impossible, Sowell's argument would be stronger if it identified the mechanisms of transmission or cited evidence for the ongoing utility of the behaviors central to his interpretation" (2008, 51). Yet, Model (2008) suggests that Sowell provided no such evidence. Moreover: "Even if their slave heritage transmitted a strong work ethic to many West Indians, in the post-emancipation period the structure of opportunity changed" (Model 2008, 51). Assuming that Sowell is correct in his own observation that: "Peonage virtually re-enslaved the black population of the West Indies, as in the southern United States [, during the post-emancipation period]" (1978, 47). Then, Model asks: "Would not these changes have affected Caribbean blacks' values?" (2008, 51). The conclusion being: "This logic leaves Sowell's readers wondering under what conditions people adopt new values and under what conditions they retain old ones" (2008, 51).

Moreover, according to Model, the underlying assumption of cultural homogeneity of the West Indies is equally problematic. That is to say, "social and economic conditions varied substantially across the Caribbean . . . In particular, provision grounds were not universally provided . . . Put simply: if some West Indian slaves had the opportunity to participate in a market economy, would not their descendants be more prosperous than the descendants of West Indian slaves who did not have this opportunity?" (2008, 51–52).

Instead, Model's work provides convincing evidence that any difference in attainment between native-born Blacks and Black immigrants is primarily due to selectivity of migration (see below). Hamilton's more recent analysis (2020) came to a similar conclusion.

The Contemporary Argument

The "all Black society" hypothesis (Domingo 1925; Ottley 1943; Reid 1939, 1969; Ueda 1980; Waters 1993, 1997, 1999; Vickerman 1999) rests exclusively on the racial demographic composition of the Caribbean, on one hand, and that of the United States, on the other. Domingo (1925, 347–48) provided an early statement: "Forming a racial majority in their own countries and not being accustomed to discrimination expressly felt as racial, they rebel against the 'color line' as they find it in America."

Specifically, the relative "success" of Caribbean immigrants in the U.S. labor market is attributed by proponents of this argument to an assumed greater achievement-orientation and work ethic ascribed to socialization in a favorable Caribbean cultural environment—one in which they were the racial majority and that consequently provided them access to high skill occupations with greater responsibilities. Compared to U.S. Blacks, the demographic argument predicts greater skills among Blacks in the West Indies because of their larger proportion in the skilled labor force. The result is a variety of hypothesized psychological benefits including greater perseverance and ambitiousness among Caribbeans (Domingo 1925; Glazer and Moynihan 1963; Osofsky 1963; Foner 1985).

In the case of Black Jamaicans, for example:

Their numerical preponderance has imparted a degree of self-confidence that has helped them to cope with persistent subjugation. Socialization in a society made up mainly of blacks has made having black role models seem normal. At the same time, there has always been an awareness that the various elites who have dominated the society have felt a certain nervousness at being surrounded by a large number of blacks. (Vickerman 1999, 40–41)

The argument being that there are strong psychological and related benefits associated with growing up a member of the dominant race in a predominantly Black society.

Whether or not Black African immigrants are likely to be advantaged or disadvantaged by their cultural attributes remains open for debate (see Dodoo 1997; Corra and Kimuna 2009; Corra and Borch 2014). Is the socioeconomic attainment of Black African immigrants in the United States enhanced by their cultural traditions? Or is it hindered by that tradition? The key reasons given for the cited success of Caribbean immigrants in the United States—being socialized in a society where they were the racial majority and one free of the legacies of a U.S. style slavery—suggest that African immigrants should be as likely as Caribbean immigrants to succeed in the U.S. labor market. Yet, a countercultural proposition emphasizes differences between African cultures and Western culture and holds that such differences make the transition to the United States or Europe more difficult for African immigrants (than, say, the descendants of ex-slaves from the Caribbean, whose ancestors were stripped of their African heritage and forced to accept Western languages and religion) (Corra and Kimuna 2009). Following this proposition, African immigrants in the United States should be disadvantaged rather than advantaged by their cultural traditions.

Yet another cultural proposition can be drawn from the distinction of African countries into those that were "settler colonies" and those that were "non-settler colonies" (Corra and Kimuna 2009). In some African countries (e.g., Kenya, Zimbabwe, South Africa), the colonial power dispatched settlers who established farms/plantations. By contrast, in (most) other African countries, the colonial power concentrated on extracting resources (mines, mostly). The expectation would be that cultural exchange was greater when settlers were present than when they were not. Hence, African emigrants from "settler colonies" might have a cultural advantage in the English-speaking world over emigrants from "non-settler colonies."[3]

Finally, as indicated in chapter 1 of this book, many recent immigrants from Africa are from Arab and/or Muslim-majority countries. And, as Hamilton (2020) recently observed, new arrivals from countries like Ethiopia, Somalia, and Sudan have religious practices and customs that markedly differ from those of the United States. Such customs and practices could open them for intense threefold discrimination: as Muslims, as Blacks, and as immigrants (Hamilton 2020).

Summary

Historical or contemporary, scholars argue that recent evidence provides little or no support for the cultural argument, at least when it comes to comparisons between native-born and Black immigrants (Model 2008; Hamilton 2019, 2020). Being one of the most comprehensive analyses to date on this topic, Model's 2008 work explicitly tested hypotheses drawn from the cultural perspective and found no support (see specifically chapter 5 of that book). Instead, Model found the selectivity of migration to be a key explanatory variable (see chapter 4 of her book, as well as her 2018 commentary).

Hamilton's more recent analysis points to several shortcomings, including the failure to explicitly take account of the historical context (pre–Civil Rights vs. post–Civil Rights) of African immigration to the United States, and selectivity and social class differences between immigrants and natives. With respect to the historical context, for example, Hamilton notes that:

> The black immigrants who are the focus of much of the extant literature on the social incorporation of black immigrants, those who arrived in the United States after 1965, experienced a profoundly different context than their predecessors. The Immigration and Nationality Act of 1965 signaled a less xenophobic stance toward immigrants from non-Western nations, and at the same time the civil rights movement was creating a less overtly discriminatory context for minorities in the United States. Although improving economic conditions for black Americans was the primary motivation of the civil rights movement, generations of immigrants of many hues also benefited from the Civil Rights Act of 1964, which outlawed discrimination based on race, color, religion, sex, or national origin and ended racial segregation in schools, workplaces, and the public sphere.

Indeed, Hamilton (2020) notes that all Blacks living in the United States during the pre–Civil Rights era faced virtually the same amount of extreme degrees of racial hostility. His analyses of the two time periods (pre– and post–Civil Rights movement) demonstrates that any socioeconomic differences between Black immigrants and African Americans emerged post–Civil Rights era, suggesting differential exposures to a legacy of institutional racism as a key variable.

An additional cultural hypothesis related to African immigrants is differences between those from countries that were "settler colonies" and those that were "non-settler colonies" (Corra and Kimuna 2009). Following this hypothesis, immigrants from countries like South Africa and Kenya, for example, would be predicted to be advantaged in the U.S. labor market. By contrast, those from other parts of Sub-Saharan Africa would be predicted to be disadvantaged. Finally, differences in religious practices and customs common among some recent immigrants from Africa might be disadvantageous.

SELECTIVITY OF MIGRATION

Proponents of "migration selectivity" argue that persons who migrate have markedly different qualities from those who do not. Migrants (especially economic ones) were initially assumed to be more ambitious, diligent, and motivated than their non-migrant counterparts. Hence, if traits are evenly distributed, then, on the average, persons who migrate should exhibit more positive traits than those in the country of origin and the country of destination.

More specifically, "migration selectivity" is the proposition that migrants (especially economic ones) generally constitute a highly selective group, with positively valued traits (i.e., qualifications, skills, and motivation) that make them highly marketable in a competitive labor market. In turn, these favorable traits are said to translate (after a period of adjustment) into postmigration success.

It follows that when the question is how immigrants compare with their native counterparts in terms of socioeconomic attainment, the general hypothesis is positive selectivity for immigrants, attributed to a human capital advantage said to be traceable to "migration selectivity" (Chiswick 1979; Butcher 1994). Here, the assumption is that immigrants are not from a sample of randomly selected individuals from their countries of origins. Rather, they are a highly selected group that systematically differ in some way from the larger population from which they emigrated.

It also follows that a key variable of selectivity is said to be the motive for immigration. At least since Everett Lee's "A Theory of Migration" (1966), researchers have hypothesized that "politically motivated emigrants" are less positively selected (pushed) than "economically motivated emigrants (pulled) (Borjas 1994; Chiswick 1978, 1999; Jasso and Rosenzweig 1990a and b; Tesfai 2019). According to Lee: "Migrants responding primarily to plus factors at destination tend to be positively selected. . . . Migrants responding primarily to minus factors at origin tend to be negatively selected" (1966, 56). Economic measures like the prospects of better occupational outcomes at the host country are plus factors; whereas emigration due to political repression is a minus factor. Hence, selection can be positive—the selected individuals are highly motivated, ambitious, and/or exhibit greater levels of education than the average individual at origin—or negative—the selected individuals possess less of these qualities. The economist Barry Chiswick (1978, 900–901) put it more succinctly: "Economic theory suggests that migration in response to economic incentives is generally more profitable for the more able and more highly motivated. This self-selection in migration implies that for the same schooling, age and other demographic characteristics immigrants to the United States have more innate ability or motivation relative to the labor market than native-born persons." Chiswick (1979) further estimates a "catching up" or "overtaking" point for immigrants at 10–15 years after immigration, with a key caveat being that this estimate is said to apply to those of similar ethnic or racial background to the immigrant.

Besides motive for migration, additional factors said to influence selectivity include "generation" and "migration costs" or "intervening obstacles." With respect to generation, for example, some scholars have hypothesized transferability of positive selectivity from the immigrant generation to subsequent generations (e.g., offspring of immigrants) (Carliner 1980; Neidert and Farley 1985), though how far the generational transfer extends remains to be fully established. And when it comes to migration itself, the higher the costs or the greater the obstacles to immigration, the more positively selected the migrant. According to Guillermina Jasso (2004, 262): "The greater the obstacles to migration, the higher the quality of the immigrant; pioneer immigrants are, thus, of higher quality than the relatives who follow."

It also follows that "early birds" are said to be more positively selected than latecomers (Model 2008). This is so because: "The overcoming of a set of intervening obstacles by early migrants lessens the difficulty of the passage for later migrants" (Lee 1966, 55). Thus, early migrants are said to be more selective than latecomers.

Scholars also make an additional distinction: between primary and secondary or "tied" movers. A good example of a primary mover is someone who migrates voluntarily with the expectation of enhancing economic gains. Whereas a secondary mover is one that relocates because of being related to a primary mover (e.g., as a husband or wife). Here, positive selectivity is said to apply more to the former than the latter.

And, as noted above, among Blacks in the United States, much of early research focused on comparisons between Caribbean immigrants and native-born Blacks (Domingo 1925; Harrison 1992; Butcher 1994; Waters 1994a). According to an early observer:

"The foreign-born black men and women, more so even than other groups of immigrants, are the hardiest and most venturesome of their folk. They were dissatisfied at home and it is to be expected that they would not be altogether satisfied with limitation of opportunity here when they have staked so much to gain enlargement of opportunity" (Domingo 1925, 347).

Both Harrison's (1992) and Waters's (1994a) early statistical analyses, for example, show a relative advantage in attainment for Caribbean immigrants (as compared with African-Americans), a finding they attribute to migration selectivity.[4] Several subsequent quantitative assessments of the relative performance of first-generation, English-speaking Caribbean immigrants and African Americans point to selectivity as an important explanatory factor (Model 1991, 1995, 2008; Butcher 1994; Kalmijn 1996; Hamilton 2019, 2020).[5]

African Immigrants

With respect to selectivity, relatively few studies have examined the migration experience of African immigrants in the United States (for notable exceptions, see Butcher 1994; Model and Ladipo 1996; Dodoo 1997; Dodoo and Takyi 2002; Model 2008, 2018; Corra and Kimuna 2009; Borch and Corra 2010; Hamilton 2019, 2020). Because migration theory links selectivity to the duration and costs of migration, a testable hypothesis is that African immigrants in the United States are an even more positively selective group than, say, Caribbean immigrants. Furthermore, U.S. Census data show Africans as one of the most, if not the most, highly educated of all immigrant groups in the United States (Butcher 1994; Logan and Deane 2003; Anderson and Connor 2018). It follows that, because of the professed centrality of education as an indicator of potential achievement and economic mobility in contemporary U.S. society, African immigrants should arguably occupy an advantaged position in the American labor market (Dodoo 1997).

Yet, early data reported by Butcher (1994) indicated an African immigrant disadvantage, a finding she attributed to the fact that "many of the African immigrants are in the United States to attend graduate school" (1994, 268). Yet Dodoo's (1997) objection is that Butcher's (1994) "employed only" comparisons also show a disadvantage for African immigrants, a finding that he argues is inconsistent with that conclusion.

In a comparison of occupational statuses among minority and majority group members in London and New York, Model and Ladipo (1996) show that, compared to African Americans and Caribbean immigrants, a sizeable part of the occupational status disadvantage of Africans in New York is attributable to discrimination. They then suggest an analysis of earnings as the "ultimate determinant of living standards" (Model and Ladipo 1996, 506).

Analyses of earnings by Dodoo (1997) and Corra and Kimuna (2009), however, found an African male and female immigrant disadvantage, respectively, relative to Caribbean immigrants. Comparing male and female African Americans and Black immigrants from Africa and the Caribbean, Corra and Borch's more recent cross-sectional and temporal analyses (2014), however, found "a sizeable earnings advantage for immigrants" (p. 103). Controlling for a host of human capital variables, however, "reduced the gap between the earnings of African immigrants and native-born blacks, although the difference still remained statistically significant" (Corra and Borch 2014, 103). Notably, Corra and Borch found no such attenuation for immigrants from the Caribbean.

A Counterproposition to Positive Selectivity for African Immigrants

A more recent counter proposition to positive selectivity for African immigrants is that recent immigrant flows from developing countries to the United States, relative to earlier ones, are less selective (Borjas 1985). Hence, such immigrants are said to have a reduced chance of success in the U.S. labor market. Proponents of this argument (negative selectivity for recent immigrants) point to the 1965 "family reunification and refugee" act, the U.S. immigration law that encouraged family and refugee-based migrations, as the impetus to such "low-quality" immigrant flows (Borjas 1985). Borjas, for example, points to the lower "duration of stay effects" of more recent immigrant groups as an indicator of waning immigrant quality. Others, however, argue that, once relevant measures are controlled, the duration of stay variable can be a good indicator of assimilation.

More specifically, the works of Roy (1951) and Borjas (1987) suggest negative selectivity for African immigrants due to Africa's economic stagnation, relative high unemployment, and inequality (presumably the economically unsuccessful being those forced to migrate). Borjas (1988), for example, links immigrant quality to differences in the level of income inequality in host as compared to country of origin. According to Borjas, immigrants will come from the less industrious when income inequality is greater at origin than destination and come from the more industrious when income inequality is lower at origin than destination.

In a series of analyses, Borjas (1985, 1987, 1991, 1994, 1995) reported finding waning immigrant quality among recent immigrants. He attributed this to changes in the mix of sending countries. Because immigrants from countries with high income inequality make up an increasing proportion of recent immigrants to the United States, a greater proportion are said to be negatively selected.

The series of analyses that Borjas reported (1985, 1987, 1991, 1994, 1995) also suggested that immigrants from Europe and Canada to the United States did not experience any declines in immigrant quality. This led him to the conclusion that Europeans and Canadians were positively selected; whereas immigrants from much of the world were negatively selected. He then predicted that, after a decade or so in the United States, the earnings of immigrants from Europe and Canada would overtake those of their native White counterparts, while the earnings of immigrants from the rest of the world would never surpass those of their native counterparts.

Taken together, Borjas's work suggests negative selectivity for African immigrants to the United States. Because income inequality is greater in Africa than in the United States, the prediction is that African immigrants are negatively selected. Moreover, his work more generally suggests that most non-White migrants are negatively selected, in our case, Black African immigrants.

Dodoo (1997), however, argues that, while the very adverse economic conditions noted are the "push" factors of massive African emigration, they have led to a phenomenon widely known as the "brain drain"—the outflow of large numbers of highly skilled, achievement-oriented Africans from Africa to the developed world. Hence, rather than negative selectivity, Dodoo argues, such economic stagnation should lead to positive African immigrant selectivity.

INTERSECTIONALITY

Lopez's (2003) analysis extends this work by closely examining the "raced" and "gendered" processes of immigrant adaptation. Her work suggests that race and gender are important dimensions to a fuller understanding of immigrant adaptation (also see Borch and Corra 2010, and, more recently, Elo et al. 2015). Gender differences in socioeconomic attainment among immigrants, for example, have been attributed to a purported greater selectivity among immigrant men. Chiswick (1977), for example, uses this line of reasoning to explain the slightly greater earnings advantage of sons whose only foreign-born parent was a father as compared to those whose only foreign-born parent was a mother. Accordingly, a testable hypothesis is that male African immigrants will exhibit greater levels of socioeconomic measures than their female counterparts.

And, as noted in chapter 1 of this book, specific questions relate to differences in entry status. Are African immigrants more or less likely than other immigrant groups to be admitted as political or family-based immigrants? Alternatively, are African immigrants more or less likely than other immigrant groups to be admitted based on employment and skills-based preferences? What about African immigrants themselves, are some groups more or less likely to be admitted into the United States based on one entry status or the other? What socioeconomic inferences can be drawn from these?

For example, if, as suggested by some previous studies, that a higher proportion of some groups of African immigrants have political rather than economic motives to relocate (Gordon 1998), then a testable hypothesis is that such immigrants will be less selective than their economically motivated counterparts. More specifically, the type of visa an immigrant holds is hypothesized to influence immigrant incorporation (Jasso 2004; Jasso, Rosenzweig and Smith 2000).

Summary

To summarize, a general proposition from selectivity theory is positive selectivity for immigrants that is attributed to a human capital advantage said to be traceable to migration selectivity (Chiswick 1979; Butcher 1994). Yet, the extent to which immigrants are positively selected is said to depend on a variety of variables, including motives for the move and obstacles associated with it. For African immigrants to the United States, distance, duration, and added costs of migration suggest positive selectivity. Moreover, voluntary immigration from Africa being a relatively recent phenomenon also suggests positive selectivity for African immigrants. Accordingly, the more recent immigration of Africans suggests that they are likely to be "primary" as opposed to "secondary" movers. And since early birds are predicted to be more selective than latecomers, a testable hypothesis is that African immigrants are a highly selective group.

Other propositions, by contrast, suggest negative selectivity for African immigrants. Given the fact that income inequality is greater in many African countries than in the United States, for example, one proposition is that African immigrants from such countries are negatively selected. Moreover, the high levels of political instability in Africa suggest negative selectivity for African immigrants, or at least some groups of African immigrants. Finally, since African immigrants themselves are differentiated by a variety of qualities including differences in entry status, selectivity predictions are expected to vary by those attributes.

DEMAND-SIDE ARGUMENTS

Demand-side arguments attribute group differences in attainment to differential treatment (discrimination) in the host country. Some groups are more desirable (or perhaps just more welcome) to members of the host country and others are not. Hence, it is the differential treatment of members of groups as such that is said to determine group outcomes. And the now well-known "residual method" of measuring discrimination (Smith 2003) is said to be differentials that persist after productivity-related attributes are taken into account (Becker 1971).

Queuing theory, for example, conceives the labor market as an imaginary line of potential workers, arranged in such a way that members of the most desirable group are at the beginning of the queue and members of the least desirable are at the end (Hodge 1973; Lieberson 1980). Desirability may be a function of several social attributes, including race, nativity, and national origin. Gender is not a factor in the queue because men and women are assumed to occupy separate queues. "Queuing, or the relative position a group holds in the eyes of employers, comes to the fore when otherwise similar workers compete for the same reward. Employers are expected to give first preference to members of the group they esteem the most, moving down the queue as the supply of more favored groups dwindles . . . In a single labor market at a single moment in time, queuing is simply a way of describing the amount of discrimination or favoritism particular groups encounter" (Model 1997, 540).

Model and Ladipo (1996), for example, use Queuing Theory to explain differences in attainment between African Americans and Puerto Ricans, on one hand, and non-White immigrants, on the other. They argue that the presence of large numbers of African Americans and Puerto Ricans in the New York labor market allows for the relegation of those two minority groups to the bottom of the employment queue and the upgrading of non-White immigrants above them.

Specifically, the so-called "White favoritism hypothesis" is said to rest on three key variables (Model 2008). First, relations between Whites and immigrants are said to be characterized by a "comfort factor" argued to promote amicable interactions between them. Such amicable relations are said to lead to favorable impressions of the immigrants. And one key variable is said to be the immense optimism that immigrants have about their prospects for success in the United States—after all, this is the point of immigration. From the perspective of Black immigrants, it is the believe that "opportunities exist in the U.S. and that their own black skin has not, and will not, prevent them from taking advantage of those opportunities. It is this belief that while racism might exist, it can surely be overcome with determination and hard work that propelled the immigrants to move from a majority black society to the U.S. in the first place" (Waters 1997, 19). Here again, the two culprits are said to be the positive selectivity of migration and socialization in a favorable Caribbean cultural environment—one in which they were the racial majority (Model 2008).

By contrast, the legacy of racism and the persistence of racial discrimination in the lives of native-born Blacks is said to inevitably be a cause for greater pessimism and the belief that racism and racial discrimination cannot be overcome with determination and hard work. The result is proposed to be native-born Black–White interactions that are said to be fraught with reservation and mistrust.

A second variable said to promote White favoritism for immigrants is what has been termed "Anglophilia." This concept refers to U.S. cultural legacies of associating positive evaluations with individuals and practices associated with Great Britain. Thus, immigrants from the English-speaking Caribbean, for example, are said to garner favorable impressions among American Whites (Arnold 1984).

A third variable said to influence White favoritism of immigrants is the "coloniality of power" (Grosfoguel 2003, 2004; Grosfoguel and Georas 2000). This perspective distinguishes groups into "colonial/racialized subjects," "colonial immigrants," and immigrants with neither legacy. The first are members of groups that are said to have been "colonized" and incorporated into a society. In the United States, these are said to include African Americans, Puerto Ricans, Native Americans, and other "oppressed groups that have been incorporated into the U.S. empire" (Grosfoguel 2003, 148). Colonial immigrants are those from regions with colonial powers other than the ones they have settled, but who are nevertheless disadvantaged by the subordinate political and economic positions associated with the colonial legacy of their regions of origins. According to Model (2008), British West Indians, for example, "are 'colonial immigrants' if they settle in the United States, but 'colonial/racialized subjects' if they settle in Britain" (p. 66). Colonial/racialized subjects and colonial immigrants' contrast with immigrants, who come from places with neither of the two legacies. Accordingly, colonial/racialized subjects are said to face the most barriers to full incorporation into the host society, followed by colonial immigrants. Immigrants with neither legacy are expected to experience the least barriers to full incorporation.

From the discrimination/demand-side perspective, then, the "Caribbean immigrant success" in the U.S. labor market is assumed to be due to a purported perception that Whites and employers view immigrants as persons with "good" work ethics (Foner 1985; Hossfeld 1994; Waters 1994a). For example, evidence revealed in Waters's (1994b) study suggest that immigrants find ways, other than their accents, to communicate their foreign heritage to employers because of this perceived employer preference of immigrant workers (also see Foner 1985; Kasinitz 1992).

An important question that is yet to be fully addressed is whether Africans also benefit from this purported favorable impression of immigrants. Like their native-born counterparts, there is some evidence that Black African immigrants face substantial discrimination in the U.S. labor market (Scroggins 1989; Takougang 1995; Apraku 1996; Kposowa 2002). Over half a century ago, Du Bois (1962) observed that the primary bases of prejudice toward Africans are degrading assumptions and stereotypes held by people of European descent. Some recent scholars also argue that the ubiquity of negative portrayals of Africa in academic, political, media, and other such entities may also serve to undermine the valuation of Africans in the United States (Hawk 1992; Zaffiro 1992; Mpanya 1995). While the extent of such discrimination, if any, is yet to be known, "it is not inconceivable that Africans may be received differently, and perhaps less favorably, than both Caribbean and American blacks" (Dodoo 1997, 530).

SUMMARY

To summarize, a general conclusion from the foregoing is "White favoritism" of immigrants that implies labor market success. Yet, the extent to which immigrants are fully incorporated is said to be influenced by several factors, including whether they are associated with "colonial/racialized subjects," "colonial immigrants," or immigrants with neither legacy. Like their West Indian counterparts, African immigrants to the United States are arguably colonial immigrants. Thus, their status in the United States is predicted to be intermediary—between groups considered "colonial/racialized subjects" (e.g., native-born Blacks, Puerto Ricans, and Native Americans) and immigrants with neither legacy.

Yet, as noted above, whether Africans also benefit from a purported favorable impression of immigrants remains to be fully demonstrated. As noted elsewhere in this book (see chapter 1), recent approaches to the study of migration emphasize the "context of reception" to the host society and the modes of incorporation of different groups into its labor market (Portes and Böröcz 1989; Portes and Rumbaut 2001, 2006). Like their native-born counterparts, some evidence suggests that Black African immigrants face substantial discrimination in the U.S. labor market (Scroggins 1989; Takougang 1995; Apraku 1996; Kposowa 2002). Moreover, the idea of "Anglophilia" suggests variation of favorability among African immigrant groups based on colonial and linguistic heritage. African immigrants from English-speaking countries who were former colonies of Great Britain (e.g., South Africa, Kenya, Nigeria, and Ghana), for example, might arguably garner more favorable impressions than those from countries without such legacies (e.g., Senegal and Togo).

Finally, much recent arrivals from Africa are from majority Muslim and/or Arabic speaking countries. Intersectionality theory (see chapter 1) suggests that immigrants from such countries might be open to intense threefold discrimination: as Muslims, as Blacks, and as immigrants (Hamilton 2020). In a similar manner, immigrant status, gender, and linguistic heritage (e.g., Arab origins/non-Arab origins) may combine in unique ways that differentially influence attainment among African immigrants. It is not inconceivable, for example, that some African females are encumbered by immigrant status, gender, and linguistic heritage interacting to place them at the bottom of the American stratification hierarchy. Alternatively, it may be the case that such interactions negatively affect African American women more than female African immigrants.

In short, there is scholarship suggesting that Black Africans face discrimination in the U.S. labor market relative to Whites. However, some scholars would also predict that Black Africans face less discrimination than native-born Blacks. Cited reasons include "Anglophilia," the "comfort factor," and the "coloniality of power."

OUTLINE OF THE REMAINING CHAPTERS OF THE BOOK

The next three chapters provide empirical examinations of several of the questions raised in this and the two previous chapters. The chapter to immediately follow (chapter 4) begins these explorations by providing an African immigrant intra-group comparison. What key qualities differentiate African immigrants from one another? What do these attributes suggest about disparities in socioeconomic attainment among African immigrants? Chapter 5 follows this up with comparisons between African immigrants and other immigrant groups. How do African immigrants compare in socioeconomic attainment with other immigrant groups? What variables influence differences in attainment, if any, between African and other immigrant groups? The final empirical chapter of the book (chapter 6) examines differences between African immigrants and the various U.S. native groups. How do African immigrants compare in socioeconomic status with native-born Americans? In chapter 7, I conclude the book with a synopsis of key findings and conclusions that can be drawn from them.

NOTES

1. See, for example, Glazer and Moynihan 1963; Sowell 1978, 1981; Chiswick 1979; Lewis 1983; Foner 1985; Butcher 1994; Hossfeld 1994; Waters 1994a and b, 1997, 1999; Dodoo 1997; Portes and Rumbaut 2001, 2006; Corra and Kimuna 2009; Corra and Borch 2014; Hamilton 2019, 2020.

2. See, for example, Portes and Rumbaut 2001, 2006; Borch and Corra 2010; Thomas 2014; Kusow, Kimuna and Borch 2018; Hamilton 2019, 2020.

3. Here, I note a possibly contrasting hypothesis that Professor Model, in a personal communication, brought to my attention. She observed that settler colonies could have possibly meant more communication between colonizer and colonized, but possibly not. For this argument, Professor Model brought to my attention the article, "Racial Intermarriage in the Americas," co-authored by Edward Telles and Albert

Esteve, and recently published in *Sociological Science* (2019, 6, 293–230). In this article, these two authors hypothesize that partnerships between colonizer and colonized were more common in "extraction colonies" like Cuba and Brazil than "settler colonies" like the United States because few White women traveled to "extraction colonies." The argument then, is that even if these mixed-race partnerships were short-term, extraction colonies became more tolerant of intermarriage because a large mixed-race population resulted from the contact between colonizer and colonized.

4. Notably, one study (Kalmijn 1996) also reported generational differences in attainment between immigrant and second and later-generation Caribbean Blacks; with the later generations generally indicating higher socioeconomic status. Implicitly, this is said to mean, at least for second and later generation British Caribbeans, further gains on African Americans as compared to those gains for the immigrant's generation.

5. One study (Butcher 1994) uncovered an unexpected but interesting and important finding that is worth noting: remarkable similarity between native-born Black "movers" (men who had moved out of their state of birth to another) and Black Jamaican and other Caribbean immigrant men "on a variety of employment and wage measures" (p. 265; also see Model 2008). This finding suggests positive selectivity for both immigrants and native-born "movers," suggesting migration to be the key variable, and not nativity.

Chapter 4

An Intra-Group Comparison of African Immigrants in the United States

Gendered Variations?

The introductory chapters of this book (chapters 1 and 2) noted that recent increases in the flow of African immigrants to the United States are accompanied with a growing diversity among this group. And, as also noted in those chapters, a key goal of this book is to provide a detailed sociodemographic/ socioeconomic portrait of these "new African Americans" (Millman 1997, 172) or "new Americans" (Barone 2001). What key qualities differentiate these immigrants from one another? And what do these differences suggest about prospects of their incorporation into U.S. society? This chapter focuses on examining these and related issues.

As noted in chapter 3 of this book, theory and research suggest that the type of U.S. visa immigrants hold impacts their incorporation into U.S. society (Jasso 2004; Jasso, Rosenzweig and Smith 2000). I begin the discussion of this chapter with this issue, and Table 4.1 provides data that offers initial insights as it pertains to African immigrants. That table displays African immigrants that obtained "legal" status by countries of birth for the years 1996,1998–2019, as reported by the U.S. Department of Homeland Security, *Yearbook of Immigration Statistics*.[1] Data is given on each of fourteen African countries, those countries taken together, and the continent of Africa as a whole. As the reader would notice, most of these are listed previously in Table 2.1 as top sending countries from Africa to the United States. They are included in the list here because each was a top ten sending country for at least one of the years in the *Yearbook of Immigration Statistics* examined in Table 4.1 (1996,1998–2019).

Table 4.1 African Immigrants by Entry Status and Selected Sample of Countries of Birth, 1996, 1998–2019.

Country	Total	Family-Sponsored Preferences (Percent)	Employment-Based Preferences (Percent)	Immediate Relatives of U.S. Citizens (Percent)	Refugees and Asylees (Percent)	Diversity (Percent)	Total
Nigeria	264,130	16.89	12.71	48.26	1.85	20.28	100
Ethiopia	243,131	10.86	4.37	30.62	27.19	26.96	100
Egypt	184,181	13.30	10.22	29.68	14.38	32.42	100
Ghana	159,346	16.49	9.42	50.39	1.71	21.99	100
Kenya	126,117	8.87	9.56	32.06	24.88	24.64	100
Somalia	124,087	2.82	0.80	8.75	85.63	2.00	100
Morocco	90,039	9.98	7.06	45.37	0.33	37.25	100
Liberia	85,235	10.32	4.43	22.40	42.25	20.60	100
Cameroon	65,157	10.69	7.18	24.77	23.72	33.63	100
Congo, Democratic Republic	61,172	3.57	2.75	5.78	55.79	32.11	100
South Africa	67,636	6.82	41.89	38.60	3.41	9.28	100
Sudan	65,231	3.96	2.39	13.96	53.03	26.65	100
Sierra Leone	43,478	11.91	6.18	33.47	27.36	21.08	100
Tanzania	25,291	8.49	9.41	28.62	46.97	6.51	100
Total	1,604,231	11.09	8.88	32.71	23.96	23.35	100

Source: U.S. Department of Homeland Security, *Yearbook of Immigration Statistics*, 1996, 1998–2019.

The table gives totals on five main admission categories, as classified by the U.S. Immigration and Nationality Act: "Family-sponsored preferences," "Employment-based preferences," "Immediate relatives of U.S. citizens," "Refugees and asylees," and "Diversity." Recalling from chapter 2 of this manuscript that the U.S. Immigration and Nationality Act provides several broad classes of admission for foreign nationals to gain legal permanent residency (LPR) status in the United States. Those classified as immediate relatives of U.S. citizens include spouses, children, and parents of U.S. citizens age 21 and older. Those admitted based on family-based preferences include relatives/family members not included in the immediate relatives class of admission (e.g., married or unmarried adult sons/daughters of U.S. citizens, brothers/sisters of such citizens, etc.). Specific subcategories in the family-based preferences include "Family First Preference" (unmarried sons/daughters, over the age of 21, of U.S. citizens), "Family Second Preference" (spouses and unmarried children of permanent residents), "Family Third Preference" (married sons/daughters of U.S. citizens), and "Family Fourth Preference" (brothers and sisters of U.S. citizens). Admissions based on employment are given to those seeking to provide needed skills in the U.S. workforce or invest in new U.S. jobs, along with their dependents. Refuge is granted to two sets of immigrants who have been persecuted or have a "well-founded" fear of persecution, refugees and asylees. Refugees are those admitted outside the United States with their immediate relatives, while asylum is given to those seeking refuge, but are already inside the United States, and their immediate relatives. Finally, those gaining LPR based on the Diversity program come from countries with relatively low levels of immigration to the United States. As noted previously in chapter 2 of this book, the Immigration Act of 1990 introduced a Diversity Visa Lottery Program designed to increase the number of immigrants from countries underrepresented in the United States (for a fuller description of these classifications, see descriptions at the DHS site: https://www.dhs.gov/immigration-statistics/lawful-permanent-residents/ImmigrantCOA).

NOTABLE VARIATIONS IN LEGAL ADMISSION STATUS

As can be seen in Table 4.1, African immigrants do indeed exhibit notable variations in legal admission status. In the years 1996,1998–2019, collectively, about 33 percent of admissions from the fourteen countries listed in Table 4.1 were granted based on Immediate Relatives of U.S. Citizens, the same percentage for the entire continent; and the highest percentage for many countries is in this category as well. Moreover, within the Immediate

Relatives of U.S. Citizens category, there is a notable spread in percentages, ranging from about 6 percent of admissions for the Democratic Republic of Congo (DRC) to about 50 percent for Ghana. As discussed in chapter 1, countries like Ghana have been top sending nations of immigrants to the United States for a much longer period than countries like the DRC. Thus, the spread in percentages under the Immediate Relatives of U.S. Citizens category noted here is likely to be reflective of duration of presence in the United States, at least in large numbers.

As also illustrated in Table 4.1, the Refugees and Asylees admission category has one of the greatest spreads in percentage. Whereas less than 1 percent of immigrants from Morocco, and about 2 percent from Nigeria and Ghana, were granted legal status as refugees and asylees, well over 80 percent of immigrants from Somalia and well over 50 percent from the Democratic Republic of Congo and Sudan were granted legal status under this category. This contrasts with only about 24 percent of immigrants from the top fourteen countries, as well as from the continent as a whole, that were granted legal status under the refugee and asylee category.

Focusing on the largely skill-based categories of employment and diversity, we see that the highest admissions are in the latter. Except for three countries—Somalia (about 2%), Tanzania (about 7%), and South Africa (about 9%), immigrants from all countries show percentages in the diversity admission category that are higher than 20 percent. And countries like Egypt, Morocco, Cameroon, and the Democratic Republic of Congo show percentages that are greater than 30 percent (about 32%, 37%, 34%, and 32%, for these four countries, respectively). The average for the fourteen countries and the entire continent is notably around 22 percent. For most countries, admissions under the employment-based preference category are in the single digits, ranging from less than 1 percent for Somalia to about 12 percent for Nigeria. Notably, over forty percent of immigrants from South Africa (about 42%) were granted legal status under employment-based preferences. About 8 and 7 percent of immigrants from the fourteen countries and from the entire continent of Africa, respectively, were granted legal status under this admission category.

Taken together, the data presented in Table 4.1 reveal significant variations in legal admission status for African immigrants. Notable among these are that well over 80 percent of immigrants from Somalia were granted legal status under the Refugee and Asylee category, more than 50 percent of immigrants from the Democratic Republic of Congo and Sudan, and about 47 percent of immigrants from Tanzania acquired legal status under this entry category. By contrast, more than 40 percent of immigrants from South Africa acquired legal status under employment-based preferences; whereas all other countries, except for Nigeria, Egypt, and Kenya, show percentages in the single digits as employment-based preference admittees. Finally, immigrants from many African countries were admitted under the diversity category (over 20% for most countries, and well over 30% for several).

The foregoing patterns, then, are suggestive of several questions worth noting here. Exactly what might we make of the averages discussed above? Do they suggest anything about varying socioeconomic profiles among African immigrants in the United States? How about the diversity and trajectories of such profiles? The section to immediately follow gives an initial assessment of some of these and related questions.

DIVERSITY IN SOCIOECONOMIC PROFILE

Table 4.2 reports a comparison of various African immigrant groupings on four socioeconomic measures: rates of unemployment, self-employment, average occupational prestige,[2] and calculated mean annual earnings. Moreover, as indicated in the introductory chapters of this book (chapters 1–3), current stratification literature suggests several key variables that can influence how immigrants do in contemporary U.S. society, including race, gender, and linguistic heritage (e.g., English vs. Arab).[3] It follows that Table 4.2 also displays socioeconomic information on these variables, as well as on immigrants from the different regions of Africa and the entire continent taken together.

Table 4.2 African Immigrants in the United States: A Comparison of Immigrants on Four Economic Indicators by Year, 1980, 1990, 2000, 2010, and 2019.

1980

Region of Origins	% Unemployed	% Self-Employed	Occupational Prestige[a]	Annual Earnings[b]	N
Central	3.39	3.39	29.51	$31,491.90	118
East	4.28	8.45	36.03	$44,893.20	982
North	4.27	10.27	34.25	$52,946.00	2503
South	1.55	12.44	40.12	$65,729.90	579
West	6.24	4.09	31.27	$33,963.00	1539
Other[c]	5.88	4.95	29.67	$37,099.90	323
Race					
Black	6.03	3.72	31.42	$33,019.30	1989
White	3.66	10.58	34.94	$54,657.30	3497
Other[d]	5.20	9.14	37.37	$45,372.00	558
Sex					
Male	4.47	11.24	39.17	$55,166.10	3647
Female	4.76	3.55	26.15	$28,510.20	2397

Region of Origins	% Unemployed	% Self-Employed	Occupational Prestige[a]	Annual Earnings[b]	N
Linguistic Heritage					
Arab[e]	4.33	10.15	34.33	$53,232.50	2472
English[f]	5.00	6.84	35.42	$43,432.90	2441
Africa	4.58	8.19	34.00	$46,607.75	6044

1990

Region of Origin	% Unemployed	% Self-Employed	Occupational Prestige[a]	Annual Earnings[b]	N
Central	6.16	5.80	33.72	$42,453.90	276
East	4.10	10.73	15.65	$50,731.00	2413
North	4.64	13.04	36.42	$66,228.90	3580
South	1.64	17.70	42.21	$85,783.60	1096
West	6.41	6.35	35.28	$41,333.30	3199
Other[c]	5.42	8.41	31.50	$43,739.70	535
Race					
Black	6.02	6.10	33.89	$40,274.20	5164
White	3.87	14.49	37.85	$70,699.90	5016
Other[d]	3.16	15.45	38.68	$64,675.40	919
Sex					
Male	4.51	13.17	39.90	$64,473.70	6736
Female	5.27	6.81	30.17	$37,426.90	4363
Linguistic Heritage					
Arab[e]	4.68	13.07	36.45	$66,455.60	3565
English[f]	4.73	10.22	37.72	$54,152.7	5345
Africa	4.81	10.67	36.08	$55,433.61	11099

2000

Region of Origin	% Unemployed	% Self-Employed	Occupational Prestige[a]	Annual Earnings[b]	N
Central	4.45	7.91	31.93	$44,078.00	898
East	4.02	8.02	33.72	$54,654.10	5024
North	3.88	10.84	34.58	$68,127.10	5720
South	2.29	13.58	41.69	$96,691.70	2055
West	4.34	7.98	36.34	$52,128.00	8323
Other[c]	4.15	8.59	31.58	$49,907.20	4051
Race					
Black	4.55	7.06	33.96	$47,873.30	14723
White	2.92	12.68	38.33	$83,046.90	6879

Other[d]	3.78	10.58	33.16	$60,064.20	4469
Sex					
Male	3.72	11.93	38.17	$68,514.70	14683
Female	4.34	5.56	30.86	$43,376.90	11388
Linguistic Heritage					
Arab[e]	3.90	10.71	34.04	$65,621.20	6255
English[f]	3.68	9.14	37.91	$62,331.70	12694
Africa	3.99	9.15	34.98	$58,946.44	26071

2010

Region of Origin	% Unemployed	% Self-Employed	Occupational Prestige[a]	Annual Earnings[b]	N
Central	10.84	7.71	33.50	$44,616.20	415
East	8.67	9.06	32.84	$49,003.70	2308
North	8.23	12.57	32.59	$63,098.10	1726
South	3.37	19.22	43.30	$104,344.00	593
West	8.92	7.27	35.56	$49,624.30	3149
Other[c]	9.95	8.04	28.95	$42,847.70	784
Race					
Black	9.50	7.33	33.06	$45,358.90	6233
White	6.30	14.38	36.30	$79,041.60	2191
Other[d]	6.53	16.70	37.62	$69,904.00	551
Sex					
Male	8.61	12.65	37.06	$63,922.00	4776
Female	8.45	6.19	30.79	$42,179.50	4199
Linguistic Heritage					
Arab[e]	8.12	12.97	32.07	$60,957.60	1797
English[f]	8.13	8.82	38.23	$60,676.30	4295
Africa	8.53	9.63	34.13	$54,760.39	8975

2019

Region of Origin	% Unemployed	% Self-Employed	Occupational Prestige[a]	Annual Earnings[b]	N
Central	3.83	6.38	32.30	$46,162.70	941
East	3.74	8.65	35.09	$56,637.10	2890
North	3.29	9.78	34.79	$65,683.90	2189
South	2.13	12.53	42.24	$110,359.00	798
West	3.79	8.31	35.91	$55,717.10	4141
Other[c]	3.62	9.71	30.60	$54,870.60	525
Race					

Region of Origin	% Unemployed	% Self-Employed	Occupational Prestige[a]	Annual Earnings[b]	N
Black	3.87	8.16	34.26	$51,419.30	8148
White	2.60	10.83	37.71	$83,235.10	2771
Other[d]	3.89	9.56	40.36	$91,954.00	565
Sex					
Male	3.21	11.98	38.04	$70,161.20	5917
Female	3.93	5.57	32.57	$48,639.70	5567
Linguistic Heritage					
Arab[e]	3.46	9.91	34.31	$63,749.40	2402
English[f]	3.36	8.46	38.29	$66,990.60	5801
Africa	3.56	8.87	35.39	$60,681.40	11484

a. Socioeconomic Index, Hauser and Warren.

b. Limited to persons with calculated annual incomes of $500 or more, computed in constant 2019 dollars.

c. Includes immigrants from Africa whose region and/or country of birth is not identified, in IPUMS terminology, "Africa, ns."

d. A catchall category that includes individuals reporting various race combinations like two major races, three or more races, etc.

e. Includes immigrants from countries with Arab listed as an official language by the U.S. Central Intelligence Agency's *World FactBook* (https://www.cia.gov/the-world-factbook). They include Algeria, Chad, Comoros, Egypt, Eritrea, Libya, Mauritania, Morocco, Somalia, Sudan, Tunisia, and Western Sahara.

f. Includes immigrants from countries with English listed as an official language by the U.S. Central Intelligence Agency's *World FactBook* (https://www.cia.gov/the-world-factbook). They include Gambia, Ghana, Liberia, Nigeria, Sierra Leone, Kenya, Malawi, Mauritius, Tanzania, Uganda, Zambia, Zimbabwe, Cameroon, Botswana, Lesotho, Namibia, South Africa (Union of), and Swaziland.

Source: Author's calculations based on samples of the 1980, 1990, and 2000 Decennial U.S. Censuses and the 2010 and 2019 American Community Surveys (ACS), as represented in the Integrated Public Use Microdata Series (IPUMS) (Ruggles et al. 2020). Data limited to persons 25 to 64 years old, and who are not living in group quarters and/or institutions.

Notable Regional Variations

Yet again, data presented in Table 4.2 are illustrative of substantial variations in the socioeconomic profiles of African immigrants. First, as can be seen from that table, regional differences are evident. Immigrants from Southern Africa are shown to exhibit a particularly unique status. Such immigrants generally report lower unemployment rates, higher rates of self-employment and occupational prestige, and notably higher annual income than immigrants from any other region. The unemployment percentages for this group, for example, range between a low of about 2 percent in 1980 and 1990 to a high of about 3 percent in 2010. Similarly, self-employment for this group ranges from a low of about 12 percent in 1980 to a high of about 19 percent in 2010. The occupational prestige measures for immigrants from Southern Africa are equally impressive, ranging from a low of about forty in 1980 to a high of about forty-three in 2010. Especially notable for this group is its calculated annual income, which ranges from a low of $65,729 in 1980, to a high of about $110,359 in 2019.

Compare these figures with those for the next closest regional group, immigrants from North Africa. The unemployment percentages for this group range between a low of about 3 percent in 2019 to a high of about 8 percent in 2010. Whereas self-employment for this group ranges from a low of about 10 percent in 2019, to a high of about 13 percent in 1990.

Note especially the difference in calculated annual earnings between immigrants from North Africa and those from Southern Africa. While calculated annual income for the former ranges from a low of about $52,946 in 1980 to a high of $68,127 in 2000, that for the latter ranges from a low of about $65,729 in 1980 to a high of about $110,359 in 2019. Focusing on the high end of the income measures, this means a more than $40,000 difference between these two groups that favors immigrants from Southern Africa.

The Salience of Race, Gender, and Linguistic Heritage

The emerging literature on African immigrants continues to also show that the usual variables of race, gender, and linguistic heritage are significant determinants and/or correlates of socioeconomic outcomes for African immigrants.[4] As with that literature, here as well these variables are shown to be salient. As can be seen in Table 4.2, the information on race suggests that being Black is consistently associated with less favorable measures than being White.[5] Black African immigrants reported appreciably higher percentages of unemployed persons, lower rates of self-employment, lower measures of occupational prestige, and notably lower measures of calculated annual income. Note, for example, that reported percentages of self-employment are two to three times higher among White Africans than among Black Africans. And the difference in calculated income is especially noteworthy: for a difference in earnings of a low of about $21,638 in 1980 to a high of about $ 35,174 in 2010. Here, I note that this is despite the fact that, for most groups, annual income values are shown to have declined in 2010, possibly because of the economic downturn from the 2008 recession. Yet, despite such declines, these values show a widening of the racial earnings gap among these groups of African immigrants. Also notable is that all of the foregoing differences were not restricted to Black-White comparisons but are true for Black-"Other" comparisons, with the former showing noticeably less favorable measures than the latter.

As the emerging literature on African immigrants is also showing (see Model 2008; Corra and Kimuna 2009; Borch and Corra 2010; Corra and Borch 2014; Elo et al. 2015), gender also continues to show as a distinguishing characteristic. Here, the reader may recall from Table 2.3 (chapter 2 of this book) that between 1980 and 2019, the proportion of African immigrants who are female (relative to those who are male) increased from roughly 40/60 to nearly 50/50.

Consistent with the extent literature, on average, measures shown for African immigrant men are noticeably more favorable than those shown for women. For example, percentages of self-employment show notable disparities between men and women, with men reporting self-employment rates that are two to three times higher than those reported by women. Similarly, the lowest occupational prestige score shown for men is about thirty-seven, while the highest is about forty. By contrast, the lowest occupational prestige score for women is about twenty-six, while the highest is about thirty-three.

Moreover, as with race, notable disparities in gender are shown for the income averages for men and women, with the greatest variation occurring in 1990 ($64,474 vs. $37,427), and the least occurring in 2010 ($63,922 vs. $42,180). Here, I again call the reader's attention to the fact that, for most groups, annual income values are shown to have declined in 2010, possibly because of the economic downturn from the 2008 recession. This overall decline may account for the closing of the gender gap between these group of immigrants in earnings in 2010.

Finally, the extent literature is also clear that linguistic heritage is a differentiating variable (see Model 2008; Corra and Kimuna 2009; Hamilton 2020). And here too, we find this variable to be a differentiating characteristic for African immigrants. Unlike averages shown for race and gender, however, variations shown for this variable are nuanced. The measures indicate favorable averages for immigrants from Arab-speaking countries on two of the four variables noted in Table 4.2 (unemployment and self-employment) and favorable ones for immigrants from English-speaking countries on one measure (occupational prestige). For the annual income measure, we see those variations favoring one group over the other varied by year, with immigrants from Arab-speaking countries showing higher annual earnings for the first three of the five time periods (1980, 1990, and 2000), and immigrants from English-speaking countries showing higher income for the other two (2010 and 2019). Yet, as already noted above, except for immigrants from Central and Southern Africa, and the group of immigrants from unidentified regions of Africa, in 2010, annual income values are shown to have declined for all groups displayed in Table 4.2. And for most groups, they only rose slightly in 2019. Again, I suspect this was due to the economic downturn resulting from the 2008 recession.

Here, the reader may benefit from race-linguistic heritage figures on our sample not reported in Table 4.2, but that are nevertheless instructive. Almost 80 percent (77.70%) of African immigrants from Arab-speaking countries self-identified as White. By contrast, only about 18 percent (17.58%) of African immigrants from English-speaking countries self-identified as White. Compare these with the figures for Black Africans. Only about 12 percent (11.52%) of Arab-speaking African immigrants self-identified as Black.

By contrast, 72 percent (71.57%) of Black African immigrants are from English-speaking countries.

I note these here because some scholars have argued that race (i.e., being "Black" or "White") frequently trumps other variables in labor market disparities in the United States. For example, in their cross-national comparative study, *Strangers No More*, Alba and Foner (2015) hypothesize that in the United States, color (i.e., "blackness") is a greater disadvantage than religion (i.e., "Muslim-ness"), whereas the converse is true in Europe (I am grateful to Professor Suzanne Model for bringing this important point to my attention). In the language of early race scholar E. C. Hughes (1945), race in the United States is a "master status characteristic." Here, the issue of linguistic heritage may be compounded by race and religion, for example, a sizeable proportion of Arab-speaking immigrants from Africa are Muslims, whereas immigrants from English-speaking African countries are more religiously diverse (see statistics from the World Atlas at https://www.worldatlas.com/articles/african-countries-with-islam-as-the-religion-of-the-majority.html).

The next question to address is exactly how stable are these patterns? How do the patterns withstand statistical scrutiny? The section to immediately follow continues our probe on the relative positions of African immigrant subgroups in the United States by providing data on multivariate logistic and general linear regression estimates on labor market disparities. And, in doing so, that section more fully examines the stability of the foregoing patterns.

AN INTRA-GROUP COMPARISON OF AFRICAN IMMIGRANTS IN THE UNITED STATES: STATISTICAL ANALYSES OF LABOR MARKET DISPARITIES

The probe now shifts from the general examination of averages to more nuanced statistical analyses of disparities. I do this by examining labor market disparities in five areas: labor force participation; unemployment; self-employment; occupational prestige; and hourly earnings. And, in doing so, variations that are statistically "significant" and those that are not can be distinguished.

Disparities in Labor Force Participation, Unemployment, and Self-Employment

Table 4.3 reports results of three multivariate logistic regression models examining disparities in labor force participation, unemployment, and self-employment between the groups of African immigrants discussed above. The first estimate reported in that table is a logistic regression model that predicts the probability that members of a subgroup of African immigrants will not be in the labor force, relative to comparable group(s), and controlling for a host of work-related attributes. Stated differently, that model predicts the likelihood that members of a group will be completely out of the labor force—unemployed and not looking for a job, relative to comparable group(s). The second model predicts the relative probability that members of a group will not be employed; that is, will be in the labor force, actively looking for a job but not employed. The third model is also a logistic regression model, and it predicts the likelihood of members of a group not being self-employed, relative to their comparison group(s).

Moreover, for these logistic regression models, I only report the likelihood ratios, and not the parameter estimates themselves since the former are more amenable to interpreting. The odds ratios are either equal to, more or less than 1.00. Since the three are logistic regression models predicting the likelihood of (1) not being in the labor force, (2) not being employed, or (3) not being self-employed, odds ratios less than 1.00 indicate a lesser likelihood for a given group relative to the group(s) with which it is being compared. By contrast, odds ratios greater than 1.00 indicate a greater likelihood, while odds ratios of 1.00 indicate that the group average is the same as the comparable group(s). Because being in the labor force, employed, and self-employed are each desirable, on each of these measures a number below 1.00 implies a favorable estimate for the group relative to the comparable group(s). In other words, as dummy variables, the odds ratios convey the likelihood relative to the reference category for each variable (e.g., each racial group relative to Whites).

Finally, by convention in the social sciences, a single asterisk (*) denotes significance at the 0.05 level, double asterisk (**) indicates significance at the 0.01 level, and triple asterisk (***) denotes a significance level at the 0.001 level. Estimates with none of these designations are considered not statistically significant.

Results of the data presented in Table 4.3 are also reported by samples separated by sex. Since men and women are said to experience the U.S. labor market differently (see Model 2008; Corra and Kimuna 2009; Borch and Corra 2010; Corra and Borch 2014), sets of results are reported each on the male and female African immigrant samples.[6]

Gendered Variations by Region and Linguistic Heritage

Beginning with the region of origins variable, we see notable variations in estimates that are gendered. Noting from that table that the reference group here is immigrants from Southern Africa, the estimates in Table 4.3 do indeed show that immigrants from that region occupy a unique position, at least

Table 4.3 An Intra-Group Comparison of African Immigrants in the United States: Logistic Regression Estimates of Three Economic Indicators, Combined 1980, 1990, 2000, 2010, and 2019 Samples of the IPUMS.

Male Sample[a] Female Sample[b]

Demographic	Probability Modeled = Not in Labor Force	Probability Modeled = Not Employed	Probability Modeled = Not Self-Employed	Probability Modeled = Not in Labor Force	Probability Modeled = Not Employed	Probability Modeled = Not Self-Employed
	Odds Ratio	Odds Ratio	Odds Ratio	Odds Ratio	Odds Ratio	Odds Ratio
YEAR[c]						
1980	2.584***	2.335***	0.953	1.688***	1.709***	1.61***
1990	0.936	1.117	0.68***	1.519***	1.572***	1.023
2000	2.405***	2.109***	0.914	1.839***	1.759***	1.008
2010	1.139	1.757***	0.909	1.14*	1.423***	0.949
2019	omitted category					
REGION						
Central	1.38*	1.51***	2.372***	0.638*	0.694***	1.271
East	1.185	1.214*	1.317***	0.735***	0.759***	1.049
North	2.165***	2.10***	2.948***	1.003	1.151	1.891*
West	1.144	1.266**	1.59***	0.64***	0.714***	1.012
Unidentified[d]	1.316*	1.529***	1.857***	0.747***	0.789**	1.167
South	omitted category					
RACE[e]						
Black	1.578***	1.593***	1.488***	0.709***	0.787***	1.959***
Other[f]	1.098	1.142*	0.937	0.932	0.965	1.128
White	omitted category					
LANGUAGE						
English[g]	0.918	0.789	1.249***	0.79***	0.789***	1.008

Demographic	Probability Modeled = Not in Labor Force	Probability Modeled = Not Employed	Probability Modeled = Not Self-Employed	Probability Modeled = Not in Labor Force	Probability Modeled = Not Employed	Probability Modeled = Not Self-Employed
Non-English	omitted category					
Arab[b]	0.656*	0.77*	0.545***			
Non-Arab	omitted category			0.899	0.878	0.97
REFUGEE						
Ref.> Average[i]	0.86**	0.856	1.251***	0.838***	0.916*	1.392***
Ref. =/<Average						
N	35,502	35,502	35,502	27,730	27,730	27,730

a. In addition to the variables listed in the table, all models also controlled for number of years of schooling, number of years of work experience plus its squared term, number of years in the United States, marital status, a set of regional variables including Midwest, West, and South (reference category = Northeast), an English deficiency measure, two dummy variables controlling for whether an earned college degree was received in the United States or abroad, and metropolitan status.

b. Models controlled for all variables included for the male sample, plus two relationship variables: number of own children currently living in the household; and number of own children under age 5 in the household.

c. Reference year = 2019.

d. Includes immigrants from Africa whose region and/or country of birth is not identified, in IPUMS terminology, "Africa, ns."

e. Reference group = White.

f. catchall category that includes individuals reporting various race combinations like two major races, three or more races, etc.

g. Includes immigrants from countries with Arab listed as an official language by the U.S. Central Intelligence Agency's *World FactBook* (https://www.cia.gov/the-world-factbook). They include Algeria, Chad, Comoros, Egypt, Eritrea, Libya, Mauritania, Morocco, Somalia, Sudan, Tunisia, and Western Sahara.

h. Includes immigrants from countries with English listed as an official language by the U.S. Central Intelligence Agency's *World FactBook* (https://www.cia.gov/the-world-factbook). They include Gambia, Ghana, Liberia, Nigeria, Sierra Leone, Kenya, Malawi, Mauritius, Tanzania, Uganda, Zambia, Zimbabwe, Cameroon, Botswana, Lesotho, Namibia, South Africa (Union of), and Swaziland.

i. Calculated from the U.S. Department of Homeland Security's 1996, 1998–2019 *Yearbook of Immigration Statistics*, as countries with percentages of individuals granted refugee or asylee status that was greater than that of the overall continent of Africa. They include Sudan, Liberia, Sierra Leone, Ethiopia, Somalia, Tanzania, and the Democratic Republic of Congo.

Source: Author's calculations based on samples of the 1980, 1990, and 2000 Decennial Censuses, and the 2010 and 2019 American Community Surveys (ACS), as represented in the Integrated Public Use Microdata Series (IPUMS) (Ruggles et al. 2020). Data limited to persons 25 to 64 years old, and who are not living in group quarters and/or institutions.

among African immigrant men. For the male sample, we see that estimates for the three logistic regression models predict immigrants from Southern Africa with a greater likelihood of being in the labor force, being employed, and being self-employed, respectively, than immigrants from virtually all other regions. And, it is worth noting, this finding importantly controls for race. The only two estimates that depart from this pattern are those for East and West Africa, and on only the first measure—labor force participation, estimates for which are not statistically significant, and suggest that immigrants from these two regions had similar labor force participation rates as immigrants from Southern Africa.

For the female sample, by contrast, the estimates for the region variable are almost opposite to those for males. In four out of five comparisons, we see that immigrants from Southern Africa are predicted to have a greater likelihood of not being in the labor force, and to be unemployed. The only notable exception to this is that both estimates (labor force participation and unemployment) for immigrants from North Africa are not statistically significant (i.e., are not statistically different from those for immigrants from Southern Africa).

Moreover, for the female sample, only one estimate for self-employment, that for immigrants from North Africa, is statistically significant. In other words, for females, the self-employment rates for all regional groups are the same as that for immigrants from Southern Africa, with the single exception of immigrants from North Africa. Female immigrants from North Africa are predicted to have a lower likelihood of being self-employed than their counterparts from Southern Africa.

Furthermore, being from a country with English designated as an "official" language is estimated to be significant among men in only one of the estimates, self-employment. Male immigrants from "English speaking" countries are predicted to exhibit a greater likelihood of being self-employed than their male counterparts from non-English speaking countries. Here again, gender differences existed, in that both the labor force participation and unemployment estimates for females are shown to be significant, while the self-employment estimate is not. Accordingly, female immigrants from English-speaking countries are estimated to be less likely than their non-English-speaking counterparts to not be in the labor force and to be unemployed.

The "Arab" speaking dimension, however, is shown to be more predictive among men than among women. All three estimates for males (labor force participation, unemployment, and self-employment) are shown to be statistically significant for the male sample, while none is shown to be statistically significant for the female sample. While all estimates show male immigrants from Arab-speaking countries to have a lesser likelihood of not being in the labor force, to be unemployed, and to not be self-employed than their non-Arab-speaking counterparts, Arab-speaking females are predicted to have the same rates of labor force participation, unemployment, and self-employment as their non-Arab-speaking counterparts.

Finally, it may be recalled from previous chapters of this book that migration theory and research suggest that how well immigrants do may be uniquely tied to whether they are "economic" or "political" migrants. The hypothesis there is that "politically motivated emigrants" are less positively selected (pushed) than "economically motivated emigrants" (pulled) (Lee 1966; Borjas 1994; Chiswick 1978, 1999; Jasso and Rosenzweig 1990a and b; Tesfai 2019). To test this hypothesis, I calculated from the U.S. Department of Homeland Security's 1996, 1998–2019 *Yearbook of Immigration Statistics* a measure of countries with percentages of individuals granted refugee or asylee status greater than that of the overall continent of Africa (see associated notes in Table 4.3 and Table 4.4 for a list of these countries). I included this measure as a dummy variable in the logistic and regression models reported here (1 = countries higher than the overall average and 0 = those with averages equal to or less than the overall average).

As can be seen in Table 4.3, the higher-than-average refugee measure is almost consistently significant, with immigrants from such countries less likely to not be in the labor force and to be unemployed, but more likely to not be self-employed. And estimates for this measure, unlike other measures reported thus far, are consistent across male and female samples. That is to say, the estimates virtually show the same effects, and direction of effects, for both samples.

Race as a Consistent Predictor of Labor Force Participation, Unemployment, and Self-Employment, with Notable Variations by Gender

Notwithstanding the foregoing variations, estimates presented in Table 4.3 show the most consistent takeaway from the results is the highly significant and consistent gendered salience of race, specifically being Black (relative to being White), in predicting disparities in labor force participation, unemployment, and self-employment. All six logistic regression estimates presented in Table 4.3 are shown to be highly significant, with Black immigrant men predicted to exhibit a greater likelihood than their White counterparts to not be in the labor force, to be unemployed, and to not be self-employed. Whereas the reverse is predicted for female Black immigrants. As shown in Table 4.3, Black men are about twice as likely as their White counterparts to not be in the labor force, about twice as likely to be unemployed, and about twice as likely to not be self-employed. By contrast, Black African females are estimated to be less likely than their White counterparts to not be in the labor force and to be unemployed, but to also be more likely to not

Table 4.4 An Intra-Group Comparison of African Immigrants in the United States: General Linear Regression Estimates of Two Economic Indicators, Combined 1980, 1990, 2000, 2010, and 2019 Samples of the IPUMS.

	Male Sample[a]		Female Sample[b]	
	Occupation	Hourly Earnings[c]	Occupation	Hourly Earnings[c]
Demographic Year[d]				
1980	7.76***	0.2185***	1.32**	-0.001
1990	-1.27**	0.034	-4.62***	0.058
2000	-3.352***	-0.038**	-4.67***	-0.074***
2010	-3.87***	N.A.	-5.13***	N.A.
2019				
Region				
Central	-2.94***	-0.234***	-0.24	-0.037
East	-0.73	-0.154***	0.21	-0.013
North	-3.72***	-0.257***	-1.32	-0.002
West	-3.13***	-0.215***	-1.22*	-0.047***
Un. Id.[e]	-2.92***	-0.188***	-0.94	-0.034
SOUTH	Omitted Category			
Race[f]				
Black	-4.76***	-0.188***	0.278	-0.036
Other[g]	-2.26**	-0.128***	-1.24**	-0.0417
WHITE	Omitted Category			
Language.				
English[h]	3.04***	0.086***	4.421***	0.085***
Non-English	Omitted Category			
Arab[i]	0.71	0.045	-0.92	-0.066
Non-Arab	Omitted Category			
REFUGEE				
Ref.> Ave.[j]	-0.80**	-0.032*	-0.72*	-0.036*
Ref. =/<Ave.	Omitted Category			
D.F.	26	25	28	27
R-Square	0.29005	0.182231	0.23567	0.12979
N	35,502	25,809	27,730	16,007

* Statistically significant at the .05 level; ** Statistically significant at the .01 level; *** Statistically significant at the .001 level

a. In addition to the variables listed in the table, all models also controlled for number of years of schooling, number of years of work experience plus its squared term, number of years in the United States, marital status, a set of regional variables including Midwest, West, and South (reference category = Northeast), an English deficiency measure, two dummy variables controlling for whether an earned college degree was received in the United States or abroad, and metropolitan status.

b. Models controlled for all variables included for the male sample, plus two relationship variables: number of own children currently living in the household; and number of own children under age 5 in the household.

c. Estimates limited to persons with reported annual earnings of $500 or more.

d. Reference year = 2019.

e. Includes immigrants from Africa whose region and/or country of birth is not identified, in IPUMS terminology, "Africa, ns."

f. Reference group = White.

g. A catchall category that includes individuals reporting various race combinations like two major races, three or more races, etc.

h. Includes immigrants from countries with Arab listed as an official language by the U.S. Central Intelligence Agency's *World FactBook* (https://www.cia.gov/the-world-factbook). They include Algeria, Chad, Comoros, Egypt, Eritrea, Libya, Mauritania, Morocco, Somalia, Sudan, Tunisia, and Western Sahara.

i. Includes immigrants from countries with English listed as an official language by the U.S. Central Intelligence Agency's *World FactBook* (https://www.cia.gov/the-world-factbook). They include Gambia, Ghana, Liberia, Nigeria, Sierra Leone, Kenya, Malawi, Mauritius, Tanzania, Uganda, Zambia, Zimbabwe, Cameroon, Botswana, Lesotho, Namibia, South Africa (Union of), and Swaziland.

j. Calculated from the U.S. Department of Homeland Security's 1996, 1998–2019 *Yearbook of Immigration Statistics*, as countries with percentages of individuals granted refugee or asylee status that was greater than that of the overall continent of Africa. They include Sudan, Liberia, Sierra Leone, Ethiopia, Somalia, Tanzania, and the Democratic Republic of Congo.

Source: Author's calculations based on samples of the 1980, 1990, and 2000 Decennial Censuses, and the 2010 and 2019 American Community Surveys (ACS), as represented in the Integrated Public Use Microdata Series (IPUMS) (Ruggles et al. 2020). Data limited to persons 25 to 64 years old, and who are not living in group quarters and/or institutions.

be self-employed. In other words, Black women are more likely than White women to be in the labor force and to be employed. But they are also more likely than their White counterparts to not be self-employed.

Compare these with estimates for the "Other" category of race, for the male sample, which is significant for only one of the three logistic regression estimates (unemployment). Male immigrants of "other" races are predicted to be more likely than their White counterparts to be unemployed but are predicted to have reported similar levels of labor force participation and self-employment as White Africans. No such difference is found among "Other" African women and their White counterparts. Female African immigrants of "other" races reported similar levels of labor force participation, unemployment, and self-employment as their White counterparts.

Finally, here I note that all logistic regression models showed parallel results (not reported in Table 4.4, but available upon request) in other areas, with most groups moving in tandem with their statistical counterparts. Married individuals, those with greater years of education and work experience, those with a college degree, both foreign and domestic, are shown to have been more favorable measures of labor force participation, employment, and self-employment than their statistical counterparts. Distinctions existed between those with U.S. degrees versus those with foreign degrees. Among men, both degrees are shown to be significant predictors of labor force participation and unemployment, with stronger effects for a U.S. degree than a foreign degree. Moreover, Wald tests of significance (not reported in Table 4.3) revealed estimates for the two types of degrees to differ significantly from one another. And for self-employment among men, those with foreign degrees are predicted to be less likely to be self-employed. Similar effects are shown for females, except those immigrants with U.S. and foreign degrees are shown to have similar levels of self-employment—the difference between the two is not statistically significant.

Additional Notable Variations

To test for differences that might have existed between other groups (e.g., differences between other regional groupings, i.e., immigrants from Central Africa vs. those from East, North, and West; immigrants from East vs. those from North and West; and immigrants from North vs. those from West), I conducted a series of Wald tests, results of which I report here. The Wald tests allow for evaluating whether coefficients for estimates included in any given logistic regression model are statistically significant. Here, it means comparisons not delineated in our models, and not reported in Table 4.3, but that might nevertheless be instructive.

As above, results of those tests are somewhat gendered. Looking at the regional groupings, for example, those comparisons indicate that thirteen of eighteen coefficients for the male sample are shown to be statistically significant.[7] Whereas only seven coefficients for the female sample are shown to be statistically significant.

For labor force participation, three coefficients are shown to be statistically significant among men: that for North Africa, relative to Central Africa, Chi-Square = 10.2773, odds ratio = 1.569, P = 0.0013; North Africa, relative to East Africa, Chi-Square = 13.8518, odds ratio = 1.827, p = 0.0002; and West Africa, relative to North Africa, Chi-Square = 15.2436, odds ratio = 0.528, p = <.0001. These values suggest that male immigrants from North Africa had lower labor force participation rates (more likely to not be in the labor force) than their counterparts from Central, East, and West Africa.

For the unemployment estimates, the Wald tests reveal all but one of the six coefficients for males to be statistically significant: those for immigrants from East Africa versus those from Central Africa, Chi-Square = 5.4079, odds ratio = 0.804, p = 0.02; North Africa versus Central Africa, Chi-Square = 7.3723, odds ratio = 1.39, p = 0.0066; West Africa versus Central Africa, Chi-Square = 3.9454, odds ratio = 0.838, p = 0.047; North Africa versus East Africa, Chi-Square = 15.2124, odds ratio = 1.729, p = <.0001; and West Africa versus North Africa, Chi-Square = 12.7416, odds ratio = 0.603, p = 0.0004. These values indicate a distinction in unemployment rates between male immigrants from East and West Africa, on one hand, and those from Central and North Africa, on the other. The former is shown to display unemployment rates that are lower than those for the latter, although unemployment rates for immigrants from North Africa are also shown to be higher than those from Central Africa.

The coefficients for self-employment follow similar patterns, with male immigrants from East and West Africa exhibiting a unique position from those of their counterparts from Central and North Africa. The Wald tests show estimates for the former to be more favorable than those for the latter: East Africa versus Central Africa, Chi-Square = 17.9774, odds ratio = 0.555, p = <.0001; West Africa versus Central Africa, Chi-Square = 8.6927, odds ratio = 0.67, p = 0.0032; North Africa versus East Africa, Chi-Square = 20.5924, odds ratio = 2.238, p = <.0001; and West Africa versus North Africa, Chi-Square = 11.6276, odds ratio = 0.539, p = 0.0006. Here, it is worth noting that the coefficient for West Africa (relative to East Africa) is also statistically significant, Chi-Square = 9.1335, odds ratio = 1.207, p = 0.0025, suggesting higher self-employment rates among immigrants from East Africa, relative to those from West Africa. Whereas the coefficient for North Africa (relative to Central Africa) is not statistically significant.

The Wald tests reveal a similar, but somewhat different pattern for the female sample. For the labor force participation variable, four coefficients are shown to be statistically significant: that for North Africa, relative to Central Africa, Chi-Square = 15.929, odds ratio = 1.572, p = <.0001; North Africa versus East Africa, Chi-Square = 5.3534, odds ratio = 1.366, p = 0.0207; West Africa versus East Africa, Chi-Square = 7.6825, odds ratio = 0.872, p = 0.0056; and West Africa versus North Africa, Chi-Square = 10.6736, odds ratio = 0.638, p = 0.0011. Like the male sample, these values suggest favorable estimates for immigrants from East and West Africa, on one hand, and those from North Africa, on the other hand.

Moreover, the unemployment coefficients for females indicate three regional comparisons to be statistically significant, mostly suggesting unfavorable measures for immigrants from North Africa: North Africa versus Central Africa, Chi-Square = 21.4117, odds ratio = 1.657, p = <.0001; North Africa versus East Africa, Chi-Square = 10.3729, odds ratio = 0.66, p = 0.0013; West Africa versus North Africa, Chi-Square = 13.1503, odds ratio = 0.621, p = 0.0003. In other words, for all three comparisons, immigrants from North Africa are shown to have had higher unemployment rates.

And finally for self-employment among females, only two coefficients are shown to be statistically significant: East Africa versus North Africa, Chi-Square = 4.819, odds ratio = 0.555, p = 0.0281; and West Africa versus North Africa, Chi-Square = 5.2068, odds ratio = 0.535, p = 0.0225. Both indicate higher rates of self-employment among immigrants from East and West Africa, relative to those from North Africa.

Taken together, the Wald tests reveal a unique position for immigrants from East and West Africa, on one hand, and those from Central, and especially North, Africa, on the other hand. Those tests generally indicate that labor force participation and self-employment rates are more favorable for the former, relative to the latter; whereas unemployment rates were generally higher for the latter. The tests indicate some slight variations by gender, but these patterns are shown to generally hold across male and female samples.

The Other-Black comparisons of race are equally instructive on the gendered salience of race. All six coefficients for "Other" are shown to be statistically significant, but again gendered: labor force participation for males, Chi-Square = 35.2778, odds ratio = 0.696, p = <.0001; unemployment, Chi-Square = 37.3975, odds ratio = 0.717, p = <.0001; and self-employment, Chi-Square = 57.8914, odds ratio = 0.63, p = <.0001. Compare these with the same three coefficients for the female sample: labor force participation, Chi-Square = 30.321, odds ratio = 1.315, p = <.0001; unemployment, Chi-Square = 17.805, odds ratio = 1.225, p = <.0001; and self-employment, Chi-Square = 35.2492, odds ratio = 0.576, p = <.0001. In other words, except for the coefficient for self-employment, these estimates show results for men and women that are opposite to one another. While men of "Other" races are shown to be less likely than their Black counterparts to not be in the labor force, to be unemployed, and to not be self-employed, female "Others" are shown to be more likely than their Black counterparts to not be in the labor force and to be unemployed. Such women, however, are less likely than their Black counterparts to not be self-employed.

Finally, for the language measures (Arab- and English-speaking), the reader will have noticed in Table 4.3 that each is in reference to everyone else not included in each of those categories, that is, for immigrants from Arab-speaking countries, the reference is everyone else that is not; and for those from English-speaking countries, the reference is everyone else that is not. Accordingly, to specifically compare immigrant groups by linguistic heritage, I recoded those two variables to obtain a three-category measure that represented (1) immigrants from Arab-speaking countries; (2) immigrants from English-speaking countries; and (3) those from neither. Models comparing these three again yielded results that are gendered. When male immigrants from English-speaking countries are the reference category for the other two male groups, only three of the six comparisons are found to be statistically significant and in favor of the latter: one for labor force participation (relative to Arab-speaking, odds ratio = 0.714, p = 0.0264); and two for self-employment (relative to Arab-speaking, odds ratio = 0.437, p = <.0001; and relative to non-Arab, non-English-speaking, odds ratio = 0.801, p = 0.0005). These estimates indicate that, for males, immigrants from English-speaking countries are estimated to be more likely than their counterparts from Arab-speaking countries to not be in the labor force and to not be self-employed. They are also more likely than their counterparts from non-Arab-speaking countries to not be self-employed.

For females, by contrast, only two of the six estimates are shown to be statistically significant, and only in the area of labor force participation and unemployment, and only between this group and immigrants from non-Arab-speaking countries: labor force participation, odds ratio = 1.265, p = <.0001; and unemployment, odds ratio = 1.267, p = <.0001. In other words, unlike those for their male counterparts, significant estimates here are in favor of immigrants from English-speaking countries.

Equally Gendered Variations by Region and Linguistic Heritage in Occupational Prestige and Hourly Earnings

Table 4.4 displays general linear regression estimates for the groups discussed above. Reported in that table, the first estimate is from a general linear regression model estimating occupational prestige for the different groups. Whereas the second is a regression estimate of hourly earnings for the same groups. Moreover, following previous research (see, e.g., Borch and Corra 2010; Corra and Borch 2014), the log of hourly earnings is used in the earnings models. Use of a logged dependent variable allows interpretation of coefficients as percentage changes in the dependent variable, once the appropriate calculations are made, while also mitigating any skewness in data generally associated with earnings measures. Accordingly, the estimates for hourly earnings reported in Table 4.4 represent values with such calculations taken into account and can therefore be interpreted as percentage of hourly earnings, as a measure of the effect of each given independent variable. As an example, consider the first value of -0.234 displayed under the hourly earnings column in Table 4.4 for male immigrants from Central Africa. This value can be interpreted as African immigrants from Central Africa having had hourly earnings that are significantly lower than those calculated for male immigrants from Southern Africa to the point of about 24 percent lower. As above, results are reported by samples separated by sex.[8]

Looking at the regression estimates of occupational prestige and hourly earnings presented in Table 4.4, we see that they are equally illustrative of the patterns indicated by the logistic regression estimates presented above. For the region variable, we again see estimates that vary by gender. For example, nine of the ten regional estimates for males are negative and highly significant, while only one of the ten estimates for females is significant. Recalling that the regional comparisons are each relative to immigrants from Southern Africa, the one exception among men is immigrants from East Africa, for which the estimate for occupational prestige is not statistically significant. In other words, while immigrant men from Southern Africa are predicted to have held occupations with similar levels of prestige compared with their male counterparts from East Africa, the former are nevertheless predicted to have hourly earnings that are significantly higher than those of the latter.

In short, among men, immigrants from Southern Africa are estimated to have held occupations with higher prestige than all other regional groups, except for those from East Africa. Immigrants from Southern Africa are also predicted to have earned significantly more than all of their other regional counterparts. The hourly earnings of male immigrants from Southern Africa, for example, are predicted to be about 23 percent higher than those of immigrants from Central Africa, 15 percent higher than that of immigrants from East Africa, 25 percent higher than that of immigrants from North Africa, 21 percent higher than that of immigrants from West Africa, and about 18 percent higher than that of immigrants from "other" regions of Africa.

For the female sample, we see virtually no regional difference on both occupational prestige and hourly earnings. Again, only one estimate is shown to be statistically significant, with immigrant women from West Africa the only group predicted to hold occupations with lower prestige than their counterparts from Southern Africa, but no such difference existed in hourly earnings.

By contrast, the regression estimates for Blacks are even more telling about the gendered nature of these results. Among men, those estimates show that Blacks held occupations with significantly lower prestige than those held by their White counterparts and earned significantly less. The hourly earnings of Black African immigrant males, for example, are predicted to be about 19 percent less than those of their White counterparts. No such differences in occupational prestige and earnings, however, is estimated to have existed among Black and White females.

Comparing these with the estimates for the "Other" category of race, we see again predictions that vary by gender. While Black men in the "Other" race category are predicted to have held occupations with lower prestige than their White counterparts, and to have earned less, among females, only the estimate for occupational prestige is shown to be statistically significant. In other words, disparities in occupations held by Blacks and Whites, as well as related earnings, were limited to differences among men.

As above, I note here that all general linear regression models showed parallel results (not reported in Table 4.4, but available upon request) in other areas, with most groups moving in tandem with their statistical counterparts. Married individuals, those with greater years of education and work experience, those with a college degree, both foreign and domestic, are shown to have held occupations with higher prestige, and to have earned more, than their statistical counterparts. Distinctions existed between those with U.S. degrees versus those with foreign degrees. For both male and female samples, both degrees are shown to be significant predictors of occupational prestige and earnings, with stronger effects for a U.S. degree than a foreign degree and estimates for the two that differ significantly from one another.

ADDITIONAL COMPARISONS BY REGION, RACE, AND LINGUISTIC HERITAGE: FURTHER GENDERED DISPARITIES

To test whether disparities in occupational prestige and earnings discussed above extended to other regional and racial comparisons, I ran the two models again with the other regions (Central, East, North, and West) and the "Other" category of race, each as the omitted category for region and race, respectively. Those comparisons again revealed the gendered nature of variations. For the region of origins variable, for example, three comparisons of occupational prestige estimates (East Africa vs. Central Africa; East Africa vs. North Africa; East Africa vs. West Africa) for males are shown to be statistically significant: East Africa versus Central Africa, parameter estimate = 2.202, p = <.0001; East Africa versus North Africa, parameter estimate = 2.985, p = 0.0004; East Africa versus West Africa, parameter estimate = 2.40, p = <.0001. And the three estimates for hourly earnings to be statistically significant include: East Africa vs. Central Africa, parameter estimate = 0.106, p = 0.0008; East Africa vs. North Africa, parameter estimate = 0.1142, p = 0.0055; and East Africa vs. West Africa, parameter estimate = 0.0779, p = < .0001.. In other words, male immigrants from East Africa are predicted to have reported occupations with higher prestige than immigrants from the other three regions (Central, North, and West Africa). They are also estimated to have earned more.

It follows that, the foregoing regional comparisons among men suggest that, to immigrants from Southern Africa, we may also add immigrants from East Africa, as occupying a unique position among African immigrants. recalling from Table 4.4 that only one of the two East Africa–Southern Africa estimates for men (hourly earnings) is shown to be statistically significant, the estimates discussed here suggest that these two groups are similarly advantaged in the U.S. labor market, at least among men.

For the female sample, by contrast, only one of the regional estimates for occupational prestige is shown to be statistically significant, while none for hourly earnings is shown to be so. For occupational prestige, the one significant comparison is that shown for East Africa versus West Africa, parameter estimate = 1.42, p = 0.0002. In other words, for occupational prestige estimates comparing female immigrants from Central, East, North, and West Africa, with one another, East African females had an advantage only over immigrants from West Africa. All other comparisons are shown to not be statistically significant. And, importantly, none of the regional estimates for hourly earnings, comparing immigrants from Central, East, North, and West Africa, each with the other, are shown to be statistically significant.

The "Other"-Black comparisons reveal similar gendered patterns. For males, occupational prestige, parameter estimate = 2.501, p = <.0001; hourly earnings, parameter estimate = 0.074, p = <.0001. Whereas for females, only the estimate for occupational prestige is significant, parameter estimate = -1.51, p = 0.0002. In other words, for male immigrants, those from "Other" regions of Africa reported occupations with higher prestige, and earned more, than their Black counterparts; whereas for female immigrants, while those from "Other" regions of Africa reported occupations with lower prestige than their Black counterparts, they did not earned less.

Finally, as with the logistic regression estimates discussed above, here as well, for the language measures (Arab- and English-speaking), I ran models comparing three groups, (1) immigrants from Arab-speaking countries; (2) immigrants from English-speaking countries; and (3) those from neither. Unlike the logistic regression comparisons discussed above, these models yielded results that are gender-consistent. For the male sample, three of the six comparisons are found to be statistically significant, and all in favor of immigrants from English-speaking countries: for occupational prestige, relative to immigrants from Arab-speaking countries, estimate = -2.3246, p = 0.0035; and relative to immigrants from non-Arab-speaking countries, estimate = -3.0371, p = <.0001. For hourly earnings, relative to non-Arab-speaking countries, estimate = -0.08, p = <.0001. And among females, four estimates are found to be significantly different, and all in favor of immigrants from English-speaking countries: for occupational prestige, immigrants from Arab-speaking countries, relative to those from English-speaking countries, estimate = -5.1328, p = <.0001, and those from non-Arab-speaking countries, relative to those from English-speaking countries, estimate = -4.2107, p = <.0001; and for hourly earnings, immigrants from Arab-speaking countries, relative to those from English-speaking countries, estimate = -0.14, p = 0.0047, immigrants from non-Arab-speaking countries, relative to those from English-speaking countries, estimate = -0.08, p = <.0001. Here, I note that none of the comparisons between immigrants from Arab-speaking countries and those from non-Arab-speaking countries are shown to be statistically significant.

Taken together then, if there is an advantage for immigrants from English-speaking countries, it is shown to be in the area of occupational prestige and earnings: Such immigrants are shown to hold occupations with higher prestige than their counterparts from Arab and non-Arab-speaking countries. They are also estimated to have earned more. The next section extends the foregoing analyses to country-level comparisons.

AFRICAN IMMIGRANTS IN THE UNITED STATES: EXAMINING LABOR MARKET DISPARITIES AT THE COUNTRY-LEVEL

Following Hamilton (2020), data presented in Table 4.5, Table 4.6, and Table 4.7 extend the foregoing analyses to a selected number of twelve countries. Again, the reader will notice that many of these countries appear in previous tables as ten major immigrant sending countries from Africa to the United States. Importantly, however, the twelve countries here represent notable diversity in race, linguistic heritage, religion, and related sociocultural qualities. And, as noted in chapter 1 of this book, many recent immigrants from Africa are from Arab and/or Muslim-majority countries. As Hamilton (2020) recently observed, new arrivals from countries like Ethiopia, Somalia, and Sudan have religious practices and customs that markedly differ from those of the United States. Such customs and practices could open them for intense threefold discrimination: as Muslims, as Blacks, and as immigrants (Hamilton 2020). Notably, to the nine primary source countries of African immigrants to the United States examined by Hamilton (2020)—Nigeria, Ethiopia, Ghana, Kenya, Liberia, Somalia, Cameroon, Sierra Leone, and Sudan, I add Egypt, Morocco, and South Africa to increase the number of individuals self-identifying as "White." Collectively, these three countries represent almost 75 percent (74.4%, to be exact) of individuals self-identifying as "White" in our sample. Moreover, Egypt and Morocco are two source countries with the largest number of Arab-speaking immigrants in the United States.

Table 4.5 gives summary statistics on four work-related "economic" measures, while Table 4.6 provides logistic regression estimates on labor force participation, unemployment, and self-employment. Finally, Table 4.7 displays general linear regression estimates on disparities in occupational prestige and hourly earnings.

Country-Level Differences That Are Gendered

As can be seen in Table 4.5, country-level disparities do indeed exist, with notable differences by sex. With few exceptions, for the male sample, the data presented in Table 4.5 suggests that countries cluster into three groupings. Four countries, Nigeria, Egypt, South Africa, and Kenya, appear to uniquely exhibit most favorable summary measures. Overall, these four show the lowest unemployment percentages for males, the highest rates of self-employment, the highest average occupational prestige scores, and the highest annual income. The average occupational prestige score for each of

Table 4.5 A Comparison of Top Sending Countries from Africa to the United States on Four Economic Indicators, Combined 1980, 1990, 2000, 2010, and 2019 Samples of the IPUMS.

Male Sample

Country	% Unemployed	% Self-Employed	Occupational Prestige	Annual Earnings[a]	N
Nigeria	5.02	10.2	40.23	$57,763.30	6032
Egypt/United Arab Rep.	3.97	15.96	42.38	$81,106.90	5744
Ethiopia	4.04	11.24	34.16	$48,281.20	2873
South Africa (Union of)	2.14	19.61	47.72	$124,411.00	2524
Ghana	4.54	7.56	36.04	$53,760.00	2751
Morocco	4.02	15.8	34.74	$63,802.50	1766
Somalia	7.83	10.00	29.26	$36,440.30	690
Sierra Leone	7.63	5.41	35.89	$49,473.60	695
Kenya	3.63	12.41	42.13	$73,415.10	1515
Liberia	5.84	4.31	34.45	$46,981.60	1044
Sudan	6.52	11.16	33.67	$51,307.70	690
Cameroon	7.34	6.82	38.21	$52,944.10	572

Female Sample

Country	% Unemployed	% Self-Employed	Occupational Prestige	Annual Earnings[a]	N
Nigeria	5.69	4.93	36.06	$46,035.20	3938
Egypt/United Arab Rep.	4.51	5.34	28.85	$44,780.50	3971
Ethiopia	6.06	3.71	27.98	$35,638.00	2590
South Africa (Union of)	2.24	10.37	36.47	$54,007.60	2458
Ghana	6.33	5.03	29.87	$40,087.40	1989
Morocco	4.8	7.08	25.55	$38,220.50	1271
Somalia	10.9	3.09	19.08	$22,578.20	679
Sierra Leone	4.71	2.98	32.05	$39,624.50	637
Kenya	4.15	6.25	36.14	$44,929.90	1375
Liberia	5.83	4.01	31.04	$38,447.50	1097
Sudan	9.41	2.35	23.06	$33,664.70	425
Cameroon	6.25	3.32	36.17	$44,064.10	512

a. Limited to persons with calculated annual incomes of $500 or more, computed in constant 2019 dollars.

Source: Author's calculations based on samples of the 1980, 1990, and 2000 Decennial Censuses, and the 2010 and 2019 American Community Surveys (ACS), as represented in the Integrated Public Use Microdata Series (IPUMS) (Ruggles et al. 2020). Data limited to persons 25 to 64 years old, and who are not living in group quarters and/or institutions.

these, for example, is above forty, and the self-employment percentages are among the highest (10% for Nigeria, 12% for Kenya, 16% for Egypt, and 20% for South Africa). The average annual earnings of immigrant males from Kenya ($73,415.10), Egypt ($81,106.90), and South Africa ($124,411.00) are especially noteworthy among this group. Note that the country with the lowest annual income among this group is Nigeria, with an average annual income of immigrants of $57,763.

As can also be seen in the summary statistics presented in Table 4.5, for males, a second group of countries falls in the mid-range, with relative low unemployment percentages for immigrants, high self-employment, occupations with relatively high average prestige, and immigrants with relatively high income. These countries include Ghana, Morocco, and Ethiopia. Among all the countries listed in Table 4.5, Morocco, for example, shows one of the highest self-employment percentages (about 16%), and one of the highest average annual incomes ($63,802.50). Similarly, Ghana shows one of the highest average occupational prestige scores (36), and annual income ($53,760).

A third grouping among men includes countries that exhibit relatively low on some measures, medium on some, and high on some. These include Cameroon, Liberia, Sierra Leone, Somalia, and Sudan. Cameroon, for example, is among countries with one of the highest percentages of unemployment (7%), yet it also shows average annual income that is relatively high ($52,944.10). Likewise, Sierra Leone registers one of the highest percent unemployed (7%) and lowest self-employment percent (about 5%), but also exhibits a relatively high average occupational prestige score (about 36).

The female sample, by contrast, exhibits patterns that are not as clearly demarcated by country groupings. Instead, measures indicate that some specific countries exhibit specific patterns. Immigrants from South Africa, for example, appear to have occupied an especially distinct position among females. Such immigrants reported the lowest unemployment percentage among women (2%), the highest percent self-employment (10%), the highest average occupational prestige score (37), and the highest calculated average annual income ($54,007.60). Immigrants from Somalia and Sudan, by contrast, exhibit the least favorable summary measures among these women.

Logistic and Linear Regression Estimates: Gendered Country-Level Disparities

With notable variations, the regression estimates presented in Table 4.6 and Table 4.7 are in accord with the foregoing findings. For both logistic and linear regression estimates presented in these two tables, immigrants from South Africa are the reference category, with which all countries are compared. And as can be seen in Table 4.6, the logistic regression estimates show that, in general, immigrants from South Africa exhibited work-related measures that were uniquely favorable, especially among men. Among men, the self-employment estimates are the clearest. When it comes to

Table 4.6 Logistic Regression Estimates of Three Economic Indicators for Top Ten Sending Countries from Africa to the United States, Combined 1980, 1990, 2000, 2010, and 2019 Samples of the IPUMS.

Male Sample[a] Female Sample[b]

Demographic	Probability Modeled = Not in Labor Force	Probability Modeled = Not Employed	Probability Modeled = Not Self-Employed	Probability Modeled = Not in Labor Force	Probability Modeled = Not Employed	Probability Modeled = Not Self-Employed
	Odds Ratio	Odds Ratio	Odds Ratio	Odds Ratio	Odds Ratio	Odds Ratio
Year[c]						
1980	2.30***	2.09***	0.81*	1.61***	1.65***	1.44*
1990	0.92	1.08	0.64***	1.43***	1.47***	0.90
2000	2.37***	2.06***	0.89*	1.80***	1.72***	1.09
2010	1.14	1.79***	0.92	1.12	1.42***	1.03
2019	omitted category					
Nigeria	1.43**	1.52***	1.49***	0.72***	0.83*	0.95
Egypt/United Arab Rep.	1.51***	1.61***	1.35***	1.09	1.21***	1.99***
Ethiopia	1.16	1.15	1.32***	0.77***	0.87	1.38
Ghana	1.06	1.14	2.03***	0.67***	0.79*	0.88
Morocco	1.27*	1.37***	1.20***	1.16*	1.29***	1.40**
Somalia	1.33	1.62***	1.33	1.03	1.34**	1.35
Sierra Leone	0.94	1.22	2.24***	0.46***	0.53***	1.70*
Kenya	1.18	1.18	1.31*	0.70***	0.74***	0.98
Liberia	1.14	1.32*	3.88***	0.54***	0.66***	1.16
Sudan	1.70***	1.84***	1.35*	1.38**	1.77***	2.70**
Cameroon	1.51*	1.80***	1.98***	0.67*	0.78	1.34
SO AFRICA	omitted category					

Demographic	Probability Modeled = Not in Labor Force	Probability Modeled = Not Employed	Probability Modeled = Not Self-Employed	Probability Modeled = Not in Labor Force	Probability Modeled = Not Employed	Probability Modeled = Not Self-Employed
Race[d]						
Black	1.39***	1.47***	1.42***	0.66***	0.72***	2.29***
Other[e]	1.09	1.2*	0.973	0.96	1.01	1.28
WHITE	omitted category					
N	26700	26700	26700	20804	20804	20804

* Statistically significant at the .05 level; ** Statistically significant at the .01 level; *** Statistically significant at the .001 level

a. In addition to the variables listed in the table, all models also controlled for number of years of schooling, number of years of work experience plus its squared term, number of years in the United States, marital status, a set of regional variables including Midwest, West, and South (reference category = Northeast), an English deficiency measure, two dummy variables controlling for whether an earned college degree was received in the United States or abroad, and metropolitan status.

b. Models controlled for all variables included for the male sample, plus two relationship variables: number of own children currently living in the household; and number of own children under age 5 in the household.

c. Limited to persons with calculated annual incomes of $500 or more, computed in constant 2019 dollars.

d. Reference group = White.

e. A catchall category that includes individuals reporting various race combinations like two major races, three or more races, etc.

Source: Author's calculations based on samples of the 1980, 1990, and 2000 Decennial Censuses, and the 2010 and 2019 American Community Surveys (ACS), as represented in the Integrated Public Use Microdata Series (IPUMS) (Ruggles et al. 2020). Data limited to persons 25 to 64 years old, and who are not living in group quarters and/or institutions.

Table 4.7 General Linear Regression Estimates of Two Economic Indicators for Top Ten Sending Countries from Africa to the United States, Combined 1980, 1990, 2000, 2010, and 2019 Samples of the IPUMS.

Male Sample[a] Female Sample[b]

Year and Country	Occupational Prestige	Hourly Earnings[c]	Occupational Prestige	Hourly Earnings[c]
1980	8.17***	0.221***	2.73***	0.016
1990	-1.63**	0.029	-4.10***	0.041
2000	-3.06***	-0.031*	-4.36***	-0.058***
2010	-3.62***	0.000	-4.59***	0.000
2019	Reference Category			
Nigeria	-2.10***	-0.232***	-0.91	-0.053
Egypt/United Arab Rep.	-5.17***	-0.277***	-6.23***	-0.129***
Ethiopia	-3.71***	-0.246***	-4.92***	-0.122***
Ghana	-3.13***	-0.193***	-4.22***	-0.088*
Morocco	-8.04***	-0.308***	-7.21***	-0.161***
Somalia	-5.36***	-0.298***	-7.72***	-0.220***
Sierra Leone	-2.90****	-0.227***	-2.04*	-0.120**
Kenya	0.44	-0.137***	0.83	-0.025
Liberia	-4.10***	-0.247***	-3.32***	-0.114**
Sudan	-5.60***	-0.289***	-8.64***	-0.213***
Cameroon	-2.10*	-0.254***	-0.73	-0.066
SO AFRICA	Reference Category			
Black	-5.66***	-0.190***	0.95	-0.012
Other	-3.66***	-0.147***	-1.67**	-0.032
WHITE	Reference Category			
D.F.	29	28	31	30
R-Square	0.29522	0.18554	0.24293	0.12867
N	26,700	19,681	20,804	12,146

* Statistically significant at the .05 level; ** Statistically significant at the .01 level; *** Statistically significant at the .001 level

a. In addition to the variables listed in the table, all models also controlled for number of years of schooling, number of years of work experience plus its squared term, number of years in the United States, marital status, a set of regional variables including Midwest, West, and South (reference category = Northeast), an English deficiency measure, two dummy variables controlling for whether an earned college degree was received in the United States or abroad, and metropolitan status.

b. Models controlled for all variables included for the male sample, plus two relationship variables: number of own children currently living in the household; and number of own children under age 5 in the household.

c. Limited to persons with calculated annual incomes of $500 or more, computed in constant 2019 dollars.

Source: Author's calculations based on samples of the 1980, 1990, and 2000 Decennial Censuses, and the 2010 and 2019 American Community Surveys (ACS), as represented in the Integrated Public Use Microdata Series (IPUMS) (Ruggles et al. 2020). Data limited to persons 25 to 64 years old, and who are not living in group quarters and/or institutions.

self-employment, the estimates show that male immigrants from all eleven countries reported self-employment rates that were significantly lower than those reported by their counterparts from South Africa. And with only a few exceptions, immigrants from South Africa are estimated to be more likely than those from other countries to be in the labor force and to be employed. Here, notable exceptions include Ethiopia (both estimates are not statistically significant), Ghana (both estimates are not statistically significant), Somalia (the labor force participation estimate is not statistically significant), Sierra Leone (both estimates are not statistically significant), Kenya (both estimates are not statistically significant), and Liberia (the labor force participation estimate is not statistically significant).

Yet again, for the female sample we see patterns that are not as consistent. Among women, immigrants from only four countries (Egypt, Morocco, Sierra Leone, and Sudan) are estimated to report self-employment rates that are significantly lower than that reported by immigrants from South Africa. The remaining estimates are not statistically significant.

Unlike their male counterparts, the estimates for labor force participation and unemployment vary noticeably by country, with some countries estimated to report less favorable estimates than immigrants from South Africa (e.g., Morocco and Sudan), and others estimated to have reported more favorable ones (e.g., Nigeria, Ghana, Sierra Leone, Kenya, and Liberia).

Taken together, the estimates for occupational prestige and hourly earnings reported in Table 4.7 are very much in accord with patterns discussed above. With only a few exceptions, immigrants from South Africa are estimated to have held occupations with higher prestige, and to have earned more than their counterparts from the other eleven countries. Gender differences are shown, but the general conclusion is that immigrants from South Africa are estimated to exhibit more favorable measures than immigrants from the other countries. A notable exception, for example, is immigrants from Kenya. For both samples, no statistically significant differences are estimated between the prestige of occupations held by immigrants from Kenya and those from South Africa. Male immigrants from Kenya are nevertheless predicted to have earned less than their counterparts from South Africa, while no such difference is shown among women.

The Salience of Race That Is Also Gendered

As with previous estimates, the logistic and linear regression estimates indicate race to be the most consistent and statistically significant predictor of labor market disparities, as indicated by labor force participation, unemployment, self-employment, occupational prestige, and hourly earnings. But also as with previous estimates, gender differences are shown. All six logistic regression estimates for Black reported in Table 4.5 are highly significant, and indicate that, for males, Black immigrants from all countries are estimated to be more likely than their White counterparts to not be in the labor force and to be unemployed, and less likely to be self-employed. By contrast, among women, Black immigrants are estimated to be less likely than their White counterparts to not be in the labor force and to be unemployed, but more likely than their White counterparts to not be self-employed. In other words, female Black immigrants are more likely than their White counterparts to be in the labor force and to be employed, but also less likely to be self-employed. Here, it is also worth noting, that only one of the six logistic regression estimates for the "Other" category, that for unemployment among males, is statistically significant. The remaining five estimates for this category are not statistically significant.

Other Theoretically Relevant Country-Level Comparisons

It may be recalled from Table 4.6 and Table 4.7 that the omitted category (the reference group) for the country-level estimates is immigrants from South Africa. Yet, using South Africa as the benchmark does not mean other theoretically relevant comparisons do not exist. To test some of these, I again ran a series of Wald tests, results of which I report here.

For example, the previous chapter noted several hypotheses on African immigrants that can be drawn from theory and research. One such hypothesis is the expectation that "settler societies" may produce more successful immigrants than "extractive societies." The distinction being from differing colonial legacies, wherein in some African countries the colonial power dispatched settlers who established farms/plantations, while in some the colonial power concentrated on extracting resources. Deducing from this distinction, and the assumption that cultural exchange was greater when settlers were present than when they were not, it is hypothesized that African emigrants from formerly "settler colonies" will have a cultural advantage in the English-speaking world over emigrants from "non-settler colonies." One good example of a country with a "settlement" heritage is Kenya, while a good example of "extraction" is Nigeria.

To test this hypothesis, I ran a series of Wald test to see if estimates for Kenya and Nigeria, for example, are significantly different from one another. Those tests revealed results that vary by measure and gender. Among men, estimates for both labor force participation and unemployment are shown to be statistically significant, and favoring immigrants from Kenya, whereas those for self-employment are not.[9] And both general linear estimates for occupational prestige and hourly earnings are shown to be statistically significant and in favor of immigrants from Kenya, relative to those from Nigeria.[10] Moreover, with respect to occupational prestige, all other additional country-level male comparisons (additional to South Africa, already discussed above) are shown to be statistically significant and in favor of immigrants from Kenya. And for hourly earnings, except for immigrants from Cameroon, Liberia, and Sierra Leone, whose earnings are shown to not differ significantly from those of immigrants from Kenya, all other country comparisons are statistically significant and in favor of Kenyans.

By contrast, among females, all three logistic regression estimates comparing Kenyans and Nigerians are not statistically significant. And only the estimates for occupational prestige, and not hourly earnings, are significantly different from one another, suggesting that, while immigrants from Kenya held occupations with higher prestige than those held by immigrants from Nigeria (estimate = 1.20, $p = 0.0506$), no statistically significant differences in hourly earnings existed between these two groups. Yet, other country-level comparisons revealed that, except for immigrants from Cameroon, all country estimates for occupational prestige and hourly earnings are significantly different from those of Kenya, and in favor of immigrants from Kenya. It follows that the Wald tests revealed here do proffer some support for the "settler societies" versus "extractive societies" hypothesis, at least as it comes to comparisons between Kenya and the other countries examined here, and albeit stronger effects among men than women.

The reader will also recall from chapter 3 the hypothesis linking immigrant quality to differences in the level of income inequality in host as compared to country of origin (Borjas 1988). Recalling from that chapter, according to Borjas, immigrants will come from the less industrious when income inequality is greater at origin than destination and come from the more industrious when income inequality is lower at origin than destination.

To test this hypothesis, I first obtained information on Gini coefficients in Africa from the World Bank for the countries listed in the tables of this section.[11] The Gini index of income inequality measures the extent to which the distribution of income among individuals or households within an economy deviates from a perfectly equal distribution. Thus, it measures the extent of discrepancy between the actual distribution of income and a hypothetical situation in which each individual or household receives the same percentage of income, and ranges from 0 (perfect equality) to 100 (perfect inequality). Thus, for the countries listed in the above tables, those values indicate South Africa, Cameroon, and Ghana, in that order, to have the highest Gini indices (66.0, 46.6, and 43.5, respectively) (among African countries, indices range from a low of 27.6 for Algeria to a high of 63.0 for South Africa). By contrast, Nigeria, Ethiopia, Sudan, and Egypt have the lowest indices (35.1, 35, 34.2, and 31.5, respectively). From the same source, I also obtained the

2019 Gini index for the United States, which is shown to be 41.5. It follows that compared with the United States, South Africa, Cameroon, and Ghana have higher Gini indices, while Nigeria, Ethiopia, Sudan, and Egypt have lower indices.

Thus, to test the effect of income inequality hypothesis, I ran a series of Wald tests to see if estimates for Ghana, for example, are significantly different from those for Nigeria and Egypt. Following Borjas, and using the foregoing values, a testable hypothesis is that estimates for immigrants from Ghana will be significantly different from those for immigrants from Nigeria and Egypt and favoring the latter two. Those tests revealed results that vary by measure and gender. Among men, all three logistic regression estimates (labor force participation, unemployment, and self-employment) are shown to be statistically significant, and favoring immigrants from Ghana on the first two dimensions, and Egypt and Nigeria on the last.[12] In other words, while immigrants from Ghana are estimated to have higher rates of labor force participation and employment than immigrants from Egypt and Nigeria, they are predicted to have lower rates of self-employment than those two groups. Moreover, the two general linear regression estimates on occupation and hourly earnings are similarly split, with Nigerians estimated to have reported occupations with higher prestige than Ghanaians (parameter estimate = 1.821, $p = 0.0054$), while immigrants from Egypt are estimated to have held occupations with lower prestige than their Ghanaian counterparts (parameter estimate = -0.869, $p = 0.0003$). Comparisons of estimates for the hourly earnings measure, however, revealed both Nigerians and Egyptians to have earned less than Ghanaians (estimate for Nigeria = -0.048, $p = 0.0131$, while estimate for Egypt = -0.104, $p = 0.0003$). It follows that, at least for the male sample, the findings of the Wald tests are notably mixed on the immigrant quality–income inequality proposition. Results of the Wald tests discussed here indicate that Ghanaians are favored over Egyptians and Nigerians on some dimensions while the latter two are favored on others.

For the female sample, the Wald tests indicate the Egyptian-Ghanaian logistic regression comparisons to be significantly different from one another,[13] and not the Nigerian-Ghanaian ones. In other words, for one of the comparisons (Egypt-Ghana), Ghanaians are shown to have higher rates of labor force participation and employment, while no such differences existed between Ghanaians and Nigerians. Similarly, for occupational prestige, those tests indicate that Nigerians held occupations with higher prestige than Ghanaians (parameter estimate = 3.31, $p = <.0001$), while Egyptians held occupations with lower prestige (parameter estimate = -5.32, $p = <0.001$). Finally, and by contrast, the Wald tests indicate no statistically significant difference in the hourly earnings of Nigerians and Egyptians, on one hand, and Ghanaians, on the other. It follows that, the Wald tests on comparisons for females are even more inconsistent on the immigrant quality–income inequality proposition.

One final comparison is worth noting here. The reader will recall from above that theory and research suggest that the type of U.S. visa immigrants hold impacts their incorporation into U.S. society (Jasso 2004; Jasso, Rosenzweig, and Smith 2000). And recalling from data presented in Table 4.1, the Refugees and Asylees admission category of African immigrants illustrates one of the greatest spreads in percentage. Again, whereas less than 1 percent of immigrants from Morocco, and about 2 percent from Nigeria and Ghana, are shown to have been granted legal status as refugees and asylees, well over 80 percent of immigrants from Somalia and well over 50 percent from Sudan are shown to have been granted legal status under this category.

Accordingly, I conducted a final set of Wald tests to see if estimates for countries like Morocco, Nigeria, and Ghana are different from those for immigrants from Somalia and Sudan. And suffice it to say that those tests reveal this to be the one area where findings for men and women are shown to be clearly consistent. Virtually all comparisons that I examined (e.g., Ghana vs. Somalia and Sudan; Cameroon vs. Somalia and Sudan) revealed estimates that favor immigrants from other countries over those from Somalia and Sudan.[14]

SUMMARY

Taken together, the findings in this chapter suggest at least three key patterns. First, African immigrants do indeed exhibit diverse paths to U.S. legal permanent residency, paths that are shown to be related with socioeconomic outcomes. Hence, analyses of African immigrant incorporation into U.S. society will benefit substantially from taking such diversity into account. Second, the data discussed in this chapter have illustrated substantial regional, country, and demographic variations in the socioeconomic profiles of African immigrants. This finding, yet again, highlights the need for analyses of labor market disparities among African immigrants to consider the immense diversity among this group of immigrants. Third, despite the significant variation illustrated in the information presented in this chapter, the data also suggest some notably stable patterns associated with race/ethnicity, gender, and linguistic heritage, with each seeming to produce notable distinctions. In fact, this is one significant and consistent finding: race/ethnicity, gender, and linguistic heritage are key predictors of socioeconomic attainment among these immigrants, with race and gender being the most consistently salient of these. Again, analyses of labor market disparities among U.S. African immigrants should consider the increasing diversity in the racial, ethnic and gender composition of the African immigrant population in the United States.

THEORETICAL ANALYSIS

The previous chapter of this book (chapter 3) noted several hypotheses on U.S. African immigrants that can be drawn from theory and research. Selectivity theory, for example, proposes that "politically motivated emigrants" are less positively selected (pushed) than "economically motivated ones" (pulled) (Lee 1966; Borjas 1994; Chiswick 1978, 1999; Jasso and Rosenzweig 1990a and b; Tesfai 2019). Following directly from this proposition, scholars have further hypothesized a direct association between the type of U.S. visa an immigrant holds and his or her speedy (or not) incorporation into U.S. society (Jasso 2004; Jasso, Rosenzweig and Smith 2000). Linking this hypothesis to the data on African immigrants analyzed in this chapter, results show patterns that are consistent with this hypothesis. Results reported in this chapter, for example, have shown that African immigrants from countries with higher-than-average percentage of refugees and asylees to the United States also exhibit less favorable socioeconomic outcomes.

Selectivity theory also suggests that "early birds" will be more positively selected than latecomers (Model 2008). According to Everett Lee: "The overcoming of a set of intervening obstacles by early migrants lessens the difficulty of the passage for later migrants" (Lee 1966, 55). Thus, early migrants are predicted to be more selective than those that follow. The results reported in this chapter are also suggestive of support for this hypothesis. In general, those reports show that African immigrants from the top sending countries in the last twenty or so years exhibit more favorable socioeconomic measures than the overall African immigrant population.

Other perspectives also suggest several hypotheses that can be revisited here. One variable, for example, said to promote White favoritism for immigrants is "Anglophilia"—U.S. cultural legacies of associating positive evaluations with individuals and practices associated with Great Britain and or the English-speaking world. Moreover, another proposition drawn from the distinction between African countries that were "settler colonies" and those that were not (Corra and Kimuna 2009) suggests that African immigrants from the former would have a cultural advantage in the English-speaking world over immigrants from the latter. As noted in chapter 3 of this book, in some African countries (e.g., Kenya, Zimbabwe, South Africa) the colonial power dispatched settlers who established farms/plantations. By contrast, in (most) other African countries, the colonial power concentrated on extracting resources (mines, mostly). The expectation is that cultural exchange was greater when settlers were present than when they were not.

Results presented in this chapter lend some support to the foregoing hypotheses. Immigrants from English-speaking countries, for example, are shown to exhibit favorable socioeconomic outcomes than those from Arab-speaking and non-Arab-speaking countries, at least on some dimensions. Similarly, immigrants from countries like South Africa and Kenya are shown to exhibit measures that are more advantageous than average. In short, though the main objective of this chapter was to examine variations in socioeconomic attainment among African immigrants of varying backgrounds, and some of these hypotheses have not been directly tested, the findings are arguably suggestive.

Finally, as noted in chapter 1 of this book, recent theoretical approaches to the study of immigration suggest that the multicolored nature of U.S. society along ethnoracial lines means that immigrants experience a segmented form of assimilation. The hypothesis here, as it relates to African immigrants, is that the socioeconomic trajectories of some immigrants (i.e., Blacks) may not mirror the pattern of quick (largely European) incorporation into the U.S. labor market that informed early theorizing. Consistent with this hypothesis, we see that the profiles of Black and White immigrants from Africa exhibit markedly different trajectories of attainment. Consistently, Black immigrants are shown to exhibit measures that are less favorable than those held by Whites and other immigrants, although this was shown to be somewhat gendered. The next chapter continues this probe by analyzing disparities among immigrants from major sending regions (e.g., Africa, Asia, Europe, etc.) to the United States.

NOTES

1. These files are available in excel and PDF, and are downloadable at https://www.dhs.gov/immigration-statistics/yearbook.

2. The measure of occupational prestige here is the average score of prestige assigned to occupations, using the Hauser and Warren Socioeconomic Index (SEI). The Hauser and Warren Socioeconomic Index is a measure of occupational status that is based upon the earnings and educational attainment associated with categories of occupations, as specified in the census documents. Importantly, the average of prestige scores for occupations is different for men and women. For more information, see R. M. Hauser and J. R. Warren "Socioeconomic Indexes for Occupations: A Review, Update, and Critique," *Sociological Methodology* 27 (1997): 177–298; and K. Nakao and J. Treas, "Updating Occupational Prestige and Socioeconomic Scores: How the New Measures Measure Up," *Sociological Methodology* 24 (1994): 1–72.

3. See, for example, Model 2008; Dodoo and Takyi 2002; Corra and Kimuna 2009; Borch and Corra 2010; Corra and Borch 2014; Thomas 2014; Elo et al. 2015; Kusow, Ajrouch, and Corra 2018; Kusow, Kimuna, and Corra 2018[AQ12]; Hamilton 2014, 2019, 2020.

4. See, for example, Dodoo and Takyi 2002; Corra and Kimuna 2009; Borch and Corra 2010; Thomas 2014; Elo et al. 2015; Kusow, Ajrouch, and Corra 2018; Kusow, Kimuna, and Corra 2018[AQ12]; Hamilton 2014, 2019, 2020.

5. Here, it might be useful to note that of the 63,668 cases in our total sample of African immigrants, 36,257 (about 56.94%) are Black, 20,354 (about 31.97%) are White, and 7,131 (about 11.20%) are "Other" races. The latter include those that identified themselves as American Indian or Alaska Native (31 cases, or about 0.05%), Chinese (143, or about 0.22%), Japanese (5, or about 0.01%), "Other Asian or Pacific Islander" (3,046, or about 4.78%), "Other race, nec" (628, or about 0.99%), two major races (3,135, or about 4.92%), and three or more major races (74 cases, or about 0.12%).

6. I also ran all three logistic regression models on the overall sample (men and women together), with female included in the model and male as the omitted category. Not surprisingly, those estimates reveal gender to be highly salient, with women predicted to be more likely than men to not be in the labor force, to be unemployed, and to not be self-employed: labor force participation, odds ratio = 3.073, $p = <.0001$; unemployment, odds ratio = 2.686, $p = <.0001$; and self-employment, odds ratio = 2.381, $p = <.000$.

7. I did not include coefficients for the unidentified regions of Africa in this part of my analysis, since that group represents a more amorphous mix of individuals, and hence less theoretically informative. Readers interested in comparisons on this dimension of region of origins may make a request from the author.

8. As with the logistic regression models, I also ran these two models on the overall sample (men and women together), with female included in the models and male as the omitted category. Again, not surprisingly, those estimates reveal gender to be highly salient, with women predicted to have reported occupations with significantly lower prestige than men, and to have earned significantly less: occupational prestige, parameter estimate = -0.995, $p = <.000$; and hourly earnings, parameter estimate = -0.149, $p = <.000$.

9. Labor force participation, Chi-Square = 3.9887, odds ratio = 1.211, $p = 0.0458$; and unemployment, Chi-Square = 9.1352, odds ratio = 1.293, $p = 0.0025$.

10. Nigeria, parameter estimate for occupational prestige = -0.9211, p-value = <.0001; and hourly earnings, parameter estimate = -0.110, p-value = <.0001.

11. Source: https://www.indexmundi.com/facts/indicators/SI.POV.GINI/rankings/africa. According to this site, the information given at the site is: World Bank, Development Research Group. And that data is based on primary household survey data obtained from government statistical agencies and World Bank country departments. The site directs visitors for more information and methodology to please see PovcalNet (http://iresearch.worldban). Note that the values noted in the text are for varying years: Cameroon, South Africa, and Sudan are for 2014, Ethiopia is 2015, Ghana is for 2016, Egypt is for 2017, and Nigeria is for 2018.

12. For the Nigeria-Ghana comparison on labor force participation and unemployment, respectively, Chi-Square = 15.9915, odds ratio = 1.35, p = <.0001, and Chi-Square = 19.6146, odds ratio = 1.333, p = <.0001; whereas for self-employment, Chi-Square = 12.8917, odds ratio = 0.664, p = 0.0003.

And for the Egypt-Ghana comparison on labor force participation and unemployment, respectively, Chi-Square = 10.0007, odds ratio = 1.42, p = 0.0016, and Chi-Square = 12.4617, odds ratio = 1.412, p = 0.0004; whereas for self-employment, Chi-Square = 12.8917, odds ratio = 0.664, p = 0.0003.

13. For labor force participation, Chi-Square = 26.3963, odds ratio = 1.628, p = <.0001; for unemployment, Chi-Square = 22.0421, odds ratio = 1.53, p = <.0001; and for self-employment, Chi-Square = 20.4835, odds ratio = 2.264, p = <.0001.

14. Males and Ghana: For males, significant comparisons include labor force participation estimates for immigrants from Ghana versus those from Sudan, Chi-Square = 13.9545, odds ratio = 1.6, p = 0.0002, unemployment, Chi-Square = 18.6776, odds ratio = 1.61, p = <.0001, and self-employment, Chi-Square = 7.7651, odds ratio = 0.664, p = 0.0053; and hourly earnings, parameter estimate = -0.1448, p = 0.0014.

Chapter 5

African Immigrants in the United States

The Gendering Significance of Race through International Migration?

"WHEREAS some doubts have arisen whether children got by any Englishman upon a negro woman should be slave or free, Be it therefore enacted and declared by this present grand assembly, that all children born in this country shall be held bond or free only according to the condition of the mother...." (Virginia House of Burgesses/General Assembly, 1662)[1]

Be it enacted, by the governor, council and burgesses of this present general assembly, and it is hereby enacted by the authority of the same, That from and after the passing of this act, all negro, mulatto, and Indian slaves, in all courts of judicature, and other places, within this dominion, shall be held, taken, and adjudged, to be real estate ... and shall descend unto the heirs and widows of persons departing this life, according to the manner and custom of land inheritance, held in fee simple." (Virginia House of Burgesses/General Assembly, 1705)[2]

"Representatives and direct Taxes shall be apportioned among the several States which may be included within this Union, according to their respective Numbers, which shall be determined by adding to the whole Number of free Persons, including those bound to Service for a Term of Years, and excluding Indians not taxed, three fifths of all other Persons." (Constitution of the United States, Article I, Section 2)[3]

"It is difficult at this day to realize the state of public opinion in relation to that unfortunate race, which prevailed in the civilized and enlightened portions of the world at the time of the Declaration of Independence, and when the Constitution of the United States was framed and adopted.... They had for more than a century before been regarded as beings of an inferior order, and altogether unfit to associate with the white race, either in social or political relations; and so far inferior, that they had no rights which the white man was bound to respect . . . a negro of the African race was regarded by them as an article of property, and held, and bought and sold as such, in every one of the thirteen colonies which united in the Declaration of Independence, and afterwards formed the Constitution of the United States." (U.S. Supreme Court, Dred Scott v. Sandford, 60 U.S. [19 How.] 393 [1857])

"I think God made all people good, but if we had to take a million immigrants in, say Zulus, next year, or Englishmen, and put them in Virginia, what group would be easier to assimilate and would cause less problems for the people of Virginia?" (Syndicated conservative columnist Patrick J. Buchanan, quoted from Hing 1993)

"Why are we having all these people from shithole countries come here?" (Then U.S. President Donald J. Trump, quoted from the *Washington Post*, January 12, 2018)[4]

BACKGROUND

As the foregoing declarations suggest, debate over the status of persons of African origins in the United States dates to the settling of this territory that we now call the United States. As early as 1662, barely forty years after the first group of captive Africans landed in Jamestown in 1619, the Virginia House of Burgesses, deploying the so-called legal doctrine of *partus sequitur ventrem*, by statute, declared enslaved status to be passed to children through the mother. Since no doubt existed whether children can be gotten by any "negro man" upon an Englishwoman, this doctrine broadened the scope of enslaved status to children from sexual unions between Englishmen (White men) and enslaved women (Black women). Less than fifty years later in 1705, the same legislative body explicitly equated enslaved status with property by law. Enshrined in the original constitution of the United States, of course, the well-known three-fifths clause equated enslavement to three-fifths of a person.

And, notably, the sentiment reflective of the declarations continue to surface recurrently at different points in our country's history. It was famously expressed by long-time conservative columnist Patrick J. Buchanan, who was twice a candidate for the Republican presidential nomination and the presidential nominee of the Reform Party in 2000: "I think God made all people good, but if we had to take a million immigrants in, say Zulus, next year, or Englishmen, and put them in Virginia, what group would be easier to assimilate and would cause less problems for the people of Virginia?" (quoted from Hing 1993). As recent as 2018, then president Donald J. Trump, supposedly referring to Nigerian and Haitian immigrants, was reported to have asked in a meeting with lawmakers in the White House: "Why are we having all these people from shithole countries come here?" ("Trump Derides Protections for Immigrants from 'Shithole' Countries," *Washington Post*, January 12, 2018). Contemporary scholarly debates, however, center around the status of African immigrants in the United States, relative to other immigrant groups. And, for both theoretical and practical reasons, that issue is an important one. Exactly how do African immigrants in the United States compare in socioeconomic status with other immigrant groups? Examining this question is the focus of this chapter. That is to say, having examined in the previous chapter the relative positions of the various African immigrant groups in the United States with one another, this chapter explores how African immigrants compare in socioeconomic attainment with other immigrant groups.

To that end, it may be recalled from chapter 3 of this manuscript that early migration theory and research (Chiswick 1978; Carliner 1980; DeFreitas 1980) portrayed a rather linear picture of U.S. immigration and successful immigrant adaptation. After a relatively short adjustment period, immigrants are said to "catch up" and/or "overtake" comparable natives in socioeconomic attainment. Chiswick (1979) estimated the "overtaking" point for immigrants at 10–15 years after immigration.

Yet, recalling the discussion in chapter 1 of this book, voluntary immigration from Africa to the United States, at least in large numbers, is a very recent phenomenon (also see Kent 2007; Thomas 2011; Capps, McCabe, and Fix 2012; Anderson and López 2018; Tamir 2022; Tamir and Anderson 2022). And also recalling discussion in that chapter of analyses reported by Borjas (1985, 1987, 1991, 1994, 1995) that suggest waning immigrant quality among recent immigrants, a phenomenon he attributed to changes in the mix of sending countries. Directly relevant to the discussion of this chapter, Borjas specifically reported finding no declines in immigrant quality among immigrants from Europe and Canada to the United States. Accordingly, he predicted that, after a decade or so in the United States, the earnings of immigrants from Europe and Canada would overtake those of their native White counterparts, while the earnings of immigrants from the rest of the world, including Africa, would never surpass those of their native counterparts.

Following Borjas, a testable hypothesis is that African immigrants will compare less favorably in labor market qualities with immigrants from Canada and Europe. And generalizing from this, a second hypothesis is that immigrants from other regions will also compare less favorably in labor market attributes with immigrants from Canada and Europe. African immigrants may also compare more or less favorably with other immigrant groups, depending on which theoretical construct is being deployed (see chapter 3 of this book). All three of these hypotheses are investigated in this chapter.

It may also be recalled from chapter 3 that recent theoretical approaches to the study of immigration suggest that the multicolored nature of U.S. society along ethnoracial lines means that immigrants experience a segmented form of assimilation. As noted in that chapter, some recent approaches to the study of migration, for example, emphasize the "context of reception" to the host society and the modes of incorporation of different groups into its labor market (Portes and Böröcz 1989; Portes and Rumbaut 2001, 2006). Here, one key variable is said to be racial status (Borch and Corra 2010; Thomas 2014; Sáenz and Manges Douglas 2015). And in terms of migration, race comes to the forefront when the question focuses specifically on how racial status differentially influences immigrant adaptation (Dodoo and Takyi 2002; Borch and Corra 2010; Thomas 2014). According to Dodoo and Takyi (2002): "The condition of Africans [and other immigrant groups] in the diaspora proffers insight into not just their adaptation to their new countries, but also the nature of racial stratification at their destinations" (p. 913). It follows that another testable hypothesis is that Black immigrants (African and non-African alike) will compare less favorably in labor market attributes with their White immigrant counterparts. Tested in the previous chapter, of course, is the proposition that Black African immigrants will also compare less favorably in labor market attributes with their White African immigrant counterparts.

This chapter is dedicated to investigating these hypotheses and the analyses begin with disparities in educational attainment, perhaps one of the most important variables said to influence labor market outcomes in the United States. Exactly how do African immigrants compare in measures of educational attainment with other immigrant groups? How do they compare with immigrants from Canada and Europe? The section to immediately follow addresses these and related questions.

HIGHEST LEVELS OF EDUCATIONAL ATTAINMENT AMONG AFRICAN IMMIGRANT GROUPS

Table 5.1 provides summary statistics on educational attainment and reports data on (1) African immigrants as a collective group; (2) Black, White, and "Other" African immigrants viewed separately; (3) immigrants from other major sending countries/regions to the United States; and (4) Black, White, and "Other" immigrants (excluding Africans) from those countries/regions. The table reports summary statistics (averages based on the mean) on five levels of education: percentages of individuals with less than a high school education/twelve years of education; those with a high school degree/twelve years of education; those with one to three years of post-secondary education; those with a bachelor's degree/at least four years of post-secondary

Table 5.1. A Comparison of Immigrants 25 to 64 Years Old from Selected Countries and Regions of Origin on Educational Attainment, Combined 1980, 1990, 2000, 2010, and 2019 Samples of the IPUMS.

Male Sample	N	% <HS	% HS	% Some College	% College Grad[a]	% 5 Yrs or more[b]	% Total
All Africans	35759	4.95	19.59	22.30	26.56	26.60	100
White Africans	11409	4.74	16.78	18.84	28.60	31.04	100
Black Africans	20497	4.90	20.73	24.94	25.06	24.37	100
Other Africans[c]	3853	5.81	21.83	18.53	28.55	25.28	100
Caribbeans	63741	26.24	37.93	20.26	9.53	6.05	100
Canadians	33576	14.82	24.71	22.08	19.68	18.71	100
Europeans	205176	19.33	28.29	18.54	15.53	18.31	100
Australians and New Zealanders	3665	5.18	19.78	20.08	25.81	29.14	100
Asians	310202	11.38	19.50	17.87	25.21	26.04	100
Mexicans	319494	63.39	24.20	7.93	2.77	1.72	100
Central Americans	68234	46.84	29.62	14.14	5.84	3.56	100
South Americans	67914	16.27	33.88	22.68	14.45	12.73	100
Pacific Islanders	3143	21.44	39.52	25.45	9.51	4.07	100
Unidentified[d] Race[e]	61607	31.23	30.89	17.85	10.44	9.59	100
Black Immigrants	56008	22.34	38.89	21.99	10.19	6.60	100
White Immigrants	568460	32.82	26.65	15.96	11.93	12.65	100
Other Immigrants[f]	512284	31.86	23.28	14.38	15.53	14.95	100
Female Sample							
All Africans	27914	9.29	28.50	24.26	23.92	14.02	100
White Africans	8945	7.84	25.72	21.36	28.62	16.46	100
Black Africans	15760	9.70	30.42	26.36	20.95	12.58	100
Other Africans[c]	3209	11.34	26.80	22.06	25.46	14.33	100
Caribbeans	80868	25.74	36.87	21.68	10.11	5.60	100
Canadians	43595	14.81	31.56	26.83	16.15	10.65	100
Europeans	245099	19.24	36.00	20.79	12.86	11.12	100

Male Sample	N	% <HS	% HS	% Some College	% College Grad[a]	% 5 Yrs or more[b]	% Total
Australians and New Zealanders	4244	7.49	30.77	24.95	22.05	14.73	100
Asians	349942	16.38	23.99	17.71	26.73	15.18	100
Mexicans	276240	62.06	24.46	8.58	3.23	1.66	100
Central Americans	73568	44.27	31.50	15.03	6.18	3.02	100
South Americans	78715	16.97	35.76	22.59	15.16	9.52	100
Pacific Islanders	3350	24.24	42.84	22.36	7.79	2.78	100
Unidentified[d] Race[e]	65111	31.70	33.00	18.44	9.89	6.96	100
Black Immigrants	69043	20.95795374	37.92	23.74	11.07	6.313456831	100
White Immigrants	611941	31.08355217	31.85	17.97	10.94	8.159610158	100
Other Immigrants[f]	539748	30.80	25.53	15.23	18.29	10.20	100

a. Data for 1980 represent those reporting four years of post-secondary schooling; 1990, 2000, 2010, and 2019 represent those reporting having earned a bachelor's degree.

b. Data for 1980 represent those reporting five-plus years of post-secondary schooling; 1990, 2000, 2010, and 2019 include those reporting having earned a master's degree, professional degree beyond a bachelor's degree, and doctoral degree.

c. A catchall category of African immigrants reporting racial backgrounds of Asian, Native American, various race combinations like two major races, three or more races, etc.

d. Includes those identifying their birthplace as Atlantic Islands, Cuba, and birthplaces other than the United States, but not identified (in IPUMS terminology, "North America, ns," "Americas, n.s.," and "Other n.e.c.").

e. Excluding African immigrants.

f. For all immigrants, excluding Africans, a catchall category that includes individuals reporting various race combinations like two major races, three or more races, etc.

Source: Author's calculations based on samples of the 1980, 1990, and 2000 Decennial Censuses, and the 2010 and 2019 American Community Surveys (ACS), as represented in the Integrated Public Use Microdata Series (IPUMS) (Ruggles et al. 2020). Data limited to persons 25 to 64 years old, and who are not living in group quarters and/or institutions.

education; and individuals reporting five or more years of post-secondary education. And, as in previous chapters, the data is separated by sex.

As can be seen in Table 5.1, African immigrants do indeed compare very favorably with the immigrant groups listed in that table.

Consider, for example, the percentage of immigrants with at least four years of post-secondary education. Looking at entries under that column in Table 5.1, we see that percentages for the African immigrant groups are the highest shown, and this is shown to be true for both men and women. For males, about

27 percent of African immigrants reported at least four years of post-secondary education, and an additional 27 percent reported five or more years. Taken together, about 54 percent of African immigrant men reported four or more years of post-secondary education. For African immigrant females, about 24 percent reported having at least four years of post-secondary education, and an additional 14 percent reported five or more years.

Compare these with those for the two immigrant groups with the closest percentages of post-secondary years of education, immigrants from Australia and New Zealand and Asia, respectively. About 26 percent and 22 percent of male and female immigrants from Australia and New Zealand, respectively, reported at least four years of post-secondary education, and an additional 29 percent and 15 percent, respectively, reported five or more years. For Asian immigrant males and females, the percentages reporting at least four years of post-secondary education are about 25 and 28, respectively, and an additional 26 percent and 15 percent, respectively, reported five or more years.

The comparisons are even more striking when you look at the different African groups, relative to others. For example, about 29 percent of White African immigrant men and women reported having had at least four years of post-secondary education, and an additional 31 percent and 17 percent, respectively, reported five or more years of post-secondary education. This means at least 60 percent of White African men reported four or more years of post-secondary education, while 46 percent of White African women reported having such years of education.

For Black African men and women with at least four years of post-secondary education, those percentages are about 25 and 21, respectively. Taken together, about 49 percent and 34 percent of Black African immigrant men and women, respectively, reported four or more years of post-secondary education.

Compare these with the averages for immigrants from Canada and Europe. About 20 percent and 16 percent of Canadian men and women, respectively, reported having had at least four years of post-secondary education, and an additional 19 percent and 11 percent, respectively, reported five or more years. For European immigrant men and women, respectively, those values are 16 percent and 13 percent, and 18 percent and 11 percent, respectively.

Returning to the hypotheses outlined earlier in this chapter, then, African immigrants, both Black and White, do compare very favorably with other immigrant groups, at least on this one dimension of educational attainment. In fact, they compare very favorably when contrasted with immigrants from Canada and Europe, and most favorably with just about all other immigrant groups. Compared with Caribbean immigrants, for example, percentages with post-secondary years of education for all African groups are virtually two or more times those for immigrants from the Caribbean. And again, these findings are true for both Black and White African immigrants, and generally across male and female samples.

By contrast, several other immigrant groups (e.g., those from Central America, Mexico, the Caribbean, the Pacific Islands, and South America) show average levels of education that are noticeably lower than those for immigrants from Canada and Europe. Whereas some other immigrant groups (those from Asia and Australia and New Zealand) exhibit measures that are higher. Moreover, disparities by gender also exist, with almost all female groups showing lower measures of educational attainment than their male counterparts.

Finally, as to disparities in educational attainment by race, the data presented in Table 5.1 does also show these to exist. In general, educational attainment averages for Blacks are lower than those for Whites, and this is shown to be true both between Black and White African immigrants, on one hand, and other Black and White immigrants (excluding Africans), on the other hand.

Notably, when it comes to African immigrants, the foregoing findings are consistent with recent surveys (see, for example, Anderson and Connor 2018; Simmons 2018). The title of a 2018 *Los Angeles Times* piece, "African immigrants are more educated than most—including people born in U.S." (Simmons 2018), is illustrative.[5]

An Immigration Policy Center analysis just released this year (2022) reports that 42 percent of Sub-Saharan Africans ages 25 and over in the United States held a bachelor's degree or higher, compared to 33 percent of all foreign- and U.S.-born adults.[6] As examples of African immigrant groups with some of the highest education, that report highlights Nigeria and South Africa, with 64 percent and 58 percent, respectively, holding at least a bachelor's degree, followed by Cameroonians (52%), Kenyans (49%), and Ghanaians (42%).

Moreover, a 2018 New American Economy study, titled, "Power of the Purse: How Sub-Saharan Africans Contribute to the U.S. Economy," highlights the type of degrees held by these immigrants.[7] It reports that one in three of undergraduate degrees held by African immigrants was focused on science, technology, engineering, and math—"training heavily in demand by today's employers" (p. 2).

In addition, the *LA Times* piece noted above indicated that African immigrants are significantly more likely to have graduate degrees, and that a total of 16 percent of African immigrants then had a master's degree, medical degree, law degree, or a doctorate, compared with only 11 percent of the U.S.-born population.

A key question that comes to mind, then, is exactly how these educational measures translate into labor market outcomes. How do African immigrants

Table 5.2. Immigrants from Selected Countries and Regions of Origin: A Comparison on Four Economic Indicators, Combined 1980, 1990, 2000, 2010, and 2019 Samples of the IPUMS.

Male Sample	% Unemployed	% Self-Employed	Occupational Prestige[a]	Annual Earnings[b]	N
Africans	4.51	12.20	38.43	$65,571.50	35,759
White Africans	3.51	16.72	42.61	$89,788.50	11,409
Black Africans	5.17	9.14	35.91	$50,836.30	20,497
Other Africans[c]	4.00	15.08	39.42	$72,284.50	3,853
Caribbeans	6.75	8.14	29.37	$45,805.60	63,741
Canadians	3.19	16.32	40.40	$90,122.80	33,576
Europeans	3.79	16.75	36.66	$78,194.00	205,176
Australians and New Zealanders	2.26	15.83	45.06	$110,524.00	3,665
Asians	3.50	13.83	38.72	$71,471.60	310,202
Mexicans	6.05	7.96	24.52	$34,875.20	319,494
Central Americans	5.27	8.62	27.04	$38,837.70	68,234
South Americans	4.22	12.69	33.21	$55,654.70	67,914
Pacific Islanders	5.09	8.88	28.27	$46,080.90	3,143
Unidentified[d] Race[e]	5.19	13.66	31.61	$51,756.00	61,607
Black Immigrants	6.76	7.17	30.07	$46,918.30	56,008
White Immigrants	4.60	13.98	32.77	$61,238.50	568,460
Other Immigrants[f]	4.55	10.47	32.37	$54,288.10	512,284
Female Sample					
Africans	5.06	5.68	30.68	$42,311.30	27,914
White Africans	6.02	4.30	30.87	$39,753.90	8,945
Black Africans	3.71	7.56	30.59	$46,841.30	15,760
Other Africans[c]	4.08	7.20	29.98	$45,242.50	3,209
Caribbeans	6.15	4.16	26.60	$36,585.50	80,868
Canadians	2.31	7.60	31.03	$43,437.00	43,595
Europeans	3.16	7.22	26.70	$39,241.50	245,099
Australians and New Zealanders	2.17	9.24	33.75	$52,766.80	4,244
Asians	3.30	7.18	28.78	$45,684.10	349,942
Mexicans	6.23	4.90	16.27	$23,049.80	276,240
Central Americans	6.04	7.57	20.68	$27,472.30	73,568
South Americans	5.08	8.51	26.22	$35,299.40	78,715
Pacific Islanders	4.48	5.10	23.06	$31,764.60	3,350
Unidentified[d] Race[e]	4.85	5.11	24.46	$32,963.10	65,111
Black Immigrants	5.66	3.68	28.68	$38,636.50	69,043
White Immigrants	4.23	6.72	23.86	$34,755.50	611,941
Other Immigrants[f]	4.54	6.59	24.88	$38,401.90	539,748

a. Socioeconomic Index, Hauser and Warren.

b. Limited to persons with calculated annual incomes of $500 or more, computed in constant 2019 dollars.

c. A catchall category of African immigrants reporting racial backgrounds of Asian, Native American, various race combinations like two major races, three or more races, etc.

d. Includes those identifying their birthplace as Atlantic Islands, Cuba, and birthplaces other than the United States, but not identified (in IPUMS terminology, "North America, ns," "Americas, n.s.," and "Other n.e.c.").

e. Excluding African immigrants.

f. For all immigrants, excluding Africans, a catchall category that includes individuals reporting various race combinations like two major races, three or more races, etc.

Source: Author's calculations based on samples of the 1980, 1990, and 2000 Decennial Censuses, and the 2010 and 2019 American Community Surveys (ACS), as represented in the Integrated Public Use Microdata Series (IPUMS) (Ruggles et al. 2020). Data limited to persons 25 to 64 years old, and who are not living in group quarters and/or institutions.

compare with other immigrants on work-related measures? The section to immediately follow takes up these and related issues.

Gendered Regional and Country Variations in Four Work-Related Measures

Table 5.2 continues this probe by providing summary statistics on four work-related measures, as they pertain to immigrants from the major sending areas to the United States discussed above, including Africa: unemployment, self-employment, occupational prestige,[8] and calculated annual earnings.

How do African immigrants compare with other immigrant groups on these four measures? The answer to this question is nuanced by several factors, including which African group is being referenced, the specific measure in question, and whether the comparison is within or across male and female samples.

If White Africans are the reference, then African immigrants do indeed compare most favorably with all immigrant groups, including those exhibiting the most favorable measures, that is, those from Australia and New Zealand, Canada, Asia, and Europe, and especially among men. For the male sample, the average of unemployed White African immigrants of 3.51 percent is the third lowest, compared with those for immigrants from Australia and New Zealand (2.26%), Canada (3.19%), and Asia (3.50%). The unemployment percent for Europe is slightly higher than that for White African immigrants, about 3.79 percent. And the self-employment percent for White African immigrant men (16.72%) is second only to that for immigrants from Europe (16.75%). White African immigrant men also show the second highest average occupational prestige (42.61), second to immigrants from Australia and New Zealand (45.06). And only immigrants from Australia and New Zealand and Canada show calculated average annual earnings ($110,524 and $90,122, respectively) that are higher than those shown for White African immigrants ($89,788).

For the female sample, the White African immigrant–other immigrant groups divide is less pronounced. That divide shows more acutely when White African immigrants are compared with immigrants from Australia and New Zealand, favoring the latter, and less so when White African immigrants are compared with immigrants from Asia, Canada, and Europe. Comparisons with the latter three show White African immigrants favored on some dimensions (occupational prestige and annual earnings), and less on others (unemployment and self-employment).

Compared with Black African immigrants, by contrast, immigrants from Asia, Australia and New Zealand, Canada, and Europe, all show measures of unemployment, self-employment, occupational prestige, and annual earnings that are noticeably more favorable. It follows that, when it comes to Africans, these summary measures appear to suggest the Black-White distinction to be most influential. Black and White Africans compare differentially with many of these groups.

The remaining immigrant groups (with the single exception of immigrant men from South America), in contrast, all show measures that are less favorable to those for Black Africans, and more saliently among men. Compare, for example, the measures for Caribbean immigrant men (6.75% unemployment, 8.14% self-employment, 29.37 mean occupational prestige, and $45,805 calculated average annual earnings), with those of African men as a group (4.51% unemployment, 12.2% self-employment, 38.43 average occupational prestige, and $65,571 in calculated average annual earnings). The difference in calculated annual earnings between African immigrant men and Caribbean immigrant men, for example, is about $19,766; and the difference between that for African immigrant women ($42,311) and Caribbean immigrant women ($36,585) is $5,726.

In short, the summary statistics shown in Table 5.2 do indeed show grouping clusters that can be identified, albeit more saliently among men. One group, which includes African immigrants, consists of immigrants from Asia, Europe, and Canada. Averages for these four are generally more favorable, relative to immigrants from a second cluster consisting of those from the Caribbean and Central and South America. Immigrants from Mexico and Australia and New Zealand seem to be in their own categories, with immigrants from Mexico showing the least favorable measures, relative to all other groups, and immigrants from Australia and New Zealand showing the most favorable measures.

Yet, taken together, an important takeaway from the foregoing is the notable salience of race (i.e., disparities stemming from the Black-White distinction). The section to immediately follow takes a closer look.

RACIAL DIFFERENCES THAT VARY BY GENDER

As in previous sections of this book, here again we see race differences that are shown to be gendered. Among men, Black immigrants (excluding Africans) are shown to exhibit less favorable summary statistics on all measures, relative to their White counterparts. Compare, for example, the self-employment percentage for White men (about 14%), which is twice that for Black men (about 7%). Note that the average occupational prestige score for Black men (about 30) is only slightly lower than that for White men (about 33). Yet, the calculated average annual earnings of Black men ($46,918) are $14,320 less than that for White men ($61,238).

Among women, by contrast, the Black-White distinction appears to exhibit a bifurcated pattern. Black women do indeed show average percent unemployed (6%) that is slightly higher than that for their White counterparts (about 4%) and show a self-employment percentage (about 4%) that is notably lower than that for White women (about 7%). Yet, Black women held occupations with higher average prestige (about 29) than their White counterparts (about 24). The calculated average annual earnings for Black women ($38,636) are also noticeably higher than that calculated for White women ($34,755). Note that the difference in calculated average earnings between these two is about $3,881. In short, while Black women reported higher percentages of unemployed, and lower rates of self-employment, than their White counterparts, occupations held by Black women are shown to have higher average prestige than those held by White women. Moreover, Black women are shown to have also earn noticeably higher than White women.

The two sections to immediately follow examine how stable the patterns noted above are, focusing specifically on distinctions between Black and White African immigrants. Those sections provide data on multivariate logistic and general linear regression estimates on labor market disparities between Black and White African and other immigrant groups. As with the previous chapter, labor market disparities are examined in five areas: labor force participation; unemployment; self-employment; occupational prestige; and hourly earnings.

Black and White African Immigrants in the United States: The Gendered Salience of Race through International Migration

Heretofore we have examined the effects of being an immigrant from Africa on a variety of work-related summary measures. While those statistics showed distinctions between Black and White Africans, the emphasis was

Table 5.3. Black and White African Immigrants Compared with Immigrants from Other Primary Sending Areas: Logistic Regression Estimates of Three Economic Indicators, Combined 1980, 1990, 2000, 2010, and 2019 Samples of the IPUMS.

Sample = Male[a]

Demographic	Ref. Equals Black African			Ref. Equals White African		
	not in labor force Odds Ratio	not employed Odds Ratio	not self-employed Odds Ratio	not in labor force Odds Ratio	not employed Odds Ratio	not self-employed Odds Ratio
Year[b]						
1980	1.072	1.257***	1.108***	1.072***	1.257***	1.108
1990	1.383	1.711***	0.983	1.383***	1.711***	0.983
2000	3.331	3.104***	1.007	3.331***	3.104***	1.007
2010	1.25	1.947***	0.976	1.250***	1.947***	0.976
Immigrant Group						
Africa[c]	0.804***	0.752***	0.534***	1.243***	1.331***	1.871***
Other Africa[d]	0.722***	0.718***	0.563***	0.897	0.956	1.054
Canada	0.750***	0.684***	0.607***	0.932*	0.910**	1.136***
Mexico	0.774***	0.791***	1.006	0.962	1.052	1.883***
Central America	0.767***	0.749***	0.861***	0.954	0.997	1.611***
Caribbean	0.953	0.963	0.729***	1.185***	1.282***	1.365***
South America	0.769***	0.730***	0.627***	0.956	0.971	1.174***
Europe	0.703***	0.672***	0.561***	0.874***	0.895***	1.05
Asia	0.906***	0.811***	0.493***	1.126***	1.080**	0.922**
Australia & New Zealand	0.571***	0.512***	0.551***	0.710***	0.681***	1.031
Pacific Islands	0.909	0.885*	0.837**	1.130*	1.177***	1.566***
Other[e]	0.864***	0.841***	0.651***	1.074*	1.119***	1.217***
Race[f]						
Black[g]	0.985	1.073***	1.933***	0.985	1.073***	1.933***
Other[h]	0.992	0.990	1.391***	0.992	0.99	1.391***
N	1162898	1162898	1162898	1162898	1162898	1162898

Sample = Female[i]

Year[b]					
1980	1.462***	1.507***	2.248***	1.462***	1.507***	2.248***
1990	1.361***	1.441***	1.454***	1.361***	1.441***	1.454***
2000	1.837***	1.872***	1.222***	1.837***	1.872***	1.222***
2010	1.227***	1.461***	1.053***	1.227***	1.461***	1.053***
Africa[c]	1.950***	1.700***	0.523***	0.513***	0.588***	1.911***
Other Africa[d]	1.528***	1.358***	0.561***	0.784***	0.799***	1.073
Canada	1.735***	1.453***	0.499***	0.890***	0.855***	0.953
Mexico	2.148***	1.979***	0.823***	1.101***	1.164***	1.573***
Central America	1.479***	1.366***	0.504***	0.758***	0.803***	0.963
Caribbean	1.525***	1.447***	0.653***	0.782***	0.851***	1.248***
South America	1.455***	1.322***	0.427***	0.746***	0.778***	0.817***
Europe	1.673***	1.442***	0.502***	0.858***	0.848***	0.96
Asia	1.685***	1.404***	0.530***	0.864***	0.826***	1.014
Australia & New Zealand	1.810***	1.480***	0.413***	0.928**	0.871***	0.789***
Pacific Islands	1.711***	1.497***	0.764***	0.877***	0.880**	1.460***
Other[e]	1.336***	1.225***	0.692***	0.685***	0.721***	1.322***
Race[f]						
Black[g]	0.583***	0.619***	1.674***	0.583***	0.619***	1.674***
Other[h]	0.873***	0.888***	1.076***	0.873***	0.888***	1.076***
N	1238590	1238590	1238590	1238590	1238590	1238590

* Statistically significant at the .05 level; ** Statistically significant at the .01 level; *** Statistically significant at the .001 level

a. In addition to the variables listed in the table, all models also controlled for number of years of schooling, number of years of work experience plus its squared term, number of years in the U.S., marital status, a set of regional variables including Midwest, West, and South (reference category = Northeast), an English deficiency measure, two dummy variables controlling for whether an earned college degree was received in the United States or abroad, and metropolitan status.

b. Reference year = 2019.

c. Estimate is for White African immigrants, when the omitted category is Black, and Black African immigrants, when the omitted category is White (Ref. Equals Black and Ref. Equals White, respectively noted above).

d. For African immigrants, a catchall category that includes individuals reporting various race combinations like two major races, three or more races, etc.

e. Includes those identifying their birthplace as Atlantic Islands, Cuba, and birthplaces other than the United States, but not identified (in IPUMS terminology, "North America, ns," "Americas, n.s.," and "Other n.e.c.").

f. Reference group = White (not African) immigrants.

g. Black (not African) immigrants.

h. For all immigrants, excluding Africans, a catchall category that includes individuals reporting various race combinations like two major races, three or more races, etc.

i. Models controlled for all variables included for the male sample, plus two relationship variables: number of own children currently living in the household; and number of own children under age 5 in the household.

Source: Author's calculations based on combined samples of the 1980, 1990, and 2000 Decennial Censuses, and the 2010 and 2019 American Community Surveys (ACS), as represented in the Integrated Public Use Microdata Series (IPUMS) (Ruggles et al. 2020). Data limited to persons 25 to 64 years old, and who are not living in group quarters and/or institutions.

more so on the "African" rather than the "race" distinction. In this section, the Black-White African distinction is addressed more explicitly.

To that end, Table 5.3 displays estimates from three logistic regression models examining Black-White disparities in labor market outcomes, as indicated in labor force participation, unemployment, and self-employment. The three logistic regression models predict the likelihood that first Black, then White, African immigrants, relative to immigrants from other sending areas, will (1) not be in the labor force, (2) not be employed, and (3) not be self-employed. Accordingly, for each of these models, the reference/omitted category of race is first Black, then White, African immigrant. In addition to the Black-White African immigrant distinction, each model also controlled for a residual "Other" category that includes African immigrants that did not report their race as Black or White (e.g., those who reported their racial background/heritage as Asian, two or more races, etc.). The models also notably controlled for the race of the other immigrant groups (other than Africans). As above, with each of these models, I control for a standard set of social and demographic characteristics, including years of education, calculated work experience and its squared term, an English deficiency measure, marital status, region, and related measures (the reader is again directed to the Methodological Appendix of this book for details on how these were derived).

And as in the previous chapter, for ease of interpretation, for the logistic regression models, I only report the likelihood ratios, and not the parameter estimates themselves. The odds ratios are either equal to or more or less than 1.00. Accordingly, since the three estimates presented in Table 5.3 are logistic regression models predicting the likelihood of (1) not being in the labor force, (2) not being employed, or (3) not being self-employed, odds ratios less than 1.00 indicate a lesser likelihood for a given immigrant group relative to African immigrants, Black or White. By contrast, odds ratios greater than 1.00 indicate a greater likelihood, while odds ratios of 1.00 indicate that the group average is the same as that of Black or White African immigrants. And, as with estimates reported in the previous chapter, for each estimate reported in Table 5.3, statistical significance at the 0.05 level is indicated with a single asterisk (*), significance at the 0.01 level is indicated with a double asterisk (**), and a triple asterisk (***) denotes significance at the 0.001 level. Estimates with none of these designations are considered not statistically significant.

The Continued Gendered Salience of Race

Looking back at the hypotheses presented in the beginning section of this chapter, how do Black and White African immigrants compare with one another? How do they compare with immigrants from Canada and Europe?

How about immigrants from other sending countries/regions? Do Black and White African immigrants differentially compare more or less favorably with these?

As shown in the estimates displayed in Table 5.3, answers to the foregoing questions are confounded by a variety of factors, including the variable being estimated and gender. Race is indeed shown to be significantly associated with disparities between Black and White African immigrants, relative to other groups, in labor force participation, unemployment, and self-employment. Yet, as with previous results, the estimates also vary notably by gender. Focusing on the male sample for a moment, we see that when Black Africans are the reference category, with only a few exceptions, estimates indicate that all groups are estimated to have a lesser likelihood than Black Africans to not be in the labor force, to be unemployed, and to not be self-employed. Note that for the male sample, when Black is the reference category, all odds ratios shown are less than 1.0, with only one exception, the estimate for immigrants from Mexico, on self-employment, which is not statistically significant. Moreover, the estimates for labor force participation for Caribbeans and immigrants from the Pacific Islands, as well as that for unemployment for Caribbeans, are not statistically significant. Taken together, however, the results for males generally show that almost all groups of males are estimated to have labor force participation rates that were higher than those of Black Africans; to have had lower unemployment rates than Black Africans; and to have higher levels of self-employment.

Importantly, in reviewing the data presented in Table 5.3 on the relative positions of Black African males, two points are worth stating and/or restating. First, the lower likelihood of others to not be in the labor force, be unemployed, and to not be self-employed, than Black Africans, also extends to White African immigrants, as well as "Other" African immigrants. That is to say, White and "Other" African immigrants are also predicted to have lesser likelihoods than Black African immigrants to not be in the labor force, to be unemployed, and to not be self-employed. And second, the estimates control for the race of other immigrants. In other words, whether a male Canadian or Mexican immigrant also self-identified as Black, White, or Other, is accounted for in these models.

Further looking at estimates for males, compare the foregoing with the estimates when White Africans are the omitted category, that is, when White African men are the reference group to all other male groups. With those estimates, we see a less consistent pattern. In fact, it can be argued that for White African immigrants the estimates show outcomes that vary noticeably by group and the variable being measured. The labor force participation and unemployment rates for immigrants from Central America, Mexico, and South America, for example, are shown to be the same as those for White Africans—all three estimates are not statistically significant. European immigrants, by contrast, are predicted to have a lesser likelihood than White Africans to not be in the labor force and to not be unemployed. The self-employment estimate, comparing these two groups, however, is not statistically significant. Yet perhaps the one somewhat consistent finding here is in self-employment. With these estimates, White African immigrant men are predicted to be more likely than most of their male counterpart groups to not be self-employed.

Comparing the patterns for males just discussed, with those for females, reveals some particularly interesting contrasts. Black African females, compared with all other immigrant groups, for example, are consistently estimated to be less likely to not be in the labor force and to be unemployed. That is to say, Black African females are predicted to be more likely than all other groups to be in the labor force and to be employed. Note the consistently significant estimates that are all lower than 1.0.

Further among females, the estimates with Black Africans being the reference group show that all the groups are predicted to be more likely than Black Africans to not be self-employed. Note the consistently significant estimates that are more than 1.0. In other words, not only are Black African females predicted to be more likely than all groups to be self-employed, they are also predicted to be more likely to be in the labor force and to be employed. Here again, I note that this is also true for White African immigrants. That is to say, White African females are also more likely than their Black counterparts to not be in the labor force and to be unemployed, that is, are less likely to be in the labor force and to be employed. And notably, this is also true for "Other" Africans.

Looking at the estimates when White Africans are the omitted category, the female sample yet again exhibits further interesting patterns that diverge appreciably from the male sample. For example, while all estimates for African immigrants of "Other" races for males are all not statistically significant, two of the estimates for the female sample are significant. White Africans (relative to African immigrants of "Other" races) are predicted to be less likely to not be in the labor force and to be unemployed. Note the consistent and highly significant estimates for these two variables (labor force participation and unemployment) that are all below 1.0.

Further focusing on the female sample, we see that the self-employment estimates show some notable variability. When White Africans are the omitted category, we see that seven groups (Black Africans, immigrants from Mexico, the Caribbean, the Pacific Islands, those from unidentified regions [Other], Black immigrants [other than Africans], and immigrants of "Other" races) all show estimates greater than 1.0, suggesting a greater likelihood for not being self-employed than White Africans. Two additional estimates are shown to be statistically significant, those for South America and Australia

Table 5.4. Black and White African Immigrants Compared with Immigrants from Other Primary Sending Areas: General Linear Regression Estimates of Two Economic Indicators, Combined 1980, 1990, 2000, 2010, and 2019 Samples of the IPUMS.

Sample = Male[a]	Ref. Equals Black		Ref. Equals White	
Demographic	Occupational Prestige	Hourly Earnings[b]	Occupational Prestige	Hourly Earnings[b]
Year[c]				
1980	3.31***	0.0212***	3.31***	0.0218***
1990	-4.66***	-0.091***	4.66***	-0.091***
2000	-6.18***	-0.160***	-6.18***	-0.160***
2010	-5.86***	N.A.	-5.86***	N.A.
Africa[d]	4.95***	0.274***	-4.95***	-0.215***
Other Africa[e]	3.14***	0.1112***	-1.81***	-0.128***
Canada	5.45***	0.372***	0.50***	0.077***
Mexico	-2.73***	-0.059***	-7.68***	-0.261***
Central America	-1.04***	0.008	-5.99***	-0.209***
Caribbean	-0.30*	0.047***	-5.25***	-0.179***
South America	1.45***	0.120***	-3.50***	-0.121***
Europe	2.93***	0.2994***	-2.01***	0.020*
Asia	3.98***	0.224***	-0.97***	-0.040***
Australia & New Zealand	7.66***	0.520***	2.71***	0.1934***
Pacific Islands	-1.77***	0.045**	-6.72***	-0.180***
Other[f]	1.01***	0.096***	-3.94***	-0.140***
Race[g]				
Black[h]	-1.07***	-0.004	-1.07***	-0.004
Other[i]	-0.72***	-0.041***	-0.72***	-0.041***
D.F.	30	29	30	29
R-Square	0.350864	0.211387	0.350864	0.211387
N	1162898	873434	1162898	873434
Sample = Female[j]				
Year[c]				
1980	-1.63***	-0.097***	-1.63***	-0.097***
1990	-6.03***	-0.104***	-6.03***	-0.104***
2000	-6.52***	-0.154***	-6.52***	-0.154***
2010	-5.98***	N.A.	-5.98***	N.A.
Africa[d]	-0.76***	0.044***	0.76***	-0.042***
Other Africa[e]	-1.10***	0.019870115	-0.34026025	-0.023
Canada	1.30***	0.032***	2.06***	-0.011
Mexico	-6.95***	-0.197***	-6.19***	-0.231***
Central America	-4.45***	-0.148***	-3.71***	-0.184***
Caribbean	-2.25***	-0.076***	-1.49***	-0.115***
South America	-1.76***	-0.059***	-1.00***	-0.099***
Europe	-1.50***	-0.021**	-0.75***	-0.0612***
Asia	-1.05***	0.049***	-0.29	0.0046
Australia & New Zealand	2.25***	0.136***	3.01***	0.0879***

Demographic	Occupational Prestige	Hourly Earnings[b]	Occupational Prestige	Hourly Earnings[b]
Pacific Islands	-4.26***	-0.078***	-3.50***	-0.117***
Other[e]	-1.10***	-0.037***	-0.34	-0.078***
Race[g]				
Black[h]	2.806***	0.105***	2.81***	0.105***
Other[i]	-0.08	-0.025***	-0.08	-0.025***
D.F.	32	31	32	31
R-Square	0.277656	0.170343	0.277656	0.170343
N	1238590	684261	1238590	684261

* Statistically significant at the .05 level; ** Statistically significant at the .01 level; *** Statistically significant at the .001 level

a. In addition to the variables listed in the table, all models also controlled for number of years of schooling, number of years of work experience plus its squared term, number of years in the United States, marital status, a set of regional variables including Midwest, West, and South (reference category = Northeast), an English deficiency measure, two dummy variables controlling for whether an earned college degree was received in the United States or abroad, and metropolitan status.

b. Estimates limited to persons with reported annual incomes of $500 or more, computed in constant 2019 dollars.

c. Reference year = 2019.

d. Estimate is for White African immigrants, when the omitted category is Black, and Black African immigrants, when the omitted category is White (Ref. Equals Black and Ref. Equals White, respectively noted above).

e. For African immigrants, a catchall category that includes individuals reporting various race combinations like two major races, three or more races, etc.

f. Includes those identifying their birthplace as Atlantic Islands, Cuba, and birthplaces other than the United States, but not identified (in IPUMS terminology, "North America, ns," "Americas, n.s.," and "Other n.e.c.").

g. Reference group = White (not African) immigrants.

h. Black (not African) immigrants.

i. For all immigrants, excluding Africans, a catchall category that includes individuals reporting various race combinations like two major races, three or more races, etc.

j. Models controlled for all variables included for the male sample, plus two relationship variables: number of own children currently living in the household; and number of own children under age 5 in the household.

Source: Author's calculations based on combined samples of the 1980, 1990, and 2000 Decennial Censuses, and the 2010 and 2019 American Community Surveys (ACS), as represented in the Integrated Public Use Microdata Series (IPUMS) (Ruggles et al. 2020). Data limited to persons 25 to 64 years old, and who are not living in group quarters and/or institutions.

and New Zealand. Both are less than 1.0, suggesting a lesser likelihood than White Africans to not be self-employed.

What then, in summary, do the foregoing findings suggest about racial disparities in labor force participation, unemployment, and self-employment between Black and White African immigrants? At least as they compare with one another, as well as with the immigrant groups examined here, we can make at least two definitive observations. First, notable Black-White differences are shown, when Black and White African immigrants are compared with other immigrant groups. But second, the effects of race are shown to be gendered, with Black males being disadvantaged relative to their male counterparts, and

Black females being advantaged relative to their female counterparts. And this is shown to be true for when (1) Black and White African immigrants are compared; (2) both are compared with "Other" African immigrants; and (3) both are compared with other non-African immigrant groups. The section to immediately follow continues our probe by examining Black-White African immigrant labor market disparities, as they pertain to occupational prestige and earnings, and relative to other immigrant groups.

Disparities in Occupational Prestige and Hourly Earnings: Estimates from Two General Linear Regression Models

This section of the chapter examines Black-White African immigrant disparities in occupational prestige and hourly earnings, as revealed by comparisons with other immigrant groups. Table 5.4 displays estimates from two general linear regression models predicting occupational prestige and logged hourly earnings for when (1) Black Africans are the reference group to all other immigrant groups, including White Africans, and (2) when White Africans are the reference category to all, including Black Africans. In other words, for each of the two models presented in Table 5.4, the reference/omitted category of race is Black or White (first Black, then White) African immigrants. As above, in addition to the Black-White African immigrant distinction, each model also controlled for a residual "Other" category that includes African immigrants that did not report their race as Black or White. Again, for the purpose of brevity, I only report estimates comparing Black and White Africans with immigrants from the other sending areas, omitting the full results for the "Other" group (available upon request from the author). The models also notably controlled for the race of the other immigrant groups (other than Africans). And as above, with each of these two models, I control for a standard set of social and demographic characteristics, including years of education, calculated work experience and its squared term, an English deficiency measure, marital status, region, and related measures.

Looking at the estimates presented in Table 5.4, we can add a few observations to the foregoing. First, the comparisons between Black and White Africans again reveal the notable salience of race, that is somewhat gendered. Compared to their White African male counterparts, Black African males are estimated to have held occupations with less prestige. They are also estimated to earn less. By contrast, Black African women are estimated to have held occupations with higher prestige than their White counterparts. The earnings estimates, however, show that such advantage in higher occupational prestige did not translate into higher earnings for Black African women. In other words, while Black African women are estimated to have held occupations with higher prestige than their White African counterparts, such women are also predicted to have earned less. Here, I reiterate that this is even after earnings-related controls are included in the model.

"Other" male African immigrants similarly held occupations with higher prestige than their Black counterparts. They are also predicted to have earned more. Again, highlighting the salience of race, such immigrants are, by contrast, predicted to have held occupations with lower prestige than their White African counterparts, and to have earn less. Among females, "Other" Africans are predicted to have held occupations with lower prestige than their Black and White counterparts, although the estimate for when Whites are the reference group is not statistically significant. But again, the estimates show that this did not translate into higher earnings for Black women.

Compared to other immigrants, we see that some groups are estimated to have had better outcomes than Black and White Africans; whereas other groups are shown to have had worse outcomes. Immigrants from Canada and Australia and New Zealand, for example, almost consistently show more favorable estimates than Black and White African immigrants, although less so for White Africans. Other immigrant groups like those from Central America and Mexico, by contrast, almost consistently show estimates less favorable to both Black and White Africans. Here I note that this is a finding that was indicated earlier but is notably robust in the face of additional controls.

In short, the regression estimates presented in Table 5.4 reveal at least three clear patterns. First, compared with their White African counterparts, estimates for Black African immigrants are less favorable, although this is more stable among men than among women. In fact, among females, those estimates revealed that Black African women held occupations with higher prestige than White African women, but the estimates show that this did not translate into higher earnings for Black women. Second, the estimates for "Other" Africans reveal patterns very similar to those shown for the Black-White African comparison. And third, relative to other immigrant groups, African immigrants, both Black and White, compare favorably in occupational prestige and earnings, but again, this varied by sending area. Immigrants from sending areas like Canada and Australia and New Zealand, for example, show relatively more favorable estimates than Black and White Africans, although this is less so for White Africans; whereas sending areas like Mexico show relatively less favorable estimates.

Additional Notable Variations

Though the focus of this chapter is more on African immigrants, Black and White, here, as in the previous chapter, I tested for differences that might have existed between some of these groups (e.g., between Canadians and Asians, Canadians and Europeans, Canadians and Caribbeans, Europeans and Caribbeans, etc.), including Wald tests on the logistic regression estimates. I briefly report some of those results here. The reader may recall from the previous chapter that the Wald test, for example, allows for evaluating whether coefficients for estimates included in any given logistic regression model are statistically significant. Here, it means comparisons not delineated in our models, and not reported in Table 5.3 or Table 5.4, but that might nevertheless be instructive.

As above, results of those tests are somewhat gendered. However, some sending areas exhibited consistent patterns worth noting here. Top among these is immigrants from Australia and New Zealand. Overall, such immigrants exhibited favorable measures almost across the board, relative to virtually every other group.

Among men, for example, immigrants from Australia and New Zealand are estimated to be more likely than all other immigrant groups to be in the labor force, to be employed, and they are more likely to be self-employed than all groups except for immigrants from Asia, who are estimated to report higher rates of self-employment, and Europeans, the self-employment estimate for whom is not statistically significant. Male immigrants from Australia and New Zealand are also estimated to have held occupations with higher prestige than all other male groups, and they are also estimated to have earned more than all.

For the female sample, the results are similar, as they relate to immigrants from Australia and New Zealand, though not consistently. On the labor force participation dimension, for example, female Mexican immigrants are more likely than their counterparts from Australia and New Zealand to not be in the labor force, while all other groups, except immigrants from the Pacific Islands, are shown to be less likely (the estimate for Pacific islanders is not statistically significant). The unemployment measure was similarly split, with female immigrants from Mexico showing a greater likelihood than their counterparts from Australia and New Zealand to be unemployed, while those from Central and South America showing a lesser likelihood. On self-employment, all groups, except for South Americans (estimate not significant) are shown to be more likely than immigrants from Australia and New Zealand to not be self-employed. Consistent with the male sample, however, immigrants from Australia and New Zealand are estimated to have held occupations with higher prestige than all others, and to have earned more.

Canadian immigrants are shown to be similarly situated, although not as consistently. Canadian male immigrants, for example, are shown to have reported higher levels of labor force participation and employment than all other groups, except for Europeans, who are shown to have higher rates. The comparisons also show that Canadian men reported higher levels of self-employment than all other immigrant groups, except for South Americans, Asians, and Europeans (and, of course, New Zealanders). The latter two are shown to have reported higher levels of self-employment than Canadian men, while South American men are estimated to have reported similar rates. Male immigrants from Canada also held occupations with higher prestige than all other immigrant groups, except, of course, New Zealanders. They also earned more than everyone else, except for Asians and New Zealanders, who earned more.

The female sample, by contrast, exhibited a more variable pattern for Canadians. On labor force participation, for example, female groups from Asia, Central America, the Caribbean, Europe, and South America all are shown to be less likely than Canadian women to not be in the labor force, whereas Mexican women are shown to be more likely. Similarly, the unemployment comparisons showed Mexican immigrants to be more likely to be unemployed, while immigrants from Asia, Central America, and South America are all shown to be less likely to be unemployed than Canadian women. And the self-employment dimension showed a similar bifurcated pattern. Canadian women, however, are shown to have held occupations with higher prestige than the other groups, and to have earned more than all except for Asians and immigrants from Australia and New Zealand.

For Asians and Europeans, by contrast, the comparisons indicated even lesser consistency. Asian men, for example, are shown to have reported higher self-employment rates than European men, to have held occupations with higher prestige, and to have earned more. By contrast, Central American, Mexican, and South American men all reported higher levels of labor force participation than Asian men (in addition to Canadians, Europeans, and New Zealanders). And the female sample showed similar variations by sending area.

Finally, the Caribbean-Other comparisons indicated a variety of outcomes. With respect to not being in the labor force and being unemployed among men, for example, all groups are shown to be less likely than Caribbean immigrants, except for Pacific islanders, who are shown to exhibit similar rates (labor force participation estimate not significant). Self-employment rates among Caribbean men, however, are shown to be higher than immigrants from Central America, Mexico, and the Pacific Islands. The latter three are also shown to have held occupations with lower prestige than Caribbeans, and Mexicans and Central Americans also earned less. The female sample showed similar variations by measure, sending area, and significance/non-significance.

SUMMARY

This chapter sought to investigate five research hypotheses:

H1. African immigrants will compare less favorably in labor market qualities with immigrants from Canada and Europe.

H2. African immigrants will compare less (or more) favorably with other immigrant groups.

H3. Immigrants from other regions will also compare less favorably in labor market attributes with immigrants from Canada and Europe.

H4. Black immigrants (African and non-African alike) will compare less favorably in labor market attributes with their White immigrant counterparts.

H5. Black African immigrants will compare less favorably in labor market attributes with their White African immigrant counterparts.

Taken together, these hypotheses can be grouped into two main areas of inquiry. First, relative to immigrants from other sending countries and regions to the United States, the quotations given at the beginning of the chapter suggest that African immigrants will compare less favorably with other immigrant groups. It follows that one goal of the chapter was to investigate whether African immigrants do indeed exhibit socioeconomic profiles that are uniquely "African" and suggestive of across-the-board low status. Alternatively, the chapter sought to investigate whether African immigrants do indeed exhibit socioeconomic profiles that are uniquely "Black" and "White," and suggestive of differential outcomes by race (i.e., in discussions of African immigration to the United States, is being "Black" and "White" the more salient issue?). The reader may recall from the previous chapter of this book that some scholars have argued that race (i.e., being "Black" or "White") frequently trumps other variables in labor market disparities in the United States. The example noted in that chapter is Alba and Foner's (2015) cross-national comparative study, *Strangers No More*, where the authors hypothesize that in the United States, color (i.e., "blackness") is a greater disadvantage than religion (i.e., "Muslim-ness"), whereas the converse is true in Europe. Does race, as early U.S. race relations scholar E. C. Hughes (1945) asserted almost eight decades ago, continue to be a "master status characteristic" in the United States?

In investigating the first of these questions, analyses of this chapter show results that are not in accord with consistently less favorable socioeconomic profiles for African immigrants. Instead, the above statistical analyses suggest that, like all immigrant groups, African immigrants exhibit varying levels of socioeconomic status that compare favorably and less favorably with differing groups and with differing measures.

And in investigating the second of the above questions, analyses of this chapter have shown race to be a salient, consistent, and statistically significant variable in labor market disparities. Yet, here as well, this finding is shown to be nuanced by multiple factors, including gender, region/country of origins and the specific variable being measured. Regional and country differences do exist, with the salience of race being more pronounced among immigrants from Africa, Asia, and Europe.

Perhaps one of the most interesting results of the chapter, however, is that many of the findings discussed were nuanced by gender. In many parts of the chapter, patterns were shown to vary by gender. Black women, for example, are shown to exhibit relatively favorable socioeconomic measures, relative to their White counterparts, and at least on some dimensions. Thus, the title of the chapter, "African Immigrants in the United States: The Gendering Significance of Race through International Migration?"

NOTES

1. Cited from *Encyclopedia Virginia*. https://encyclopediavirginia.org/entries/negro-womens-children-to-serve-according-to-the-condition-of-the-mother-1662.

2. 1705 Virginia House of Burgesses Act, quoted from Myers 2003, 97.

3 Changed by section 2 of the Fourteenth Amendment. Quoted and cited from Myers 2003, 97.

4. Josh Dawsey, "Trump Derides Protections for Immigrants from 'Shithole' Countries," *Washington Post*, January 12, 2018, https://www.washingtonpost.com/politics/trump-attacks-protections-for-immigrants-from-shithole-countries-in-oval-office-meeting/2018/01/11/bfc0725c-f711-11e7-91af-31ac729add94_story.html.

5. The article is accessible at https://www.latimes.com/world/africa/la-fg-global-african-immigrants-explainer-20180112-story.html.

6. The report is accessible at https://www.migrationpolicy.org/article/sub-saharan-african-immigrants-united-states#English_Proficiency.

7. The report is accessible at https://research.newamericaneconomy.org/wp-content/uploads/sites/2/2018/01/NAE_African_V6.pdf.

8. The measure of occupational prestige here is the average score of prestige assigned to occupations, using the Hauser and Warren Socioeconomic Index. The Hauser and Warren Socioeconomic Index is a measure of occupational status that is based upon the earnings and educational attainment associated with categories of occupations, as specified in the census documents. Importantly, the average of prestige scores for occupations are different for men and women. For more information, see R. M. Hauser and J. R. Warren, "Socioeconomic Indexes for Occupations: A

Review, Update, and Critique," *Sociological Methodology* 27 (1997): 177–298; and K. Nakao and J. Treas, "Updating Occupational Prestige and Socioeconomic Scores: How the New Measures Measure Up," *Sociological Methodology* 24 (1994): 1–72.

Chapter 6

African Immigrants in the United States

A Comparison with Natives

"The problem of the Twentieth Century is the problem of the color line—the relation of the darker to the lighter races of men in Asia and Africa, in America and the islands of the sea." (W. E. B. Du Bois 1903, v)

As noted in chapter 1 of this book, nativity (i.e., native versus foreign-born/ immigrant) comes to the forefront of immigration theory and research when the key question is how immigrants compare with their native counterparts in terms of socioeconomic attainment.[1] Here, we may note again at the outset that, compared to Hispanic and Asian immigrants, Black immigrants in the United States have been considerably less researched and, until very recently, Black African immigrants remained a relatively understudied group (for recent exceptions, see Corra and Borch 2014; Thomas 2014; Hamilton 2020). Nevertheless, recalling again from chapter 3 of this book, early migration theory and research (Chiswick 1978; Carliner 1980; DeFreitas 1980) portrayed a rather linear picture of U.S. immigration and successful immigrant incorporation. After a relatively short adjustment period, immigrants are said to "catch up" with and/or "overtake" comparable natives in socioeconomic attainment. And, as noted elsewhere in this book, Chiswick (1979) estimated the "overtaking" point for immigrants at 10–15 years after immigration.

Yet, as also discussed in the introductory chapters of this book, recent theoretical approaches to the study of immigration suggest that the multicolored nature of U.S. society along ethnoracial lines means that immigrants experience a segmented and/or racialized form of assimilation (Portes and Zhou 1993; Sáenz and Manges Douglas 2015). One hypothesis is that socioeconomic trajectories of immigrants from non-European countries may not mirror the pattern of quick (largely European) incorporation into the U.S. labor market that informed early theorizing (Portes and Zhou 1993). Moreover, analyses reported by Borjas (1985, 1987, 1991, 1994, 1995) suggest waning immigrant quality among recent immigrants, a phenomenon he attributed to changes in the mix of sending countries. More specifically, Borjas reported finding no declines in immigrant quality among immigrants from Europe and Canada to the United States. He then predicted that, after a decade or so in the United States, the earnings of immigrants from Europe and Canada would overtake those of their native White counterparts, while the earnings of immigrants from the rest of the world, including Africa, would never surpass those of their native counterparts.

Here, it might also be recalled from chapters 1 and 2 of this book that voluntary immigration from Africa to the United States, at least in large numbers, is a very recent phenomenon (Thomas 2011; Capps, McCabe, and Fix 2012; Elo et al. 2015). Accordingly, and following Borjas, a testable hypothesis is that African immigrants will compare less favorably in labor market outcomes with natives. Yet a counter proposition is that, given their reported high levels of education (Butcher 1994; Dodoo 1997; Logan and Deane 2003), African immigrants do indeed stand to do relatively well in the U.S. labor market (Dodoo 1997; Corra and Kimuna 2009; Corra and Borch 2014). Following this proposition, African immigrants are expected to compare favorably with natives, or at least with comparable native groups. Scholars also point to the salience of race in the United States and its potential impact on the incorporation of immigrants (Thomas 2014; Sáenz and Manges Douglas 2015). It follows that another hypothesis is that Black African immigrants, as opposed to White African immigrants, may not do as well as natives, especially given the salience of race in contemporary America.

PREVIOUS STUDIES OF AFRICAN IMMIGRANTS

Several recent research studies have attempted to examine some of the foregoing hypotheses, with some mixed results (Butcher 1994; Dodoo 1997; Kposowa 2002; Kollehlon and Eule 2003; Model 2008; Corra and Kimuna 2009; Corra and Borch 2014; Hamilton 2014, 2019, 2020). One area of inquiry, for example, has been in labor market disparities between African immigrants and representative samples of native Blacks (Dodoo 1999; Corra and Kimuna 2009; Corra and Borch 2014; Dodoo and Takyi 2002). An early example is Dodoo's (1997) analysis of the 1990 U.S. population census to assess the earnings attainment of male African immigrants, their Caribbean-born counterparts, and African Americans. While finding higher average earnings for African immigrants than the other two, Dodoo (1997) also found that controls for relevant earnings-related measures erased the African immigrant advantage and elevated the earnings of Caribbean immigrants above those of African immigrants and native-born Blacks. Notably, Dodoo found "a substantial African (but not Caribbean) disadvantage, wherein university degree holders . . . receive little, if any, reward for their degrees" (1997, 527).

Corra and Kimuna's subsequent analysis (2009), by contrast, found subtle but important differences among females of the same three groups (African Americans, African, and Caribbean immigrants).[2] Distinguishing Caribbean immigrants into three categories of linguistic heritage—English, French, and Spanish, Corra and Kimuna (2009) reported noticeably higher average earnings for African, English, and French Caribbean immigrant women than that for their African American counterparts. By contrast, they report average earnings for Spanish Caribbean immigrant women that is lower than that for African American women. These patterns, however, change substantially, once earnings related measures were controlled: The African immigrant advantage is eliminated in the 1990 sample and becomes negative and significant in the 2000 sample. By contrast, the English and French Caribbean immigrant advantages (as well as the Spanish Caribbean immigrant disadvantage) in earnings remain significant for the 1990 sample, only to disappear in the 2000 sample; and for French Caribbean immigrants, become negative and significant. Corra and Kimuna's (2009) study, in short, provides a cautionary note to generalizing findings exclusively based on the experiences of male immigrants.

Importantly, a key variable that has been recently noted is the role of migration itself (both internal and international) in producing labor market disparities (Butcher 1994; Hamilton 2014, 2019, 2020). A key critique is that, unlike the native-born, immigrants are not from a sample of randomly selected individuals from their countries of origins. Rather, they are a highly selected group that, as economist Kristin Butcher (1994) suggests, are appropriately comparable to native-born "internal movers" (frequently operationalized as the native-born living in states different from their state of birth) rather than the overall native-born Black population (for similar arguments, see Tolnay 2003; Hamilton 2014, 2019, 2020). Such movers are found to exhibit similar socioeconomic profiles and/or trajectories with immigrants (Butcher 1994; Model 2008; Hamilton 2020). Using data from the 1980 U.S. Census and comparing "native Black movers" (domestic interstate migrants) with immigrant Blacks, Butcher (1994) showed very similar earnings profiles between the two groups. Results from two more recent studies (Model 2008; Hamilton 2020) are notably similar.

Here, findings from a recent study by Hamilton (2014) are worth noting. Evaluating whether arrival cohorts of Black immigrants from four sending regions—the English-speaking Caribbean, Latin America, Haiti, and

Africa—converge with the earnings of four subgroups of U.S.-born men (native Blacks taken together, native Black movers, native Black non-movers, and U.S.-born non-Hispanic Whites), Hamilton offered results that are of critical import.[3] First, he found lower weekly earnings for all cohorts of Black immigrants upon arrival in the United States, relative to both native Black groups (Blacks taken together, and native Black movers). Second, with respect to projections of convergence/divergence, Hamilton reported that: "Although the rate of earnings growth varies by birthplace, several arrival cohorts of black immigrants from English-speaking countries in Africa and the Caribbean are projected to overtake the earnings of native blacks (collectively) as their tenure of U.S. residence increases. Fewer of these arrival cohorts, however, are projected to converge with or surpass the earnings of native black movers, and no arrival cohort is projected to achieve earnings parity with native whites" (p. 977).

Moreover, Hamilton's (2014) study also included additional findings that are worth reiterating here. A key variable of distinction, for example, is linguistic heritage (i.e., immigrants from English and non-English speaking countries). He reports that "the earnings of most arrival cohorts of immigrants from the English-speaking Caribbean, after residing in the United States for more than 20 years, are projected to converge with or slightly overtake those of U.S.-born black internal migrants. The findings also show three arrival cohorts of black immigrants from English-speaking African countries are projected to surpass the earnings of U.S.-born black internal migrants."

And, as am sure readers of this book are well aware, the significance of race for socioeconomic attainment in the United States is a classic issue in stratification research (Wilson 1980, 1989; Farley 1984; Burstein 1985; Tomaskovic-Devey 1993; Cancio, Evans, and Maume 1996; Borch and Corra 2010; Thomas 2014). Importantly, the literature on the socioeconomic attainment of immigrants also points to the significance of race on the socioeconomic attainment process and suggests that Black immigrants fare worse than other immigrant groups to the United States (Chiswick 1979; Model and Ladipo 1996; Model 1997; Dodoo and Takyi 2002; Borch and Corra 2010). Disaggregating Caribbean immigrants by nation of origin/linguistic heritage—English, French, and Spanish Caribbean—and controlling for gender, an early analysis by Model (1991), for example, reports some earnings penalty for a few non-English-speaking Caribbean immigrant subgroups relative to Whites; suggesting, at least for males, race as an influential factor: "While all Caribbean-born men had lower earnings than White men, West Indian women indicated net earnings that were equivalent to those of White women" (Model 1991, 248).

Likewise, in exploring "race differences in earnings between black and white Africans in America," Dodoo and Takyi (2002) report "sizeable differences among [Black and White] immigrants who have relatively similar human capital" (p. 913). They find that "[W]hites have annual earnings 80 per cent higher than their black counterparts, and the gap in hourly wage is almost 48 percent." Notably, Dodoo and Takyi (2002) report that "more than half (53 per cent) of the race difference [between Black and White African immigrants] in wages remains unexplained by earnings-related attributes such as education, occupation, and hours worked" (p. 913).

Using U.S. Census data to compare earnings of Black and White African immigrant men and women of working age (25–64) living in the United States in 1980, 1990, and 2000, and controlling for a host of human capital variables, year, whether the person migrated before age 16, U.S. region of residence, and marital status, Borch and Corra's more recent analysis (2010) demonstrated a significant White wage premium that was larger for men than for women. They also showed that, for men, the Black-White difference appeared to have grown over time.

THE CURRENT CHAPTER

Following the foregoing growing but rich body of research, this chapter takes a closer look at how African immigrants to the United States compare in socioeconomic attainment with natives, using a variety of measures and statistical techniques. That is to say, it examines how African immigrants compare with the different U.S. native racial and ethnic groups (i.e., native-born Asians, Blacks, Hispanics, Native Americans, and Whites). Though addressing this specific issue is not the focus of this book, this chapter provides a closer look, albeit briefly.

NOTABLE EDUCATIONAL DIFFERENCES BETWEEN BLACK AND WHITE AFRICAN IMMIGRANTS AND NATIVES FAVORING IMMIGRANTS

Given the professed centrality of education as an indicator of potential achievement and economic mobility in contemporary U.S. society, I begin this chapter with differences in levels of educational attainment between Black and White African immigrants and the various native groups. Exactly how do Black and White African immigrants compare in educational attainment with natives? This section takes a closer look.

Table 6.1 provides summary statistics on educational attainment and reports data on (1) African immigrants collectively; (2) Black, White, and "Other" African immigrants viewed separately;[4] (3) native born Blacks

Table 6.1. Black and White African Immigrants Compared with Natives on Educational Attainment, Combined 1980, 1990, 2000, 2010, and 2019 Samples of the IPUMS.

Male Sample	N	% <HS	% HS	% Some College	% College Grad[a]	% 5 Yrs or more[b]	% Total
All Africans	35,759	4.95	19.59	22.30	26.56	26.60	100
White Africans	11,409	4.74	16.78	18.84	28.60	31.04	100
Black Africans	20,497	4.90	20.73	24.94	25.06	24.37	100
Other Africans[c]	3,853	5.81	21.83	18.53	28.55	25.28	100
All Native Blacks	852,403	25.87	40.84	21.21	7.93	4.16	99.99999999
Native Black Non-Movers[d]	529,949	26.96	43.77	19.63	6.66	2.98	100
Native Black Movers[e]	322,454	24.08	36.02	23.80	10.01	6.09	100
Native Americans	75,296	24.08	41.64	23.79	6.57	3.92	100
Native Asians	264,012	9.28	21.15	20.77	27.14	21.66	100
Native White Hispanics	250,238	24.23	36.00	23.61	10.33	5.83	100
Native Non-White Hispanics	134,255	23.40	41.52	24.00	7.98	3.10	100
Native Whites	7,876,258	13.20	36.54	22.71	16.67	10.88	100
Native Others	90,387	17.74	35.87	22.26	15.02	9.11	100
Female Sample							
All Africans	27,914	9.29	28.50	24.26	23.92	14.02	100
White Africans	8,945	7.84	25.72	21.36	28.62	16.46	100
Black Africans	15,760	9.70	30.42	26.36	20.95	12.58	100
Other Africans	3,209	11.34	26.80	22.06	25.46	14.33	100
All Native Blacks	1,105,412	23.52	39.11	23.21	8.95	5.21	100
Native Black Non-Movers[d]	706,322	24.01	40.99	22.48	8.20	4.32	100
Native Black Movers[e]	399,090	22.64	35.78	24.51	10.27	6.80	100
Native Americans	82,956	23.77	39.57	26.26	6.87	3.53	100
Native Asians	306,239	13.83	24.79	19.47	28.03	13.88	100
Native White Hispanics	275,706	24.91	36.96	22.59	10.23	5.31	100

Native Non-White Hispanics	148,892	24.04	40.01	24.15	8.40	3.40	100
Native Whites	8,194,653	12.27	40.33	23.78	15.31	8.31	100
Native Others	95,555	15.88	35.30	24.36	15.70	8.76	100

a. Data for 1980 represent those reporting four years of post-secondary schooling; 1990, 2000, 2010, and 2019 represent those reporting having earned a bachelor's degree.

b. Data for 1980 represent those reporting five-plus years of post-secondary schooling; 1990, 2000, 2010, and 2019 include those reporting having earned a master's degree, professional degree beyond a bachelor's degree, and doctoral degree.

c. A catchall category of African immigrants reporting racial backgrounds of Asian, Native American, various race combinations like two major races, three or more races, etc.

d. Native Blacks reporting a current state of residence that is the same as their state of birth.

e. Native Blacks reporting their current state of residence as different from their state of birth.

Source: Author's calculations based on samples of the 1980, 1990, and 2000 Decennial Censuses, and the 2010 and 2019 American Community Surveys (ACS), as represented in the Integrated Public Use Microdata Series (IPUMS) (Ruggles et al. 2020). Data limited to persons 25 to 64 years old, and who are not living in group quarters and/or institutions.

viewed collectively and separately as native-born Black "non-movers" and "movers," and (4) other native racial and ethnic groups (native Asians, Hispanics, Whites, etc.). For native born Blacks, "non-movers" are those reporting a current state of residence that is the same as their state of birth. Whereas "movers" are native-born Blacks reporting a current state of residence that is different from their state of birth. The reader will recall that this is said to be a key variable previously noted as a differentiating factor, that is, the role of migration itself in producing disparities (Butcher 1994; Model 2018; Hamilton 2014, 2019, 2020).

Data reported in Table 6.1 are summary statistics (averages) on five levels of education: percentages of individuals with less than a high school education/twelve years of education; those with a high school degree/twelve years of education; those with one to three years of post-secondary education; those with a bachelor's degree/at least four years of post-secondary education; and individuals reporting five or more years of post-secondary education. And, as in previous chapters, the data is separated by sex.

Looking at the information presented in Table 6.1, we can make at least four substantive observations about disparities in educational attainment between our groups. First, African immigrants do indeed compare very favorably with virtually all native groups. Focusing on the second to last two columns of Table 6.1, for example, which indicate percentages for each group that reported having had at least four years of post-secondary education and five-plus years of post-secondary education, respectively, we see that African immigrants, both male and female, show the highest averages, with the single exception of native Asians. Consider the first of these two levels of educational attainment (the percent of each group with at least four years of post-secondary education). For males, about 27 percent of African immigrants reported at least four years of post-secondary education, and an additional 27 percent reported five or more years. Taken together, about 54 percent of African immigrant men reported four or more years of post-secondary education. For African immigrant females, about 24 percent reported having at least four years of post-secondary education, and an additional 14 percent reported five or more years.

Compare these with those for the native group with the closest percentages of post-secondary years of education, Asian Americans. About 27 percent and 28 percent of male and female Asian Americans, respectively, reported at least four years of post-secondary education, and an additional 22 percent and 14 percent, respectively, reported five or more years.

Summary statistics for each of Black and White Africans, on one hand, and the various native groups, on the other hand, provide striking contrasts. For example, about 29 percent each of White African immigrant men and women reported having had at least four years of post-secondary education, and an additional 31 percent and 17 percent, respectively, reported five or more years of post-secondary education. This means at least 60 percent of White African men reported four or more years of post-secondary education, while 46 percent of White African women reported having such years of education. Again, summary statistics for Asian Americans are the closest to these.

For Black African men and women with at least four years of post-secondary education, those percentages are about 25 and 21, respectively. Taken together, about 49 percent and 34 percent of Black African immigrant men and women, respectively, reported four or more years of post-secondary education. And, as with the White African-Other comparisons, percentages for Asian Americans are the only ones that approximate these.

It follows that African immigrants, both Black and White, compare very favorably with natives on this very important dimension of educational attainment. In fact, they compare most favorably with all native groups, and this is shown to be true for both the male and female samples. Notably, the closest comparisons are with Asian Americans, percentages for whom are very similar with those of Africans taken together, and Black and White Africans viewed separately. And, as noted in the previous chapter of this manuscript, these findings are consistent with recent surveys (see, for example, Anderson and Connor 2018; Simmons 2018).

A second observation that can be made is again the salience of race in these summary statistics on educational attainment. Though both Black and White African immigrants compare very favorably with all native groups on educational attainment, the immigrant-native distinctions are highest when White Africans are compared with natives.

A third observation that can be made is the clear distinction by internal–non-internal migration, that is, comparisons between native born Black "movers" and "non-movers." While only about 7 percent of male Black non-movers are shown to have reported at least four years of post-secondary education, 10 percent of Black male movers reported this to have been the case. Moreover, the percent of male Black movers with five-plus years of post-secondary education (6.10%) is twice that for Black non-movers (2.98%). And the same pattern is shown for the female sample.

Finally, a fourth observation is the salience of gender, but yet again in a very interesting way. We see at least three discernable patterns. First, a clear gendered distinction existed between one set of groups that includes male and female African immigrants (all groups) and Native White men and women, with percentages for at least four years of education and five- plus, respectively, clearly favoring males. By contrast, another set of groups, including native born Blacks (both overall, among movers, and among non-movers), non-White Hispanics, and, to a lesser extent, Asian Americans, is tending to exhibit patterns of educational attainment favoring women, at least when looking at the percentages reporting four or more years of post-secondary education. Finally, a third set of groups is also discernable, and it includes the rest, for which the gender distinction appears to exist, but not as clear as the first two.

Given the foregoing, then, a question that comes to mind is exactly how these differing levels of educational measures translate into labor market outcomes for these groups. More specifically, how do African immigrants compare with the different native groups on work-related measures? The section to immediately follow takes a further look.

African Immigrants in the United States: A Comparison with U.S. Natives on Unemployment, Self-Employment, Occupational Prestige, and Annual Earnings

Table 6.2 continues analyses of this chapter by reporting summary measures, comparing African immigrants with native born Americans, on four dimensions: (1) unemployment, (2) self-employment, (3) occupational prestige,[5] and (4) calculated annual earnings. The data are separated by sex, and include measures for immigration status and race (i.e., those for Black and White African immigrants). Another differentiation displayed is that between native born Black "internal migrants" and "noninternal migrants." Again, "Black movers" are native-born Blacks whose current state of residence is different from their state of birth, whereas "Black non-movers" are those whose current residence is the same as their state of birth (for a similar operationalization, see Hamilton 2020).

A quick glance at the summary measures presented in Table 6.2 reveals at least four clearly discernable patterns. First, African immigrants compare

Table 6.2. Black and White African Immigrants Compared with Natives on Four Economic Indicators, Combined 1980, 1990, 2000, 2010, and 2019 Samples of the IPUMS.

Male Sample	% Unemployed	% Self-Employed	Occupational Prestige	Annual Earnings[a]	N
African Immigrants	4.51	12.20	38.43	$65,571.50	35759
African Blacks	5.17	9.14	35.91	$50,836.26	20497
African Whites	3.51	16.72	42.61	$89,788.50	11409
Other Africans[b]	4.00	15.08	39.42	$72,284.50	3853
Native Blacks	6.66	3.42	26.84	$44,782.87	859369
Native Black Non-Movers[c]	8.09	4.76	25.84	$40,740.50	529949
Native Black Movers[d]	6.56	4.84	28.45	$51,091.80	322454
Hispanic Americans (White)	5.36	8.21	31.68	$52,318.71	250238
Hispanic Americans (Non-White)	6.37	6.51	29.58	$46,651.20	134255
Native Americans	9.82	8.15	27.91	$43,388.90	75296
Asian Americans	3.47	11.45	38.55	$70,585.40	264012
Native Whites (Non-Hispanic)	3.09	13.79	33.01	$67,487.00	7876258
Native Others[e]	5.17	10.82	31.71	$55,696.90	90387
Female Sample					
African Immigrants	5.06	5.68	30.68	$42,311.25	27914
Black Africans	6.02	4.30	30.87	$39,753.90	15760
White Africans	3.71	7.56	30.60	$46,841.30	8945
Other Africans[b]	4.08	7.20	29.98	$45,242.50	3209
Native Blacks	5.99	2.37	26.05	$34,179.60	1114570
Native Black Non-Movers[c]	6.42	2.26	25.23	$31,738.10	706322
Native Black Movers[d]	5.22	2.56	27.48	$38,419.00	399090
Hispanic Americans (White)	4.10	4.07	27.56	$34,835.70	275706
Hispanic Americans (Non-White)	5.21	3.83	27.14	$32,904.60	148892
Native Americans	6.21	4.22	25.60	$29,502.00	82956
Asian Americans	3.20	6.57	30.20	$46,616.70	306239
Native Whites (Non-Hispanic)	2.63	6.28	30.40	$37,040.30	8194653
Native Others[e]	4.76	6.63	28.69	$39,636.50	95555

a. Limited to persons with calculated annual incomes of $500 or more, computed in constant 2019 dollars.
b. A catchall category that includes African immigrants reporting various race combinations like two major races, three or more races, etc.
c. Native Blacks reporting a current state of residence that is the same as their state of birth.
d. Native Blacks reporting their current state of residence as different from their state of birth.
e. A catchall category that includes natives reporting various race combinations like two major races, three or more races, etc.

Source: Author's calculations based on samples of the 1980, 1990, and 2000 Decennial Censuses, and the 2010 and 2019 American Community Surveys (ACS), as represented in the Integrated Public Use Microdata Series (IPUMS) (Ruggles et al. 2020). Data limited to persons 25 to 64 years old, and who are not living in group quarters and/or institutions.

favorably with several groups on a number of dimensions. While African immigrants show average unemployment percentages that are higher than some groups (for the male sample, Asian Americans and non-Hispanic Whites; and for the female sample, Asian Americans, White Hispanics, native Whites, and native "Others"), they also show unemployment percentages that are notably lower than several native groups. Similarly, self-employment is greater among African immigrant males than among all other native group, except for non-Hispanic Whites. Moreover, with only a few exceptions, this is also true among women. Among women, it is worth further noting, two of the three self-employment percentages for the African immigrant subgroups (White and Other Africans) are the highest (about 8% and 7%, respectively). Finally, the average occupational prestige scores and earnings figures follow similar patterns, with African immigrants showing values higher or equal to most native groups.

A second clear pattern illustrated in Table 6.2 is the salience of race. This is clearly demonstrated in all comparisons, but especially when looking at Black and White African immigrants, on one hand, and natives, on the other hand. For example, we can see the salience of race quite clearly when we compare White African immigrants with all the other groups, native-born and immigrant. Compared with Black African immigrant males, White African immigrant males show the highest percent self-employed, the highest average occupational prestige, and the highest income. They also show the lowest percent unemployed. With only a few exceptions, these patterns are also true among females.

White African males, for example, show the highest average annual earnings of all groups, about $89,789. The second highest is shown for the "Other" African immigrant group of males, about $72,285. The next two highest earnings are shown for Asian Americans and non-Hispanic White males, about $70,585 and $67,487, respectively.[6] These racial differences, of course, are accentuated (or abated) by gender, with the effects shown to be more salient among men than among women.

The data presented in Table 6.2 also illustrates a third clear pattern, that of the salience of gender. On average, women reported unemployment rates that are noticeably higher than those reported by men, and they report rates of self-employment that are lower than their male counterparts. Only the unemployment percentages for native born Blacks and Native Americans depart from this pattern. Native born Black and Native American men both show a higher percentage unemployed, relative to their female counterparts. Yet, even among this group, men show measures of percent self-employed, occupational prestige, and earnings that are noticeably higher than those shown for their female counterparts.

Finally, a fourth clear pattern illustrated in Table 6.2 is that the mere fact of being a "mover" is a differentiating factor among native Blacks. The patterns noted above are accentuated by internal migration/non-migration. Looking at the native Black "internal/noninternal migration" distinction in Table 6.2, for example, we see that movers generally show measures that are more favorable than non-movers. Native born Black male movers, for example, report a lower unemployment percentage than their non-mover counterparts (about 7% vs. 8%), Yet the self-employment percentages are relatively the same (about 5% for both). Such Black male movers also show an occupational prestige average that is higher (about 29 vs. 26). Black men movers also show calculated annual earnings higher than that for their non-mover counterparts (about $51,092 vs. $40,741). Native Black female movers similarly show a lower percent unemployed than their non-mover counterparts (about 5% vs. 6%), are shown to have held occupations with higher prestige (about 28 vs. 25), and shown to have earned more (about $38,419 vs. $31,738). And while the mover–non-mover distinction here is not examined among non-Hispanic Whites, there is every reason to suppose that disaggregating movers from non-movers among non-Hispanic Whites (or any other native group, for that matter) would also show the movers to be advantaged relative to non-movers.

To summarize, the data presented in Table 6.2 are unequivocal on several points. First, as illustrated in previous chapters of this book, African immigrants do not collectively exhibit socioeconomic profiles that are uniformly favorable or unfavorable to all groups. Instead, their qualities vary on a number of important dimensions indicative of diversity rather than homogeneity. Highlighted here is the salience of race in producing disparities. Second, like their native counterparts, the usual variables of race and gender are clearly operative—African immigrant males and females (as well as the native groups) exhibit attributes that markedly differ from one another. And third, as in previous studies (e.g., Butcher 1994; Model 2008; Hamilton 2014, 2020), migration is itself a key differentiating variable, with internal (domestic) migrants showing measures that markedly differ from those shown for non-migrants and immigrants alike. And exactly how stable are these patterns? The two sections to immediately follow take a closer look.

SIMILAR PATTERNS IN DISPARITIES IN LABOR FORCE PARTICIPATION, UNEMPLOYMENT, AND SELF-EMPLOYMENT BETWEEN BLACK AND WHITE IMMIGRANTS AND NATIVES

Table 6.3 displays estimates from three logistic regression models examining disparities in labor force participation, unemployment, and self-employment between Black and White African immigrants and the various U.S. native-born groups. The three logistic regression models predict the likelihood that first Black, then white African immigrants, relative to each native group, will (1) not be in the labor force, (2) not be employed, and (3) not be self-employed. Accordingly, two estimates are given in Table 6.3 for each model. The first represents an estimate comparing each of the native groups with Black African immigrants; whereas the second compares each of the native groups with White African immigrants. It follows that for each of these models, the reference/omitted category of race is first Black, then White, African immigrant. In addition to the Black-White African immigrant distinction, each model also controlled for a residual "Other" category that includes African immigrants that did not report their race as Black or White (e.g., those who reported their racial background/heritage as Asian, two or more races, etc.) (see note 4 for details on the composition of this group). Moreover, with each of these models, I control for a standard set of social and demographic characteristics, including non-citizenship status, an English deficiency measure, years of education, calculated work experience and its squared term, marital status, region, metropolitan status, a college degree obtained in the United States or abroad, and, for the female sample, two relationship variables indicating number of children in the household.

Again, for ease of interpretation, for the logistic regression estimates presented in Table 6.3, I only report the likelihood ratios, and not the parameter estimates themselves. The odds ratios are either equal to or more or less than 1.00. Moreover, since the three are logistic regression models predicting the likelihood of (1) not being in the labor force, (2) not being employed, or (3) not being self-employed, odds ratios less than 1.00 indicate a lesser likelihood for a given native group relative to African immigrants. By contrast, odds ratios greater than 1.00 indicate a greater likelihood, while odds ratios of 1.00 indicate that the group is estimated to have the same likelihood as African immigrants. Finally, by convention in the social sciences, for each

Table 6.3. Logistic Regression Estimates on Three Economic Indicators, Combined 1980, 1990, 2000, 2010, and 2019 Samples of the IPUMS.

Male[a]	Ref. Equals Black	Ref. Equals White	Ref. Equals Black	Ref. Equals White	Ref. Equals Black	Ref. Equals White
Demographic	Probability modeled = not in labor force	Probability modeled = not in labor force	Probability modeled = not employed	Probability modeled = not employed	Probability modeled = not self-employed	Probability modeled = not self-employed
Year[b]						
1980	0.84***	0.84***	0.96***	0.96***	0.72***	0.72***
1990	1.18***	1.18***	1.31***	1.31***	1.12***	1.110***
2000	1.88***	1.88***	1.80***	1.80***	0.94***	0.94***
2010	1.49***	1.49***	2.07***	2.07***	1.01*	1.01*
2019	Omitted					
White/Black Africa[c]	0.84***	1.20***	0.80***	1.24***	0.60***	1.66***
Other Africa[d]	0.90*	1.07	0.88*	1.09	0.62***	1.02
Native Black Non-Movers[e,f]	2.11***	2.52***	2.05***	2.55***	1.99***	3.30***
Native Black Movers[f]	1.70***	2.03***	1.63***	2.03***	2.09***	3.47***
Native American	2.25***	2.69***	2.32***	2.89***	1.32***	2.18***
Native White Hispanic	1.34***	1.60***	1.24***	1.54***	1.16***	1.92***
Native Non-White Hispanic	1.58***	1.89***	1.46***	1.81***	1.39***	2.31***
Native Asian	0.98	1.18***	0.88***	1.10***	0.89***	1.48***
Native White	1.03	1.23***	0.93***	1.15***	0.73***	1.21***
Native Other[g]	1.44***	1.72***	1.33***	1.65***	0.85***	1.40***
N	9575809	9575809	9575809	9575809	9575809	9575809
Female[h]	Ref. Equals Black	Ref. Equals White	Ref. Equals Black	Ref. Equals White	Ref. Equals Black	Ref. Equals White

Demographic	Probability modeled = not in labor force	Probability modeled = not in labor force	Probability modeled = not employed	Probability modeled = not employed	Probability modeled = not self-employed	Probability modeled = not self-employed
Year[b]						
1980	1.94***	1.94***	1.88***	1.88***	1.67***	1.67***
1990	1.69***	1.69***	1.69***	1.69***	1.33***	1.33***
2000	1.72***	1.72***	1.69***	1.69***	1.15***	1.15***
2010	1.37***	1.37***	1.61***	1.61***	1.17***	1.17***
2019	Omitted					
White/Black Africa[c]	1.98***	0.51***	1.76***	0.57***	0.60***	1.68***
Other Africa[d]	1.64***	0.83***	1.479***	0.84***	0.63***	1.06
Native Black Non-Movers[e,f]	2.17***	1.10***	2.15***	1.22***	1.54***	2.58***
Native Black Movers[f]	1.93***	0.98	1.85***	1.05*	1.40***	2.35***
Native White Hispanics	2.18***	1.10***	1.96***	1.11***	1.01	1.69***
Native Non-White Hispanics	2.42***	1.23***	2.24***	1.27***	1.13***	1.90***
Native American	2.70***	1.37***	2.61***	1.48***	1.06	1.77***
Native Asian	1.45***	0.73***	1.27***	0.72***	0.74***	1.24***
Native White	1.93***	0.97	1.67***	0.95*	0.62***	1.05
Native Other[g]	2.26***	1.14***	2.09***	1.19***	0.69***	1.16***
N	10,234,124	10,234,124	10,234,124	10,234,124	10,234,124	10,234,124

* Statistically significant at the .05 level; ** Statistically significant at the .01 level; *** Statistically significant at the .001 level

a. In addition to the variables listed in the table, all models also controlled for number of years of schooling, number of years of work experience plus its squared term, number of years in the United States, marital status, a set of regional variables including Midwest, West, and South (reference category = Northeast), an English deficiency measure, two dummy variables controlling for whether an earned college degree was received in the United States or abroad, and metropolitan status.

b. Reference year = 2019.

c. Estimate is for White African immigrants, when the omitted category is Black, and Black African immigrants, when the omitted category is White (Ref. Equals Black and Ref. Equals White, respectively noted above).

d. A catchall category that includes African immigrants reporting various race combinations like two major races, three or more races, etc.

e. Native Born Blacks reporting their current state of residence as different from their state of birth.

f. Native born Blacks reporting a current state of residence that is the same as their state of birth.

g. A catchall category that includes natives reporting various race combinations like two major races, three or more races, etc.

h. Models controlled for all variables included for the male sample, plus two relationship variables: number of own children currently living in the household; and number of own children under age 5 in the household.

Source: Author's calculations based on samples of the 1980, 1990, and 2000 Decennial Censuses, and the 2010 and 2019 American Community Surveys (ACS), as represented in the Integrated Public Use Microdata Series (IPUMS) (Ruggles et al. 2020). Data limited to persons 25 to 64 years old, and who are not living in group quarters and/or institutions.

estimate reported in Table 6.3, statistical significance at the 0.05 level is indicated with a single asterisk (*), significance at the 0.01 level is indicated with a double asterisk (**), and a triple asterisk (***) denotes significance at the 0.001 level. Estimates with none of these designations are considered not statistically significant.

Looking at results presented in Table 6.3, we can see that Black and White African immigrants display patterns that are very similar, and virtually consistent across male and female samples. With only few exceptions, relative to each of the native groups, both Black and White African immigrants are estimated to be less likely to not be in the labor force and to not be unemployed. And, in general, they are also estimated to be less likely to not be self-employed.

The few exceptions concern estimates for Asian Americans and native Whites, some of which are either not statistically significant or are shown to be in the opposite direction to what is just noted. The estimate for labor force participation for Asian American males, relative to Black African men, for example, is not statistically significant, while the estimates for both unemployment and self-employment are statistically significant and in opposite directions. That is to say, while Asian American men and Black African men had similar labor force participation rates, Asian American men are estimated to have reported higher levels of unemployment than Black African men, yet they are also estimated to have reported a lesser likelihood to not be self-employed than Black African men. Similarly, while Asian American men are estimated to have a greater likelihood of not being in the labor force and of not being self-employed than White African men, they are also estimated to have a lower likelihood of being unemployed.

Native White women, by contrast, are estimated to have a greater likelihood of not being in the labor force and not being self-employed than Black African women, but they are estimated to have a lower likelihood of not being in the labor force and of not being unemployed than White African women. Native White women and Black women are estimated to have similar rates of unemployment, while native White women and White African women are estimated to have similar rates of self-employment.

Results presented in Table 6.3 also show another key pattern that is consistent across Black African immigrant–native and White African immigrant–native comparisons, and that is also virtually consistent across male and female samples. That pattern has to do with the internal-international migration distinction noted in Table 6.3. Those estimates show notable and significant variations between the two immigrant groups (Black and White Africans) and the two groups of native Blacks—movers and non-movers. With only one exception, the logistic regression estimates show that both groups of native Blacks (movers and non-movers) are predicted to have a

Table 6.4. Black and White African Immigrants Compared with Natives: General Linear Regression Estimates on Two Economic Indicators, Combined 1980, 1990, 2000, 2010, and 2019 Samples of the IPUMS.

	Sample = Male[a]				Sample = Female[b]			
Demographic	Ref. Equals Black Occupational Prestige	Ref. Equals White Occupational Prestige	Ref. Equals Black Hourly Earnings	Ref. Equals White Hourly Earnings[c]	Ref. Equals Black Occupational Prestige	Ref. Equals White Occupational Prestige	Ref. Equals Black Hourly Earnings[c]	Ref. Equals White Hourly Earnings[c]
Year[d]								
1980	3.61***	3.61***	0.06***	0.06***	−2.87***	−2.87***	−0.09***	−0.09***
1990	−3.64***	−3.64***	−0.02***	−0.02***	−6.77***	−6.77***	−0.12***	−0.12***
2000	−6.15***	−6.15***	−0.13***	−0.13***	−6.94***	−6.94***	−0.16***	−0.16***
2010	−6.13***	−6.13***	N.A.	N.A.	−5.97***	−5.97***	N.A.	N.A.
White/Black Africa[e]	4.15***	−4.15***	0.23***	−0.23***	−1.33***	1.33***	0.05***	−0.05***
Other Africa[f]	2.51***	−1.64***	0.09***	−0.13***	−1.61***	−0.28	0.01	−0.03***
Native Black Movers[g]	−4.51***	−8.66***	−0.01	−0.21***	−5.03***	−3.70***	−0.06***	−0.10***
Native Black Non-Movers[h]	−5.40***	−9.54***	−0.09***	−0.27***	−7.17***	−5.84***	−0.15***	−0.18***
Native Americans	−3.23***	−7.37***	−0.06***	−0.25***	−6.40***	−5.07***	−0.18***	−0.22***
Native White Hispanics	−1.45***	−5.60***	−0.01	−0.21***	−5.58***	−4.25***	−0.14***	−0.18***
Native Non-White Hispanics	−2.59***	−6.74***	−0.05***	−0.24***	−6.94***	−5.6***	−0.18***	−0.21***
Asian Americans	2.21***	−1.94***	0.16***	−0.07***	−2.13***	−0.80***	0.01	−0.04***
Native Whites	1.25***	−2.90***	0.12***	−0.10***	−2.87***	−1.54***	−0.09***	−0.13***
Native Others[i]	−1.19***	−5.33***	0.004	−0.20***	−5.14***	−3.81***	−0.13***	−0.171***
D.F.	27	27	26	26	29	29	28	28
R-Square	0.262243	0.262243	0.14978	0.14978	0.212524	0.212524	0.129049	0.129049
N	9575809	9575809	7324341	7324341	10,237,327	10,237,327	6458914	6458914

* Statistically significant at the .05 level; ** Statistically significant at the .01 level; *** Statistically significant at the .001 level

a. In addition to the variables listed in the table, all models also controlled for number of years of schooling, number of years of work experience plus its squared term, number of years in the United States, marital status, a set of regional variables including Midwest, West, and South (reference category = Northeast), an English deficiency measure, two dummy variables controlling for whether an earned college degree was received in the United States, and metropolitan status.

b. Models controlled for all variables included for the male sample, plus two relationship variables: number of own children currently living in the household; and number of own children under age 5 in the household.

c. Limited to persons with calculated annual incomes of $500 or more, computed in constant 2019 dollars.

d. Reference year = 2019.

e. Estimate is for White African immigrants, when the omitted category is Black, and Black African immigrants, when the omitted category is White (Ref. Equals Black and Ref. Equals White, respectively noted above).

f. A catchall category that includes African immigrants reporting various race combinations like two major races, three or more races, etc.

g. Native Blacks reporting their current state of residence as different from their state of birth.

h. Native Blacks reporting a current state of residence that is the same as their state of birth.

i. A catchall category that includes natives reporting various race combinations like two major races, three or more races, etc.

Source: Author's calculations based on samples of the 1980, 1990, and 2000 Decennial Censuses, and the 2010 and 2019 American Community Surveys (ACS), as represented in the Integrated Public Use Microdata Series (IPUMS) (Ruggles et al. 2020). Data limited to persons 25 to 64 years old, and who are not living in group quarters and/or institutions.

142   *Chapter 6*

greater likelihood than either immigrant groups to not be in the labor force, to not be employed, and to not be self-employed. And this pattern is shown to have existed for both male and female samples. The one exception is the estimate for unemployment for female native Black movers, relative to Black African immigrants, which is not statistically significant.

Moreover, Wald tests revealed the estimates for Black movers to be statistically significantly different from those of their non-mover counterparts, and this is found to be consistent across male and female samples. For all three estimates, native Black non-movers are estimated to have a greater likelihood than their native Black mover counterparts to not be in the labor force, to be unemployed, and to not be self-employed.[7]

Taken together, then, the key finding from the data reported in Table 6.3 is that relative to almost all native groups, Black and White African immigrants are estimated to be significantly more likely to be in the labor force, to be employed, and to also be self-employed. And again, few exceptions concerning Asian Americans and native Whites are noted, but these exceptions are not shown to be particularly consistent across measures and samples. And notably, the distinction between native internal migrants and non-migrants did not eliminate significant variations in estimates for African immigrants, both Black and White, relative to native-born Blacks. The section to immediately follow continues our probe by presenting general linear regression estimates on occupational prestige and hourly earnings, again comparing first Black Africans, then White Africans, with each of our native groups.

SIMILAR PATTERNS IN DISPARITIES IN OCCUPATIONAL PRESTIGE AND HOURLY EARNINGS BETWEEN BLACK AND WHITE IMMIGRANTS AND NATIVES

The two estimates presented in Table 6.4 are from general linear regression models on occupational prestige and hourly earnings, respectively. And, as in the previous two chapters, the log of hourly earnings is used in the earnings models. Again, use of a logged dependent variable allows interpretation of coefficients as percentage changes in the dependent variable, once appropriate calculations are made, while also mitigating any skewness in data generally associated with earnings measures. Accordingly, the estimates for hourly earnings reported in Table 6.4 represent values with such calculations considered and can therefore be interpreted as percentage of hourly earnings, as a measure of the effect of each given independent variable. As an example, consider the first two values of 0.23 and -0.23 displayed under the hourly earnings column in Table 6.4 for White and Black African immigrant males, respectively. The first value can be interpreted as White African immigrants having had hourly earnings that are significantly higher than that of their Black male counterparts, to the point of about 23 percent higher. The second value (-0.23) is, of course, negative because it is in reference to Black African immigrants, relative to White Africans, and is effectively the opposite/negative of the value for White African immigrants.

Estimates for occupational prestige and earnings presented in Table 6.4 show some relatively stable patterns for the immigrant-native comparisons, both Black and White, with a few divergences by gender. For the male sample, for example, Asian and Native White men are shown to have reported occupations with higher prestige than both Black and White African males. Asian American and native White males are also estimated to have earned more than their Black and White African counterparts. All other male groups, by contrast, are estimated to have reported occupations with lower prestige than Black and White African men. They are also estimated to have earned less, with one exception. The hourly earnings of White Hispanics and Black Africans are estimated to not be statistically different from one another.

For the female sample, by contrast, all native groups are shown to have reported occupations with lower prestige than both Black and White African females, including native Whites and Asian Americans. All native groups are also shown to have hourly earnings that are significantly less than those for Black and White African females, except for Asian Americans, the estimate for whom, relative to Black Africans, is not statistically significant.

Finally, the internal versus external migration distinctions did not eliminate differences between Black and White African immigrants and native Black movers and non-movers. Both groups of natives are shown to have held occupations with lower prestige than both Black and White Africans, and to have earned less. Moreover, significance tests of the native Black non-movers estimate reveal both estimates for occupational prestige and hourly earnings to be statistically significantly different from the estimates for native Black movers, favoring movers on both estimates, and across both male and female samples. In other words, native Black non-movers are estimated to have occupations with lower prestige than their mover counterparts, and they are also estimated to have earned less.[8]

SUMMARY

This chapter sought to take a closer look at the relative socioeconomic and labor market standings of African immigrants, Black and White, and those of the various U.S.-born groups. By distinguishing Black and White Africans from one another, and by separating measures for males from those for females, the chapter sought to fully account for variations by nativity, race, and gender. Summary statistics showed that African immigrants compare favorably with several groups on a number of dimensions.

In addition to nativity, analyses of the chapter also showed a race effect to immediately emerge in the summary statistics, and to continue through the more sophisticated statistical analyses. Moreover, the salience of race is clearly demonstrated in all comparisons, but especially when looking at Black and White African immigrants. For example, White Africans held occupations with higher prestige, and show earnings that are appreciably higher than Black Africans. The average annual earnings of White African immigrant males, for example, is shown to be about $38,953 more than that of their Black African immigrant counterparts ($89,789 vs. $50,836). And these patterns generally persisted under the sophisticated multivariate statistical analyses.

Yet, the data also showed effects that are mediated by gender. The summary measures, for example, showed that, on average, women reported lower employment than men, they also reported unemployment rates that are greater than those reported by men, and they report rates of self-employment that are lower than their male counterparts. The average annual earnings of White African females, for example, is about $7,087 lower than that of their male counterparts ($89,788 vs. $39,754). And, in general, the native-immigrant comparisons shown with the logistic and regression estimates followed similar patterns as these (i.e., the results for the male and female samples show notable variations).

Moreover, analyses of the chapter have also shown salient nativity, race, and gender effects favoring White Africans. The calculated annual earnings shown for White African immigrants (about $89,789 for males and about $46,841 for females), for example, are appreciably higher than all groups. White African males, for example, are generally shown to be less likely than their native counterparts to be in the labor force, to be employed, to be self-employed, to report occupations with greater prestige than almost all native male groups, and to earn more. By contrast, Black African females are estimated to hold occupations with higher prestige than all other female groups, except for native Asians, and with no exceptions, Black African females are estimated to have had hourly earnings that are significantly greater than all their native counterparts.

To summarize, key findings of this chapter include the following. First, results show repeatedly that, raw and net, White African immigrants fare better than Black African immigrants. Second, results of this chapter also show that, on several outcomes, raw and net, Black African immigrants do better than most native-born groups. In particular, Black African immigrant women's net earnings are significantly higher than all groups, including native-born non-Hispanic White women. Indeed, very few groups out-earn Black African immigrant women. The chapter to immediately follow examines implications of these and related findings noted here and in previous chapters.

NOTES

1. See, for example, Chiswick 1978, 1979; Sowell 1978; Borjas 1995; Kalmijn 1996; Waters 1999; Shaw-Taylor and Tuch 2007; Model 2008, 2018; Corra and Kimuna 2009; Mason 2010; Jasso 2011; Corra and Borch 2014; Hamilton 2020.

2. In both Corra and Kimuna's (2009) study, and that of Borch and Corra (2010), the researchers reported the earnings of Black African women, relative to native-born Black women, to decline appreciably over time. Elo et al. (2015), however, recently suggested that this was likely due to changes in the composition of the African-born population rather than a real decline in the earnings of individual Black African migrant women.

3. One cautionary note here, however, is that it should not be autamatically assumed that findings derived from studies of male immigrants will be directly generalizable to the migration experiences of female immigrants. As Corra and Kimuna (2009) observed: "The experience of Black female immigrants to the United States has been ignored in discussions of economic outcomes, mainly because they have been traditionally viewed as 'dependents,' moving as wives, mothers or daughters of male migrants" (p. 1032).

4. Here, it might be useful to note that of the 63,668 cases in our total sample of African immigrants, 36,257 (about 56.94%) are Black, 20,354 (about 31.97%) are White, and 7,131 (about 11.20%) are "Other" races. The latter include those that identified themselves as American Indian or Alaska Native (31 cases, or about 0.05%), Chinese (143, or about 0.22%), Japanese (5, or about 0.01%), "Other Asian or Pacific Islander" (3,046, or about 4.78%), "Other race, nec" (628, or about 0.99%), two major races (3,135, or about 4.92%), and three or more major races (74 cases, or about 0.12%).

5. The measure of occupational prestige here is the average score of prestige assigned to occupations, using the Hauser and Warren Socioeconomic Index. The Hauser and Warren Socioeconomic Index is a measure of occupational status that is based upon the earnings and educational attainment associated with categories of occupations, as specified in the census documents. Importantly, the average of prestige scores for occupations are different for men and women. For more information, see R. M. Hauser and J. R. Warren, "Socioeconomic Indexes for Occupations: A Review, Update, and Critique," *Sociological Methodology* 27 (1997): 177–298; and K. Nakao and J. Treas, "Updating Occupational Prestige and Socioeconomic Scores: How the New Measures Measure Up," *Sociological Methodology* 24 (1994): 1–72.

6. Although beyond the scope of this chapter, a cautionary note is worth mentioning here. If some of these large pan-ethnic groups were disaggregated, some of the patterns noted here may be noticeably different. For instance, if Asians were divided into Chinese, Korean, Indian, etc., notable earnings differences between Indian

Americans, for example, and the other groups are most definitely likely to emerge. Similar notable distinctions are also likely to surface, if Hispanics were divided into Cuban, Puerto Rican, etc.

7. Other differences also existed, including, for males, Native Americans are shown to have a greater likelihood than native Black movers to not be in the labor force and to be unemployed; but the former are less likely than native Black movers to not be self-employed. All other male groups, by contrast, are shown to be less likely than Black male movers to not be in the labor force, to not be unemployed, and to not be self-employed. Among females, significant estimates include those for Native Americans, native Others, White Hispanics, and non-White Hispanics, all of whom are shown to be more likely than native Black movers to not be in the labor force; Native Americans, White Hispanics, non-White Hispanics, and other natives are also all shown to have a greater likelihood to be unemployed. And for self-employment, African Others, Native Americans, Asians, White Hispanics, non-White Hispanics, native Whites, and native Others are all less likely than native Black movers to not be self-employed.

8. Again, other differences existed, with all other male groups estimated to have held occupations with higher prestige than movers. For males, Native Americans and non-White Hispanics are also estimated to have earned less than native Black movers, whereas all others are estimated to have earned more. For females, movers held occupations with lower prestige than native Whites and Asians, but higher prestige than all others. Female non-movers and all others earned less than movers, but Asians earned more than movers.

Chapter 7

African Immigrants in the United States

Summary and Concluding Observations

Today, African immigrants constitute a growing and increasingly visible component of the U.S. immigrant population. This book was written to accomplish four distinct, but related, objectives associated with this growth. First, I sought to take a closer look at the growth of African immigration to the United States in recent years, as well as implications that can be drawn from this growth. Exactly what has been the trend of African immigration to the United States? How has this trend changed in the last few decades? And how does this compare with the flow of other comparable immigrant groups? As to African immigration to the United States, what regions/countries have been the main sources of immigrants? And how have such sources changed (or not) over the last few decades? And exactly who are these immigrants? What qualities distinguish them from one another? What do these qualities suggest about the changing racial and ethnic composition of the United States? The first two chapters of the book sought to address these and related questions, and the findings are summarized below.

The second objective of the book was to provide a detailed sociodemographic and socioeconomic portrait of African immigrants in the United States. What key qualities differentiate these immigrants from one another? And what do these differences suggest about prospects of their incorporation into U.S. society? The third chapter of the book exclusively sought to address these and related issues, and, in doing so, it endeavored to highlight key qualities that distinguish these "new African Americans" (Millman 1997, 172) or "new Americans" (Barone 2001) from one another.

Importantly, contemporary debates on immigration from Africa to the United States center around the status of immigrants from that sending region, relative to other immigrant groups. Yet, demonstrated in chapter 1 of the book is that voluntary immigration from Africa to the United States, at least in large numbers, is a very recent phenomenon. And notably, some scholars have argued that recent immigrant flows from developing countries to the United States, relative to earlier ones, are less selective (Borjas 1985). Hence, such immigrants are said to have a reduced chance of success in the U.S. labor market. In seeking to directly address this and related issues, the third goal of the book was to examine how African immigrants compare in socioeconomic attainment with other immigrant groups.

Finally, a fourth objective of the book was to provide a comparison of socioeconomic portraits of African immigrants with the various U.S. native groups (e.g., native-born Asians, Blacks, Hispanics, and Whites). Propositions drawn from selectivity theory reviewed in chapter 3 of the book (Chiswick 1978; Carliner 1980; DeFreitas 1980) portrayed a rather linear picture of U.S. immigration and successful immigrant incorporation. After a relatively short adjustment period, immigrants are said to "catch up" with and/or "overtake" comparable natives in socioeconomic attainment. Yet, a counter proposition is that socioeconomic trajectories of immigrants from non-European countries may not mirror the pattern of quick (largely European) incorporation into the U.S. labor market that informed early theorizing (Portes and Zhou 1993). Thus, the fifth chapter of the book sought to examine how African immigrants compare in socioeconomic status with the various U.S. native-born groups (racial and ethnic groups).

A TREND OF SIZEABLE NUMERICAL INCREASES: CONCENTRATION AND DIVERSITY

The first two chapters of the book introduced the text and key related issues in the study of African immigrants in the United States. In doing so, those chapters illustrated a dramatic increase in the flow of African immigration to the United States in recent years (see Figures 2.1 and 2.2). This growth is shown to have occurred noticeably in the 1990s and accelerating in the 2000s and 2010s.

Moreover, in examining the recent flow of African immigration to the United States, those two chapters (1 and 2) illustrated two distinct qualities shown to characterize the recent dramatic increase of African immigration to the United States: that of "concentrated" immigration, on one hand, and "diversity" in immigration flows, on the other. By "concentrated immigration," it is meant the dramatic increase in the flow of immigrants from Africa to the United States is shown to also be occurring most dramatically among immigrants from a limited number of long-standing sending countries.

For example, data examined in chapter 2 revealed that, throughout the period 1996–2019, from 69 to 76 percent of immigrants from Africa granted permanent residence status in the United States came from ten sending countries. Yet, a second emerging trend was also uncovered in that chapter. The concentration of the flow of African immigrants from a limited number of long-term sending countries has been on the decline. For example, top ten sending countries are shown to have been changing over the years, with some countries reaching that threshold (and some dropping below) as time progressed. This is argued to be an indication of growing "diversity" in the flow of African immigrants to the United States in recent years.

Moreover, shifts in regional representation are also shown to be evident, with African immigrants from Northern and Southern Africa decreasing proportionately, while immigrants from the other three regions increasing or holding steady. Immigrants from Central Africa, for example, represented about 3 percent of the total number of African immigrants in the United States in 1980. By 2019, however, the percentage of immigrants from this region had increased to about 9 percent, a growth representing a threefold increase. By contrast, the percentage of immigrants from North Africa was as high as 39 in 1980. By 2019, however, that percentage had dropped dramatically to about 18, almost one-half decline.

RESULTING SOCIODEMOGRAPHIC CHANGES IN THE RACIAL/ETHNIC COMPOSITION OF THE U.S. POPULATION

Several resulting sociodemographic processes are highlighted in chapter 2 of the book, including the changing composition of the foreign-born and U.S. Black populations. Consequently, African immigrants are shown to now constitute a growing and increasingly sizeable component of the foreign-born and U.S. Black populations. For example, data presented in chapter 2 on the current makeup of the foreign-born Black population of the United States today (see Figure 2.3) revealed that, in 1980, African immigrants constituted about 8 percent of the U.S. foreign-born Black population. By 1990, that percentage is shown to have grown to about 13 percent, and to have almost tripled to about 23 percent by 2000. It is shown to have increased from there appreciably by 2010 to about 34 percent and, by 2019, noticeably so to about 42 percent.

Moreover, data also presented in chapter 2 (see Figure 2.4) on the changing composition of the U.S. Black population is similarly illustrative. Looking at the percentage of the U.S. Black population that is African immigrant, we see in chapter 2 that this percentage was under 1 percent in both 1980 and 1990 (about 0.35% and 0.78%, respectively). By 2000, however, that percentage is shown to have reached approximately 2 percent (1.86%), but almost doubled by 2010 to about 4 percent (about 3.61%). It is shown to have reached 5 percent by 2019 (about 5.1%).

Summary measures examined in chapter 1 also demonstrated that African immigrants are indeed a very diverse group, coming from countries and regions that are culturally, linguistically, politically, and/or economically distinct. Recent waves of immigrants from Africa, for example, increasingly include people of Arab ethnic origins that come mainly from North and East Africa. These trends and patterns suggest that African immigrants are indeed adding to the increasing diversity and racial/ethnic transformation that U.S. society is currently experiencing (Shaw-Taylor and Tuch 2007; Logan and Deane 2003; Capps, McCabe, and Fix 2012; Thomas 2014; Anderson 2015; Elo et al. 2015; Anderson and López 2018; Hamilton 2020). And finally, examining socioeconomic profiles of these "new African Americans" (Millman 1997, 172) or "new Americans" (Barone 2001), the first two chapters also demonstrated notable variations among African immigrants in a variety of attributes, including legal entry status, race, ethnicity and linguistic heritage, and socioeconomic status.

A PATTERN OF CHANGING RACIAL/ETHNIC AND GENDER COMPOSITION OF IMMIGRANTS

Two clear patterns shown to directly flow from the foregoing shifts have been the changing racial/ethnic composition of the African immigrant population in the United States, as well as its gender composition. First, and consistent with previous studies (Kollehlon and Eule 2003; Elo et al. 2015), the trend shown is a growing proportion of self-identified "Black" African immigrants, on one hand, and a decreasing proportion of self-identified "White" immigrants, on the other hand.

Data examined in chapter 4, for example, indicated that about 33 percent of African immigrants in the United States self-identified as Black in 1980. That percentage increased to about 44 percent by 1990, 56 percent by 2000, 69 percent by 2010, and finally 72 percent by 2018. By contrast, the percent of African immigrants identifying as White begins at almost 60 percent in 1980—about 58 percent. That percentage declines appreciably to 48 percent by 1990, declines again dramatically to 27 percent by 2000, to 25 percent by 2010, and ends up down to about 24 percent by 2018. In other words, until very recently, voluntary immigration from Africa to the United States has been disproportionately those who identified themselves as White. More recent immigration from Africa, by contrast, has increasingly included Black Africans (for similar patterns, see Borch and Corra 2010; Elo et al. 2015).

Data examined in chapter 2 also illustrated that the gender composition of the African immigrant population in the United States has, in recent years, shifted from majority male to parity—half of African immigrants living in the United States today are male and half are female. For example, data examined in chapter 2 showed that in 1980, three out of every five African immigrants living in the United States were male. By 2019, that number had declined to one out of every two—exactly half of the total African immigrant population.

DIVERSITY IN SOCIOECONOMIC PROFILE

Specifically seeking to accomplish the second objective of the book—to provide a detailed socioeconomic portrait of African immigrants in the United States, as well as variations in such portrait, analyses in the fourth chapter of the book illustrated notable differences in terms of legal entry status,[1] socioeconomic outcomes, and so forth. Between the years 1996, 1998–2019, for example, data examined in chapter 4 demonstrated that South Africa had over 40 percent of admissions under the employment-based preference category. By contrast, Somalia was shown to have had well over 80 percent of its admissions under the refugee and asylee category, while the DRC was shown to have had more than 50 percent, and reported figures for Liberia and Tanzania were shown to each average to more than 40 percent. These findings suggest that African immigrants do indeed exhibit diverse paths to U.S. legal permanent residency, paths that are shown to be related with socioeconomic outcomes. Similar variations were shown in socioeconomic measures. Percentages of employment/unemployment, self-employment, rates of ownership of dwelling, education, income, and other measures, for example, are all shown to substantially vary by country, region, and demographic profile.

The Salience of Race, Linguistic Heritage, and Gender

Consistent with the current extant literature (see Model 2008; Corra and Kimuna 2009; Kusow, Kimuna and Corra 2016; Kusow, Ajrouch and Corra 2018; Hamilton 2020), data examined in chapter 4 revealed three specific variables to be significant predictors of disparities in socioeconomic outcomes: race/ethnicity, gender, and linguistic heritage. It follows that, despite the significant variation in attainment among the various African immigrant groups, data presented in chapter 4 also suggests some noteworthy stable patterns associated with race/ethnicity, gender, and linguistic heritage.

Race, for example, is shown to be a notable quality associated with disparities in socioeconomic measures, with Black immigrants from Africa consistently shown to exhibit lower measures of socioeconomic outcomes than their White counterparts. Gender and linguistic heritage are also additional variables shown to be associated with disparities. A lower percentage of women were shown to be employed, a lower percentage were shown to be self-employed, and women were shown to exhibit noticeably lower measures of occupational prestige and are shown to have lower income than men. Yet, the multivariate sections of chapter 4 demonstrated that, net of other controls, race is more salient among men, and less so among women, and sometimes has the opposite effect to that shown for men. Finally, English-speaking was generally shown to be a favorable attribute, with individuals so designated shown to have reported higher levels of education, earnings, and other measures than immigrants from non-English-speaking countries.

SPECIFIC THEORETICALLY DRAWN TESTED INTRA-AFRICAN GROUP HYPOTHESES

In addition to reviewing summary statistics comparing the various African immigrant groups with one another, as well as statistical analyses of significant differences, chapter 4 of the book directly tested several more specific hypotheses drawn from theory and research. Migration theory and research, for example, suggest that how well immigrants do may be uniquely tied to whether they are "economic" or "political" migrants. The hypothesis being that "politically motivated emigrants" are less positively selected (pushed) than "economically motivated emigrants" (pulled) (Lee 1966; Borjas 1994; Chiswick 1978, 1999; Jasso and Rosenzweig 1990a and b; Tesfai 2019).

And data presented in chapter 4 of the book (see Table 4.1) demonstrated the Refugees and Asylees admission category of African immigrants to illustrate one of the greatest spreads in percentage. For example, whereas less than 1 percent of immigrants from Morocco, and about 2 percent from Nigeria and Ghana, are shown to have been granted legal status in the United States as refugees and asylees, well over 80 percent of immigrants from Somalia and well over 50 percent from Sudan are shown to have been granted legal status under this category.

To test the "economically motivated" versus "politically motivated" hypothesis, chapter 4 introduced a calculated measure of countries with percentages of individuals granted refugee or asylee status greater than that of the overall continent of Africa, derived from statistics from the U.S. Department of Homeland Security's 1996, 1998–2019 *Yearbook of Immigration Statistics* (see associated notes in Table 4.3 and Table 4.4 for a list of these countries).

This value was used to compare such countries with countries with averages equal to or less than the overall average for the continent. This measure was included as a controlled variable in the logistic and regression models reported in chapter 4.

Linking the "economically motivated" versus "politically motivated" hypothesis to the data on African immigrants analyzed in chapter 4, results show patterns that are consistent with this hypothesis. Results reported in that chapter, for example, demonstrated that African immigrants from countries with higher-than-average percentages of refugees and asylees to the United States also exhibit less favorable socioeconomic outcomes. Immigrants from such countries, for example, are shown to be less likely to not be in the labor force and to be unemployed, but they are also more likely to not be self-employed. Further tests examine if estimates for countries like Morocco, Nigeria, and Ghana are different from those for immigrants from Somalia and Sudan. Those tests reveal this to be the one area where findings for men and women are shown to be clearly consistent. Virtually all comparisons examined (e.g., Ghana vs. Somalia and Sudan; Cameroon vs. Somalia and Sudan) revealed estimates that favor immigrants from other countries over those from Somalia and Sudan.

Selectivity theory also suggests that "early birds" will be more positively selected than latecomers (Model 2008). According to Everett Lee: "The overcoming of a set of intervening obstacles by early migrants lessens the difficulty of the passage for later migrants" (Lee 1966, 55). Guillermina Jasso (2004, 262) similarly observed that: "The greater the obstacles to migration, the higher the quality of the immigrant; pioneer immigrants are, thus, of higher quality than the relatives who follow." Thus, early migrants are predicted to be more selective than those that follow.

Results reported in chapter 4 are also suggestive of support for this hypothesis. In general, those reports demonstrated that African immigrants from the top sending countries in the last twenty or so years exhibit more favorable socioeconomic measures than the overall African immigrant population. Recalling from the discussion above, such top sending countries tended to have also been long-standing sending countries of immigrants to the United States, and they include Nigeria, Ghana, and Egypt, among others.

Another proposition noted in chapter 3 is the so-called "White favoritism hypothesis," said to help immigrants. One variable, for example, said to promote White favoritism for immigrants is "Anglophilia"—U.S. cultural legacies of associating positive evaluations with individuals and practices associated with Great Britain and or the English-speaking world. A related proposition was drawn from the distinction between African countries that were "settler colonies" and those that were not (Corra and Kimuna 2009). In some African countries (e.g., Kenya, Zimbabwe, South Africa), the colonial power dispatched settlers who established farms/plantations. By contrast, in (most) other African countries, the colonial power concentrated on extracting resources (mines, mostly). The expectation is that cultural exchange was greater when settlers were present than when they were not. In short, this proposition suggests that African immigrants from the former would have a cultural advantage in the English-speaking world over immigrants from the latter.

Results presented in chapter 4 of the text lend some support to both foregoing hypotheses. Immigrants from English-speaking countries, for example, are shown to exhibit more favorable socioeconomic outcomes than those from non-English speaking countries, at least on some dimensions. Similarly, immigrants from countries like South Africa and Kenya are shown to exhibit measures that are more advantageous than average.

Another hypothesis drawn from the literature links immigrant quality to differences in the level of income inequality in host as compared to country of origin (Borjas 1988). According to Borjas, for example, immigrants will come from the less industrious when income inequality is greater at origin than destination and come from the more industrious when income inequality is lower at origin than destination.

Chapter 4 reported results testing this hypothesis. Results of those tests are shown to be notably mixed on the immigrant quality–income inequality proposition. Results are shown to vary appreciably by measure, gender, and country of origins.

AFRICAN IMMIGRANTS COMPARED WITH OTHER IMMIGRANT GROUPS

As noted above, a third goal of this book was to examine how African immigrants compare in socioeconomic attainment with other immigrant groups. And, in seeking to accomplish that goal, chapter 5 of the book examined two distinct but related questions. First, it sought to investigate whether African immigrants do indeed exhibit socioeconomic profiles that are uniquely "African" and suggestive of across-the-board low status. Alternatively, that chapter sought to investigate whether African immigrants do indeed exhibit socioeconomic profiles that are uniquely "Black" and "White," and suggestive of differential outcomes by race (i.e., in discussions of African immigration to the United States, is being "Black" and "White" the more salient issue?).

For example, some scholars have argued that race, that is, being "Black" or "White," frequently trumps other variables in labor market disparities in the United States. The example cited in chapter 4 is Alba and Foner's (2015) cross-national comparative study, *Strangers No More*, where the authors hypothesize that in the United States, color (i.e., "blackness") is a greater disadvantage than religion (i.e., "Muslim-ness"), whereas the converse is true in Europe.

In investigating the first of these two questions, analyses reported in chapter 5 show results that are not in accord with consistently less favorable socioeconomic profiles for African immigrants. Instead, statistical analyses reported in that chapter suggest that, like all immigrant groups, African immigrants exhibit varying levels of socioeconomic status that compare favorably and less favorably with differing groups and with differing measures.

And in investigating the second of the above questions, analyses reported in chapter 5 of this book have shown race to be a salient, consistent, and statistically significant variable in labor market disparities. When it comes to Africans, measures examined in chapter 5 suggest the Black-White distinction to be most influential. Black and White Africans compare differentially with many of these groups.

Yet, here as well, this finding is shown to be nuanced by multiple factors, including gender, region/country of origins, and the specific variable being measured. Regional and country differences do exist, with the salience of race being more pronounced among immigrants from Africa, Asia, and Europe.

And importantly, arguably one of the most interesting results reported in chapter 5 is that many of the findings discussed were nuanced by gender. In many parts of that chapter, patterns are shown to vary by gender. Black women, for example, are shown to exhibit relatively favorable socioeconomic measures, relative to their White counterparts, at least on some dimensions.

When it comes to racial status, then, the findings, in short, reveal its complexity and nuanced effects in labor market disparities! Such nuances, then, are reflective of the title of chapter 5 and this book itself, "African Immigrants in the United States: The Gendering Significance of Race through International Migration?" The question mark denotes my proposition of such a gendering process underway, but that the final outcomes of which are yet to be known.

AFRICAN IMMIGRANTS AND U.S. NATIVES: DISPARITIES MEDIATED BY NATIVITY, RACE, AND GENDER

Chapter 6 of the book sought to take a closer look at the relative socioeconomic and labor market standings of African immigrants, Black and White, and those of the various U.S.-born groups. By distinguishing Black and White Africans from one another, and by separating measures for males from those for females, that chapter sought to fully account for variations by nativity, race, and gender. And, in doing so, it sought to address the fourth objective of the book outlined above.

Four key findings reported in chapter 6 are worth noting at the outset. First, summary statistics showed that African immigrants, both Black and White, compare favorably with several groups on several dimensions. For example, the average percentage with a college degree or more for African immigrants (about 54% for males and about 38% for females) was shown to be noticeably higher than that for all native groups, including non-Hispanic Whites.

A second key finding is that, results show repeatedly that, raw and net, White African immigrants fare better than Black African immigrants, especially among men. White Africans are shown to hold occupations with higher prestige and to have earnings that are appreciably higher. The average annual earnings of White African immigrant males, for example, is shown to be about $38,952 more than that of their Black African immigrant counterparts ($89,789 vs. $50,836). And these patterns generally persisted under the sophisticated multivariate statistical analyses.

A third key finding reported in chapter 6 is that, on several outcomes, raw and net, Black African immigrants do better than most native-born groups. In particular, Black African immigrant women's net earnings are significantly higher than all groups of females, including native born non-Hispanic White women. Indeed, very few groups are shown to out-earn Black African immigrant women.

It follows that, taken together, a key finding from chapter 5 is the salience of race that is mediated by gender. Thus, again, the "gendering significance of race through international migration," wherein the effects of race are acutely salient among men, and less so among women, or sometimes take the opposite effect. Black African females, for example, are estimated to hold occupations with higher prestige than all other groups, except for native Asians and Whites; and with no exceptions, Black African females are estimated to have had hourly earnings that are significantly greater than all their native counterparts, including native Asians and Whites.

A fourth key finding reported in chapter 6 is also worth highlighting. Consistent with previous studies (Butcher 1994; Model 2008; Hamilton 2014, 2019, 2020), summary statistics reported in that chapter indicated that the mere fact of being a "mover" is a differentiating factor, at least among the native Black sample. Those statistics suggested that disparities among native Blacks are accentuated by internal migration/non-migration. Movers are shown to generally exhibit measures that are more favorable than non-movers. Yet, in contrast to previous studies (Butcher 1994; Model 2008; Hamilton 2014, 2019, 2020), the distinction between native internal migrants and non-migrants did not eliminate statistically significant variations in estimates for African immigrants, relative to native-born Blacks.

GENERAL IMPLICATIONS

A remaining question, then, is exactly what can be inferred from all the foregoing? What general implications can be drawn from the findings reported in this book? First, data examined throughout the book clearly show that African immigrants are indeed not a monolithic group. To the contrary, they come from countries and regions that are culturally, linguistically, politically, and/or economically distinct. Consequently, they exhibit notable variations in a variety of attributes, including legal entry status, race, ethnicity and linguistic heritage, and socioeconomic status. The resulting inescapable conclusion is that lumping African immigrants into one homogeneous group for theoretical and/or empirical analyses is problematic, to say the least. A direct implication is that analyses of labor market disparities among African immigrants should clearly consider the emerging immense diversity among this group of immigrants.

Beyond regional and country variations, findings of this study also suggest that research should pay close attention to the increasing diversity in the racial, ethnic, and gender composition of the African immigrant population in the United States. Yet, as with all questions associated with these variables in the United States, many of the associations with labor market disparities noted in this book are also shown to be nuanced. For example, while several of the findings show race to be a salient and statistically significant predictor of labor market disparities, many of the findings also suggest this relationship to be confounded by sending region, as well as the variable being measured (e.g., labor force participation, unemployment, occupational prestige, etc.). Studies of the labor market experiences of African immigrants must also consider such nuances.

Finally, linguistic heritage is clearly an important variable that must be considered in studies of labor market disparities among African immigrants. Such linguistic heritage should also be considered in comparisons between African and other immigrant groups.

NOTE

1. Recalling from chapter 2 of this book, the U.S. Immigration and Nationality Act (INA) provides several broad classes of admission for foreign nationals to gain legal permanent residency (LPR) status in the United States. Those classified as immediate relatives of U.S. citizens include spouses, children, and parents of U.S. citizens age 21 and older. Those admitted based on family-based preferences include relatives/family members not included in the immediate relatives class of admission (e.g., married or unmarried adult sons/daughters of U.S. citizens, brothers/sisters of such citizens, etc.). Specific subcategories in the family-based preferences include "Family First Preference" (unmarried sons/daughters, over the age of 21, of U.S. citizens), "Family Second Preference" (spouses and unmarried children of permanent residents), "Family Third Preference" (married sons/daughters of U.S. citizens), and "Family Fourth Preference" (brothers and sisters of U.S. citizens). Admissions based on employment are given to those seeking to provide needed skills in the U.S. workforce or invest in new U.S. jobs, along with their dependents. Refuge is granted to two sets of immigrants who have been persecuted or have a "well-founded" fear of persecution, refugees and asylees. Refugees are those admitted outside the United States with their immediate relatives, while asylum is given to those seeking refuge, but are already inside the United States, and their immediate relatives. Finally, those gaining LPR based on the diversity program come from countries with relatively low levels of immigration to the United States (for a fuller description of these classifications, see descriptions at the DHS site https://www.dhs.gov/immigration-statistics/lawful-permanent-residents/ImmigrantCOA).

Methodological Appendix

1. The U.S. Department of Homeland Security's *Yearbook of Immigration Statistics* is "a compendium of tables that provides data on foreign nationals who, during a fiscal year, were granted lawful permanent residence (i.e., admitted as immigrants or became legal permanent residents), were admitted into the United States on a temporary basis (e.g., tourists, students, or workers), applied for asylum or refugee status, or were naturalized" (quoted from https://www.dhs.gov/immigration-statistics/yearbook).
2. Funded by the National Science Foundation, the University of Minnesota, and the National Institutes of Health, the Integrated Public Use Microdata Series (IPUMS) are nationally representative samples of U.S. Census data specifically compiled and made available for social and economic research. Compiled and put together by the Minnesota Population Center, the series contains microdata samples (5%, 1%, etc.) of Decennial U.S. Census as far back as 1850 and up to the 2010 Decennial Census. It also currently has samples of the American Community Survey (ACS) from 2000 all the way to 2020. Conducted annually by the U.S. Census Bureau, the ACS is an annual statistical survey of a small (nationally representative) percentage of the U.S. population. For a complete description of the IPUMS dataset, including sample and variable descriptions, data compilation, and storage, see the IPUMS website at http://www.ipums.org.
3. The sample of African and Caribbean immigrants depicted in Figures 2.1 and 2.2 included those whose region of birth is reported by the U.S. Department of Homeland Security's *Yearbook of Immigration Statistics* as Africa or the Caribbean, respectively.
4. In Figures 2.3 and 2.4, Black African immigrants are defined as those who identified themselves by race as "Black" and whose birthplace is reported as Africa in the census documents.

5. In Figures 2.3 and 2.4, Black Caribbean immigrants are those who identified themselves by race as "Black" and whose birthplace is reported as the Caribbean in the census documents.
6. In Figure 2.4, foreign-born Blacks are those who identified themselves as "Black," and who reported their birthplace outside the United States.
7. For analyses reported in chapter 5, the selected sample of African immigrants included those who recorded their birthplace in any of the African countries in the census documents. All other immigrant groupings (those from Asia, Europe, etc.) were similarly selected.
8. The immigrant African regional groupings were defined as follows: those from Central Africa (including Eritrea, South Sudan, Angola, Cameroon, Central African Republic, Chad, Congo, Equatorial Guinea, Gabon, Sao Tome and Principe, and Zaire), East Africa (including Burundi, Comoros, Djibouti, Ethiopia, Kenya, Madagascar, Malawi, Mauritius, Mozambique, Reunion, Rwanda, Seychelles, Somalia, Tanzania, Uganda, Zambia, and Zimbabwe), North Africa (including Algeria, Egypt, Libya, Morocco, Tunisia, Sudan, and Western Sahara), Southern Africa (including Botswana, Lesotho, Namibia, South Africa [Union of], and Swaziland), and West Africa (including Benin, Burkina Faso, Gambia, Ghana, Guinea, Guinea-Bissau, Ivory Coast, Liberia, Mali, Mauritania, Niger, Nigeria, Senegal, Sierra Leone, and Togo).
9. For the estimates reported throughout the empirical chapters of the book (4–6), logistic regression is used when the dependent variables are dichotomous, whereas general linear regression is used when the dependent variables are continuous interval scale.

THREE DICHOTOMOUS DEPENDENT MEASURES OF DISPARITIES IN WORK STATUS

1. A dichotomous variable distinguished individuals reporting being in the labor force (1) and everyone else (0).
2. A dichotomous variable distinguished individuals "employed" if they reported (1) being in the labor force and (2) employed, with 1 indicating such employment and 0 indicating nonemployment.
3. A dichotomous variable distinguished those who reported being self-employed (1) and everyone else (0).

TWO CONTINUOUS DEPENDENT MEASURES OF ECONOMIC DISPARITIES

1. The natural logarithm of occupational prestige: Socioeconomic Index, Hauser and Warren (range equals 7.13–80.53).
2. The natural logarithm of hourly earnings, derived from annual income calculated from reported wage and salary income. To obtain hourly earnings, annual earnings are divided by the product of weeks worked per year and hours worked per week. All earnings results are limited to persons earning at least $500 annually, in constant 2019 dollars. The 2010 sample did not have the weeks worked last year variable, so hourly earnings estimates are not reported for that year.

INDEPENDENT VARIABLES

With each regression model reported in the text, I control for a standard set of social and demographic characteristics, including number of years of schooling, number of years of work experience plus its squared term, number of years in the United States, marital status, a set of regional variables including Midwest, West, and South (reference category = Northeast), an English deficiency measure, two dummy variables controlling for whether an earned college degree was received in the United States or abroad, and metropolitan status.

1. The estimation of the average number of years of schooling follows Kalmijn's (1996) formulation, where kindergarten is estimated to equal to 0 years of schooling; grades 1 to 4 equal to 2.5 years; grades 5 to 8 equal to 6.5 years; grade 9 equals to 9 years; grade 10 equals to 10 years; grade 11 equals to 11 years; grade 12 and high school graduates equal to 12 years; partial college and associate degree in an occupational program translate to 13 years; associate degree in an academic program translates to 14.5 years; bachelor's degree equals to 16 years; master's degree translates to 18 years; and professional and doctorate degrees translate to 22 years.
2. Two measures of labor market experience are the number of years of work experience, which is calculated by taking age minus respondent's years of schooling minus six, and the squared term of labor market experience.
3. Calculation of mean years in the United States is adopted from Dodoo (1997), where year of arrival is enumerated in ranges, estimated for

each respondent as the midpoint of their assigned range. From there, it is possible to calculate the number of years in the United States up to the date of the survey/census: 2016–2019 = 1.5 years; 2014–2015 = 4.5 years; 2011–2013 = 7 years; 2009–2010 = 9.5 years; 2004–2008 = 13 years; 1999–2003 = 18 years; 1994–1998= 23 years; 1989–1993 = 28 years; etc.
4. The distinction of foreign vs. U.S. degrees was adopted from Dodoo (1997), where a college degree is deemed to have been earned in the United States if the number of years of work experience is less than the number of years since migration.
5. Delineating countries as "English speaking" and "Arab speaking" comes from the U.S. Central Intelligence Agency's *World FactBook* (https://www.cia.gov/the-world-factbook).
6. A dichotomous measure delineated those deemed "deficient" in English (1) and all others (0). Those deficient in English either reported that they did not speak English or did speak English, "but not well."
7. A dichotomous variable distinguished individuals who were married (with spouse present or absent) and everyone else.
8. Following Model (2008), for the female sample, two additional relationship variables were included in logistic and general linear models: number of own children currently living in the household (1 = 1 or more, 0 = none); and number of own children under age 5 in the household (1 = 1 or more, 0 = none).

References

Alba, Richard, and Nancy Foner. 2015. *Strangers No More.* Princeton, NJ: Princeton University Press.
Alba, Richard, and Victor Nee. 1997. "Rethinking Assimilation Theory for a New Era of Immigration." *International Migration Review* 31 (4): 826–874.
American Immigration Council. 2012. "African Immigrants in America: A Demographic Overview." Accessed March 15, 2015, at https://www.americanimmigrationcouncil.org/sites/default/files/research/african_immigrants_in_america_a_demographic_overview.pdf.
Anderson, Monica. 2015. "A Rising Share of the U.S. Black Population Is Foreign Born; 9 Percent Are Immigrants; and While Most Are from the Caribbean, Africans Drive Recent Growth." Pew Research Center, Washington, DC. April 9, 2015.
Anderson, Monica, and Gustavo López. 2018. "Key Facts About Black Immigrants in the U.S." Pew Research Center, Washington, DC. January 24, 2018.
Anderson, Monica, and Phillip Connor. 2018. "Sub-Saharan African Immigrants in the United States Are also More Highly Educated than U.S. Native-Born Population." Pew Research Center, Washington, DC. April 24, 2018. Accessed June 22, 2022, at https://www.pewresearch.org/global/2018/04/24/sub-saharan-african-immigrants-in-the-u-s-are-often-more-educated-than-those-in-top-european-destinations/.
Apraku, Kofi. 1996. *Outside Looking In: An African Perspective on American Pluralistic Society.* Westport, CT: Praeger.
———. 1991. *African Émigrés in the United States: A Missing Link to Africa's Social and Economic Development.* New York: Praeger.
Arnold, Faye W. 1984. "West Indians and London's Hierarchy of Discrimination." *Ethnic Groups* 6: 47–64.
Arthur, John A. 2000. *Invisible Sojourners: African Immigrant Diasporas in the US.* Westport, CT: Praeger.
Barone, Michael. 2001. *The New Americans: How the Melting Pot Can Work Again.* Washington DC: Regnery Publishing.
Bashi, Vilna, and Antonio McDaniel. 1997. "A Theory of Immigration and Racial Stratification." *Journal of Black Studies* 27 (5): 668–682.

Batalova, Jeanne. 2020. "Immigrant Women and Girls in the United States." Migration Policy Institute. Accessed January 23, 2022, at https://www.migrationpolicy.org/article/immigrant-women-and-girls-united-states-2018.

Berger, Joseph, Bernard Cohen, and Morris Zelditch Jr. 1972. "Status Characteristics and Social Interaction." *American Sociological Review* 37: 241–255.

Berger, Joseph, Thomas L. Conner, and M. Hamit Fisek. (eds.). 1974. *Expectation States Theory: A Theoretical Research Program*. Cambridge, MA: Winthrop. Reprint. Lanham, MD: University Press of America, 1982.

Berger, Peter L. 1963. *Invitation to Sociology*. New York: Anchor Books.

Blalock, Hubert M., Jr. 1967. *Toward a Theory of Minority-Group Position*. New York: Wiley.

Bonilla-Silva, Eduardo. 2017. *Racism Without Racists: Color-Blind Racism and the Persistence of Racial Inequality in America*. Lanham, MD: Rowman & Littlefield.

Borch, Casey, and Mamadi Corra. 2010. "Differences in Earnings among Black and White African Immigrants in the United States, 1980–2000: A Cross-Sectional and Temporal Analysis." *Sociological Perspectives* 53 (4): 573–592.

Borjas, George J. 1985. "Assimilation, Changes in Cohort Quality, and the Earnings of Immigrants." *Journal of Labor Economics* 3: 463–89.

———. 1987. "Self Selection and the Earnings of Immigrants." *American Economic Review* 77: 531–553.

———. "Immigration and Self-Selection" (April 1988). NBER Working Paper No. w2566, Available at SSRN: https://ssrn.com/abstract=1638804.

———. 1991. "Immigration and Self-Selection." In *Immigration, Trade, and the Labor Market*, edited by J.M. Abowd, 29–76. Chicago: University of Chicago Press.

———. 1994. "The Economics of Immigration." *Journal of Economic Literature* 32 (4): 1667–717.

———. 1995. "Assimilation and Change in Cohort Quality Revisited: What Happened to Immigrant Earnings in the 1980s?" *Journal of Labor Economics* 13 (2): 201–45.

———. 1999. *Heaven's Door: Immigration Policy and the American Economy*. Princeton, NJ: Princeton University Press.

———. 2000. "The Economic Progress of Immigrants." In *Issues in the Economics of Immigration*, edited by George Borjas. Chicago, IL: University of Chicago Press.

Browne, Irene, and Joya Misra. 2003. "The Intersection of Gender and Race in the Labor Market." *Annual Review of Sociology* 29: 487–513.

Buchanan, Patrick J. 2002. *The Death of the West: How Dying Populations and Immigrant Invasions Imperil Our Country*. New York: St. Martin's Press.

Budig, Michelle J., and Paula England. 2001. "The Wage Penalty for Motherhood." *American Sociological Review* 66 (2): 204–225.

Burstein, Paul. 1985. *Discrimination, Jobs, and Politics*. Chicago: University of Chicago Press.

Butcher, Kristin. 1994. "Black Immigrants in the United States: A Comparison with Native Blacks and Other Immigrants." *Industrial and Labor Relations Review* 47: 265–84.

Cancio, Silvia, A., T. David Evans, and David J. Maume. 1996. "Reconsidering the Declining Significance of Race: Racial Differences in Early Career Wages." *American Sociological Review* 61 (4): 541–556.

Capps, Randy, Kristen McCabe, and Michael Fix. 2012. *Diverse Streams: Black African Migration to the United States.* Washington, DC: Migration Policy Institute.

Carliner, Geoffrey. 1980. "Wages, Earnings and Hours of First, Second, and Third Generation American Males." *Economic Inquiry* 18 (1): 87–102.

Carter, J. Scott, Shannon Carter, and Mamadi Corra. 2016. "The Significance of Place: The Impact of Urban and Regional Residence on Gender-Role Attitudes." *Sociological Focus* 49 (4): 271–285.

Carter, J. Scott, and Mamadi Corra. 2012. "Beliefs about the Causes of Racial Inequality: The Persisting Impact of Urban and Suburban Locations?" *Urban Studies Research*: 1–7. Available online at http://www.hindawi.com/journals/usr/2012/242741.

Carter, J. Scott, and Mamadi Corra. 2016. "Racial Resentment and Attitudes Toward the Use of Force by Police: An Over-Time Trend Analysis." *Sociological Inquiry* 86 (4): 496–511.

Carter, J. Scott, Mamadi Corra, and Shannon K. Carter. 2011. "Southern Intolerance Revisited: Political Conservatism and Justification for the Racial Status Quo." *Southern Studies: An Interdisciplinary Journal of the South* 18 (2): 27–48.

Carter, J. Scott, Mamadi Corra, Shannon K. Carter, and Rachel McCrosky. 2014. "The Impact of Place? A Reassessment of the Importance of the South in Affecting Beliefs about Racial Inequality." *Social Science Journal* 51: 12–20.

Carter, J. Scott, Mamadi Corra, and David Jenks. 2016. "In the Shadows of Ferguson: The Role of Racial Resentment on White Attitudes Toward the Use of Force by Police." *International Journal of Criminal Justice Sciences* 11 (2): 114–131.

Carter, J. Scott, Mamadi Corra, and Sarah Okorie. 2018. "Seeing Discrimination: Does Acknowledging Structural Determinants of Inequality Impact Support for the Use of Force by the Police among Whites?" *The Western Journal of Black Studies* 42 (1&2): 18–28.

Chiswick, Barry. 1977. "Sons of Immigrants: Are They at an Earnings Disadvantage?" *American Economic Review* 67 (4): 376–380.

———. 1978. "The Effect of Americanization on the Earnings of Foreign-Born Men." *Journal of Political Economy* 86 (5): 897–921.

———. 1979. "The Economic Progress of Immigrants: Some Apparently Universal Patterns." In *Contemporary Economic Problems,* edited by William Fellner, 357–99. The American Enterprise Institute.

———. 1986. "Is the New Immigration Less Skilled Than the Old?" *Journal of Labor Economics* 4: 168–92.

———. 1999. "Are Immigrants Favorably Self-Selected?" *American Economic Review* 89 (2): 181–5.

———. 2000. "Are Immigrants Favorably Self-Selected?" In *Migration Theory: Talking Across Disciplines,* edited by C.B. Brettell and J.F. Hollifield, 61–76. New York: Routledge.

Cho, S., Kimberlé Crenshaw, and Leslie McCall. 2013. "Toward a Field of Intersectionality Studies: Theory, Applications, and Praxis." *Signs* 38 (4): 785–810.

Cohen, Philip N., and Matt L. Huffman. 2003. "Occupational Segregation and the Devaluation of Women's Work across U.S. Labor Markets." *Social Forces* 81 (3): 881–908.

Collins, Patricia H. 2000a. "Gender, Black Feminism, and Black Political Economy." *Annals of the American Academy of Political and Social Science* 568: 41–53.

———. 2000b. *Black Feminist Thought* (2nd Edition). New York: Routledge.

Corra, Mamadi. 2009. "The State of Black America on the Heels of the Election of Barack Obama as the First African American President of the United States." *The Western Journal of Black Studies* 33 (3): 192–211.

———. 2014. "The Impact of Status Differences on Gatekeeping: A Theoretical Bridge and Bases for Investigation." *Current Research in Social Psychology* 22 (8): 27–38.

———. 2020. "Inequality and Multiracial Gatekeeping." *Sociological Focus* 53(3): 293–321.

Corra, Mamadi, and Casey Borch. 2014. "Socioeconomic Differences among Blacks in America: Over Time Trends." *Race and Social Problems* 6 (2): 103–119.

Corra, Mamadi, and J. Scott Carter. 2008. "Shadow of the Past? Assessing Racial and Gender Differences in Confidence in the Institutions of Science and Medicine." *Black Women, Gender and Family* 2 (1): 54–83.

Corra, Mamadi, J. Scott Carter, and Shannon Carter. 2011. "The Interactive Impact of Race and Gender on High School Advanced Course Enrollments." *Journal of Negro Education* 80 (1): 33–47.

Corra, Mamadi, Shannon Carter, J. Scott Carter, and David Knox. 2009. "Trends in Marital Happiness by Sex and Race, 1973–2006." *Journal of Family Issues* 30 (10): 1379–1404.

Corra, Mamadi, and Sitawa Kimuna. 2009. "Double Jeopardy? Female African and Caribbean Immigrants in the United States." *Journal of Ethnic and Migration Studies* 35 (6): 1015–1035.

Corra, Mamadi, and Michael Lovaglia. 2012. "Too Small to See? African-American Under-Enrollment in Advanced High School Courses." *Journal of Women and Minorities in Science and Engineering* 18 (4): 295–314.

Coverman, Shelley. 1986. "Occupational Segmentation and Sex Differences in Earnings." In *Research in Social Stratification and Mobility*, Vol. 5, edited by R. Robinson, 139–172. Greenwich, CT: JAI Press.

Crenshaw, Kimberlé. 1991. "Mapping the Margins: Intersectionality, Identity Politics, and Violence against Women of Color." *Stanford Law Review* 43 (6): 1241–1299.

Dawsey, Josh. 2018. "Trump Derides Protections for Immigrants from 'Shithole' Countries." *Washington Post*, January 12, 2018, https://www.washingtonpost.com/politics/trump-attacks-protections-for-immigrants-from-shithole-countries-in-oval-office-meeting/2018/01/11/bfc0725c-f711-11e7-91af-31ac729add94_story.htm.

DeFreitas, Gregory. 1980. *Relative Earnings of Black Immigrants: The American Case*. Cambridge, UK: University of Cambridge Faculty of Economics and Politics.

De la Cruz, G. Patricia, and Angela Brittingham. 2003. *The Arab Population: 2000*. Washington, DC: U.S. Census Bureau.

Diamba, Yankj K. 1999. "African Immigrants to the United States: A Socio-Demographic Profile in Comparison to Native Blacks." *Journal of Asian and African Studies* 34 (2): 210–215.

Diamba, Yankj, and Frank D. Bean. 1999. "Black and White African Women in America: Demographic Profile and Socio-Economic Assimilation." *African Population Studies* 14 (2): 97–105.

Dodoo, F. Nii-Amoo. 1991a. "Earnings Differences Among Blacks in America." *Social Science Research* 20: 93–108.

———. 1991b. "Immigrant and Native Black Workers' Labor Force Participation in the United States." *National Journal of Sociology* 5: 1–17.

———. 1991c. "Blacks and Earnings in New York State." *Sociological Spectrum* 11: 203–12.

———. 1991d. "Minority Immigrants in the United States: Earnings Attributes and Economic Success." *Canadian Studies in Population* 18: 42–55.

———. 1997. "Assimilation Differences among Africans in America." *Social Forces* 76: 527–46.

———. 1999. "Black and Immigrant Labor Force Participation in America." *Race and Society* 2 (1): 69–82.

Dodoo, F. Nii-Amoo, and Baffour K. Takyi. 2002. "Africans in the Diaspora: Black-White Earnings Differences among America's Africans." *Ethnic and Racial Studies* 25 (6): 913–41.

Domingo, Wilfrid A. 1925. "Gift of the Black Tropics." In *The New Negro: An Interpretation*, edited by Alain Locke. New York: Johnson Reprint.

Du Bois, W.E.B. 1962. Letter Communication about the Proposed Encyclopedia Africana Project. Accra, Ghana.

———. [1903] 1994. *The Souls of Black Folk*. New York: Dover Publications, Incorporated.

———. [1903] 2000. *The Souls of Black Folk*, Centennial Edition. New York: Random House Publishing Group.

Dugger, Karen. 1988. "Social Location and Gender-Role Attitudes: A Comparison of Black and White Women." *Gender & Society* 2: 425–448.

Ellison, Ralph. 1952. *Invisible Man*. New York: Random House.

Elo, Irma T., Elizabeth Frankenberg, Romeo Gansey, and Duncan Thomas. 2015. "Africans in the American Labor Market." *Demography* 52: 1513–1542.

Farley, Reynolds. 1984. *Blacks and Whites: Narrowing the Gap*. Cambridge, MA: Harvard University Press.

Fears, Darryl. 2002. "A Diverse—and Divided—Black Community." Washington Post, February 23, 2002. https://www.washingtonpost.com/archive/politics/2002/02/23/a-diverse-and-divided-black-community/3375e84c-2730-45f6-a14a-52fd563b-1dae/. Accessed July 15, 2019.

Foner, Nancy. 1985. "Race and Color: Jamaican Migrants in London and New York City." *International Migration Review* 19: 708–727.

General Assembly. "Negro Women's Children to Serve According to the Condition of the Mother" (1662). (2020, December 07). In *Encyclopedia Virginia*. https://encyclopediavirginia.org/entries/negro-womens-children-to-serve-according-to-the-condition-of-the-mother-1662.

Glazer, Nathan, and Daniel Moynihan. 1963. *Beyond the Melting Pot*. Cambridge, MA: M.I.T. Press and Harvard University Press.

Goffman, Erving. 1959. *The Presentation of Self in Everyday Life*. Anchor Books. New York, NY: Bantam Doubleday Dell Publishing Group.

Golash-Boza, and Tanya Maria. 2021. *Race and Racisms: A Critical Approach*. New York/Oxford: Oxford University Press.

Gordon, April. 1998. "The New Diaspora: African Immigration to the United States." *Journal of Third World Studies* 15 (1): 79–103.

Grace-McCaskey, Cynthia A., Susan Pearce, Lynn Harris, Mamadi Corra, and Kayla Evans. 2021. "Finding Voices in the Floods of Freedom Hill: Innovation Solutions in Princeville, North Carolina." *Journal of Environmental Studies and Sciences* 11: 341–351.

Greeley, Andrew. 1976. *Ethnicity, Denomination, and Inequality*. Beverly Hills and London: Sage.

Grosfoguel, Ramon. 2003. *Colonial Subjects*. Berkeley, California: University of California Press.

———. 2004. "Race and Ethnicity or Racialized Ethnicities?" *Ethnicities* 4 (3): 315–36.

Grosfoguel, Ramon, and Chloe S. Georas. 2000. "'Coloniality of Power' and Racial Dynamics: Notes Toward a Reinterpretation of Latino Caribbeans in New York City." *Identities* 7 (1): 85–125.

Harrison, Lawrence. 1992. *Who Prospers?* New York: Basic Books.

Hamilton, Tod G. 2014. "Selection, Language Heritage, and the Earnings Trajectories of Black Immigrants in the United States." *Demography* 51 (3): 975–1002.

———. 2019. *Immigration and the Remaking of Black America*. New York: Russell Sage Foundation.

———. 2020. "Black Immigrants and the Changing Portrait of Black America." *Annual Review of Sociology* 46: 295–313.

Hawk, Beverley. 1992. *Africa's Media Image*. New York: Praeger.

Hing, Bill Ong. 1993. "Beyond the Rhetoric of Assimilation and Cultural Pluralism: Addressing the Tension of Separatism and Conflict in an Immigration-Driven Multiracial Society." *California Law Review* 81 (4): 863–925. JSTOR, www.jstor.org/stable/3480889.

Hodge, Robert W. 1973. "Toward a Theory of Racial Differences in Employment." *Social Forces* 52: 16–31.

Hodson, Randy, and Robert Kaufman. 1982. "Economic Dualism: A Critical Review." *American Sociological Review* 47 (6): 727–739.

Hossfeld, Karen. 1994. "Hiring Immigrant Women: Silicon Valley's Simple Formula." In *Women of Color in U.S. Society*, edited by M. Zinn and B. Dill. Philadelphia, PA: Temple University Press.

Hughes, Everett C. 1945. "Dilemmas and Contradictions of Status." *American Journal of Sociology* 50: 353–359.

Hurst, Charles E., Heather M Fitz Gibbon, and Anne M. Nurse. 2017. *Social Inequality: Forms, Causes, and Consequences*. Ninth Edition. Boston: Routledge.
Ifatunji, Mosi Adesina. 2016. "A Test of the Afro Caribbean Model Minority Hypothesis: Exploring the Role of Cultural Attributes in Labor Market Disparities Between African Americans and Afro Caribbeans." *Du Bois Review: Social Science Research on Race* 31 (1): 109–138.
———. 2017. "Labor Market Disparities Between African Americans and Afro Caribbeans: Reexamining the Role of Immigrant Selectivity." *Sociological Forum* 32 (3): 522–543.
———. 2018. "Years of Since Migration: On the Motivation to Reexamine the Role of Immigrant Selectivity in Black Ethnic Labor Market Disparities." *Sociological Forum* 33 (2): 547–552.
James, Winston. 2002. "Explaining Afro-Caribbean Social Mobility in the United States: Beyond the Sowell Thesis." *Comparative Studies in Society and History* 44 (2): 218–62.
Jasso, Guillermina. 2004. "Have the Occupational Skills of New Immigrants to the United States Declined over Time? Evidence from the Immigrant Cohorts of 1977, 1982, and 1994." In *International Migration: Prospects and Policies in a Global Market*, edited by Douglas S. Massey and J. Edward Taylor. Oxford: Oxford University Press.
———. 2011. "Migration and Stratification." *Social Science Research* 40: 1292–1336.
Jasso, Guillermina, and Mark R. Rosenzweig. 1990a. *The New Chosen People*. New York: Russell Sage Foundation.
———. 1990b. "Self-Selection and the Earnings of Immigrants: Comment." *American Economic Review* 80 (1): 298–304.
Jasso, Guillermina, Mark R. Rosenzweig, and James Smith. 2000. "The Changing Skill of New Immigrants to the United States: Recent Trends and Their Determinants." In *Issues in the Economics of Immigration*, edited by George J. Borjas. Chicago: University of Chicago Press.
Kalmijn, Matthijs. 1996. "The Socioeconomic Assimilation of Caribbean American Blacks." *Social Forces* 74: 911–30.
Kane, Emily W. 1992. "Race, Gender, and Attitudes toward Gender Stratification." *Social Psychology Quarterly* 55: 311–320.
Kasinitz, Philip. 1992. *Caribbean New York: Black Immigrants and the Politics of Race*. Cornell University Press.
Katende, Charles. 1994. *Population Dynamics in Africa*. PhD diss., University of Pennsylvania.
Kaufman, Robert L. 2002. "Assessing Alternative Perspectives on Race and Sex Employment Segregation." *American Sociological Review* 67 (4): 547–572.
Kent, Mederios Mary. 2007. "Immigration and America's Black Population." *Population Bulletin* 62 (4): 1–16.
Kim, Jingsung, and Francis Kemegue. 2007. "Addressing the Low Returns to Education of African Born Immigrants in the United States." Economic Working Papers. Accessed August 5, 2010, at http://digitalcommons.bryant.edu/econwork/4/.

Kollehlon, K., and E. E., Eule. 2003. "The Socioeconomic Attainment Patterns of Africans in the United States" *International Migration Review* 37 (4): 1163–1190.

Konadu-Agyemang, Kwadwo, and Baffour K. Takyi. 2006. "An Overview of African Immigration to the US and Canada." In *The African Diaspora in North Africa: Trends, Community Building, and Adaptation*, edited by K. Konadu-Agyemang, B. Takyi, and J. Arthur, 189–289. Lanham, MD: Lexington Books.

Kposowa, Augustine J. 2002. "Human Capital and the Performance of African Immigrants in the U.S. Labor Market." *The Western Journal of Black Studies* 26: 175–183.

Kunkle, Fredrick. 2015. "Black Immigrants Is Remaking U.S. Black Population, Report Says." *Washington Post*, April 9, 2015. https://amren.com/news/2015/04/black-immigration-is-remaking-u-s-black-population-report-says/. Accessed June 2, 2015.

Kusow, Abdi, Kristine Ajrouch, and Mamadi Corra. 2018. "Socioeconomic Achievement Among Arab Immigrants in the United States: The Influence of Region of Origin and Gender." *Journal of International Migration and Integration* 19 (1): 111–127.

Kusow, Abdi, Sitawa Kimuna, and Mamadi Corra. 2016. "Socioeconomic Diversity Among African Immigrants in the United States: An Intra African Immigrant Comparison." *Journal of International Migration and Integration* 17 (1): 115–130.

Lazarsfeld, Paul, and Robert K. Merton. 1954. "Friendship as a Social Process: A Substantive and Methodological Analysis." In Freedom and Control in Modern Society, edited by M. Berger, T. Abel, and H. Charles. New York: Van Nostrand.

Lazarus, Emma. 1883. "The New Colossus." Statue of Liberty, New York.

Lee, Everett S. 1966. "A Theory of Migration." *Demography* 3: 47–57.

Lewis, Gordon. 1983. *Main Currents in Caribbean Thought: The Historical Evolution of Caribbean Society in its Ideological Aspects, 1492–1900*. Baltimore, MD: Johns Hopkins University Press.

Lieberson, Stanley. 1980. *A Piece of the Pie*. Berkeley, CA: University of California Press.

Lobo, Arun P. 2001. "US Diversity Visas Are Attracting Africa's Best and Brightest." *Population Today* 29 (5): 1–2.

Logan, B. Ikubolajeh, and Kevin J. Thomas. 2012. "The U.S. Diversity Visa Program and the Transfer of Skills from Africa." *International Migration* 50 (2): 1–19.

Logan, John R., and Glenn Deane. 2003. "Black Diversity in Metropolitan America." Lewis Mumford Center for Comparative Urban and Regional Research, University of Albany.

Lopez, Nancy. 2003. *Hopeful Girls, Troubled Boys: Race and Gender Disparity in Urban Education*. New York: Routledge.

Macionis, John J. 2019. *Sociology*. Sixteenth Edition. Boston: Pearson Education, Inc.

Mason, Patrick L. 2010. "Culture and Intraracial Wage Inequality among America's African Diaspora. *American Economic Review* 100: 309–315.

Mazuri, Ali A. 1987. *The Africans: A Triple Heritage*. New York: Little Brown & Company.

McCabe, Kristen. 2011. "African Immigrants in the United States." Migration Information Source. http://www.migrationpolicy.org/article/african-immigrants-united-states/.

McCall, Leslie. 2001. *Complex Inequality: Gender, Class, and Race in the New Economy*. New York: Routledge.

———. 2005a. "The Complexity of Intersectionality." *Signs: Journal of Women in Culture and Society* 30 (3): 1771–1800.

———. 2005b. "Gender, Race, and the Restructuring of Work: Organizational and Institutional Perspectives." In *The Oxford Handbook of Work and Organization*, edited by P. Tolbert, R. Batt, S. Ackroyd, and P. Thompson, 74–94. New York: Oxford University Press.

Meyers, David G., and Jean M. Twenge. 2019. *Social Psychology*. Thirteenth Edition. New York: McGraw-Hill Education, Inc.

Miller, Alexander O., Mamadi Corra, and Danielle Smith. 2009. "Generic Processes in the Production of Relations among Incarcerated Juvenile African American Males and Female Correctional Officers." *Sociation Today* 7 (2). Available online at http://www.ncsociology.org/sociationtoday/v72/juvenile.htm.

Millman, Joel. 1997. *The Other Americans: How Immigrants Renew Our Country, Our Economy and Our Values*. New York: Viking, Penguin Group.

Mills, C. Wright. 1959. *The Sociological Imagination*. New York: Oxford University Press.

Mishel, Lawrence, Jared Bernstein, and Sylvia Allegretto. 2007. *The State of Working America, 2006*. Ithaca, NY: Cornell University Press.

Model, Suzanne. 1991. "Caribbean Immigrants: A Black Success Story?" *International Migration Review* 25: 248–76.

———. 1995. "West Indian Prosperity: Fact or Fiction?" *Social Problems* 42: 535–53.

———. 1997. "An Occupational Tale of Two Cities: Minorities in London and New York." *Demography* 34: 539–50.

———. 2008. *West Indian Immigrants: A Black Success Story?* New York: Russell Sage.

———. 2018. "Selectivity Is Still in the Running: A Comment on Ifatunji's Labor Market Disparities." *Sociological Forum* 33 (2): 539–46.

Model, Suzanne, and David Ladipo. 1996. "Context and Opportunity: Minorities in London and New York." *Social Forces* 75: 485–510.

Mpanya, Mutombo. 1995. "Stereotypes of Hunger in U.S. Hunger Appeals." In *The Color of Hunger*, edited by David Shields, 25–33. Lanham, MD: Rowman & Littlefield.

Myers, John P. 2003. *Dominant Minority Relations in America: Linking Personal History with the Convergence in the New World*. Boston: Allyn & Bacon.

Neidert, Lisa J., and Reynolds Farley. 1985. "Assimilation in the United States: An Analysis of Ethnic and Generation Differences in Status and Achievement." *American Sociological Review* 50 (6): 840–50.

Nawyn, Stephanie J., and Julie Park. 2019. "Gendered Segmented Assimilation: Earnings Trajectories of African Immigrant Women and Men." *Ethnic and Racial Studies* 42 (2): 216–234.

Oaxaca, Ronald. 1973. "Male-Female Wage Differentials in Urban Labor Markets." *International Economic Review* 14 (3): 693–709.

Osofsky, Gilbert. 1963. *Harlem: The Making of a Ghetto*. New York: Harper & Row.

Ottley, Roi. 1943. *New World a-Coming*. Boston, MA: Houghton Mifflin.

Parrillo, Vincent N. 2019. *Strangers to These Shores: Race and Ethnic Relations in the United States*. Boston: Allyn & Bacon.

Portes, Alejandro, and József Böröcz. 1989. "Contemporary Immigration: Theoretical Perspectives on its Determinants and Modes of Incorporation." *International Migration Review* 23 (3): 606–630.

Portes, Alejandro, and Rubén G. Rumbaut. 2001. *Legacies: The Story of the Immigrant Second Generation*. Berkeley, CA: University of California Press.

———. 2006. *Immigrant America: A Portrait*. Berkeley, CA: University of California Press.

Portes, Alejandro, and Min Zhou. 1993. "The New Second Generation: Segmented Assimilation and Its Variants." *Annals of the American Academy of Political and Social Sciences* 530: 74–96.

Portes, Alejandro, and Robert Bach. 1985. *Latin Journey: Cuban and Mexican Immigrants in the United States*. Berkeley, CA: University of California Press.

Reid, Ira de A. 1939/1969. *The Negro Immigrant*. AMS Press.

Reid, John. 1986. "Immigration and the Future of the U.S. Black Population." *Population Today* 14: 6–8.

Reitz, Jeffrey G., and Sherrilyn M. Sklar. 1997. "Culture, Race, and the Economic Assimilation of Immigrants." *Sociological Forum* 12 (2): 233–277.

Reskin, Barbara F. 1988. "Bringing the Men Back In: Sex Differentiation and the Devaluation of Women's Work." *Gender & Society* 2 (1): 58–81.

Ridgeway, Cecilia L. 2000. "The Formation of Status Belief: Improving Status Construction Theory." In *Advances in Group Processes*, Vol. 17, edited by Edward J. Lawler, 77–102. Greenwich, CT: JAI Press.

———. 2014. "Why Status Matters for Inequality." *American Sociological Review* 70: 1–16.

Ridgeway, Cecilia L., and Henry A. Walker. 1995. "Status Structures." In Sociological Perspectives on Social Psychology, edited by K. Cook, G. Fine, and J. House, 281–310. Boston: Allyn & Bacon.

Ritzer, George. 2007. Contemporary Sociological Theory and Its Classical Roots: The Basics. Boston: McGraw-Hill.

Roberts, Sam. 2005. "More Africans Enter U.S. Than in Days of Slavery," *New York Times*, February 21, 2005, http://mumford.albany.edu/census/othersay/02212005NewYorkTimes.pdf.

Roos, Patricia, A. 1990. "Review of Revolving Doors: Sex Segregation and Women's Careers, by Jerry Jacobs." *American Journal of Sociology* 95: 1315–1316.

Roy, Andrew. 1951. "Some Thoughts on the Distribution of Earnings." *Oxford Economic Papers* 3: 135–46.

Ruggles, Steven, Sarah Flood, Ronald Goeken, Josiah Grover, Erin Meyer, Jose Pacas, and Matthew Sobek. 2020. Integrated Public Use Microdata Series: Version 10.0 [Machine-readable database]. Minneapolis, MN: Minnesota Population Center [producer and distributor]. https://doi.org/10.18128/D010.V10.0.

Sackett, Blair, and Annette Lareau. Forthcoming. *Seeking Refuge, Finding Inequality: Refugees Navigating Their Way*. University of California Press.

———. 2022. "Refugee Families, Institutional Knots, and Reverberating Consequences: Obstacles to Upward Mobility." Paper presented at the Russell Sage Foundation Conference on Administrative Burdens. February 24, 2022.

Sáenz, Rogelio, and Karen Manges Douglas. 2015. "A Call for the Racialization of Immigration Studies: On the Transition of Ethnic Immigrants to Racialized Immigrants." *Sociology of Race and Ethnicity* 1 (1): 166–180.

Scroggins, Deborah. 1989. "Atlanta: A Magnet for Emigres, but Racial Barriers a Surprise." *Atlanta Journal and Constitution*, August 20, 1989.

Shaw-Taylor, Yoku, and Steven Tuch. 2007. *The Other African Americans: Contemporary African and Caribbean Families in the United States*. Lanham, MD: Rowman & Littlefield Publishers.

Snyder, David. 2002. "Signs of a Boom in African Influx: Surge's Impact Seen throughout Country." *Washington Post*.

Simmons, Ann M. 2018. "African Immigrants Are More Educated Than Most—Including People Born in the U.S." *Los Angeles Times*, January 12, 2018. Latimes.com/world/Africa/la-fg-global-african-immigrants-explainer-20180112-story.html.

Smith, Stephen. 2003. *Labor Economics*, Second Edition. London, Routledge.

Sowell, Thomas. 1975. *Race and Economics*. New York: David McKay.

———. 1978. "Three Black Histories." In *Essays and Data on American Ethnic Groups*, edited by Thomas Sowell and Lynn D. Collins, 7–64. Washington DC: The Urban Institute.

———. 1981. *Ethnic America: A History*. New York: Basic Books.

———. 1983. *The Economics and Politics of Race*. New York: William Morrow.

———. 1994. *Race and Culture: A World View*. New York: Basic Books.

Takougang, Joseph. 1995. "Black Immigrants to the United States." *The Western Journal of Black Studies* 19: 50–7.

Tamir, Christine. 2022. "Key Findings about Black immigrants in the U.S." Pew Research Center, Washington, DC, January 27. Accessed June 11, 2022, at https://www.pewresearch.org/fact-tank/2022/01/27/key-findings-about-black-immigrants-in-the-u-s/.

Tamir, Kristine, and Monica Anderson. 2022. "The Caribbean Is the Largest Origin Source of Black Immigrants, but Fastest Growth Is among African Immigrants." Pew Research Center, Washington, DC, January 20. Accessed June 11, 2022, at https://www.pewresearch.org/race-ethnicity/2022/01/20/the-caribbean-is-the-largest-origin-source-of-black-immigrants-but-fastest-growth-is-among-african-immigrants/.

Tesfai, Rebbeca. 2017a. "Continued Success or Caught in the Housing Bubble? Black Immigrants and the Housing Market Crash." *Population Research and Policy Review* 36: 531–560.

———. 2017b. "Racialized Labour Market Incorporation? African Immigrants and the Role of Education Occupation Mismatch in Earnings." *International Migration* 55 (4): 203–220.

———. 2019. "Double Minority Status and Neighborhoods: Examining the Primacy of Race in Black Immigrants' Racial and Socioeconomic Segregation." *City and Community* 18 (2): 509–528.

Thomas, Kevin J. A. 2011. "What Explains the Increasing Trend in African Emigration to the US?" *International Migration Review* 45 (1): 3–28.

———. 2014. *Diverse Pathways: Race and the Incorporation of Black, White, and Arab-Origin Africans in the United States*. East Lansing, MI: Michigan State University Press.

Tolnay, S. E. 2003. "The African American 'Great Migration' and Beyond." *Annual Review of Sociology* 29: 209–232.

Tomaskovic-Devey, Donald. 1993. *Gender and Racial Inequality at Work*. Ithaca, NY: ILR Press.

Ueda, Reed. 1980. "West Indians." In *The Harvard Encyclopedia of Ethnic Groups*, edited by Stephan Thernstrom. Cambridge, MA: Belknap Press of Harvard University Press.

U.S. Department of Homeland Security (DHS). 1996–2019. *Yearbook of Immigration Statistics*. Washington, DC: DHS.

U.S. Immigration and Naturalization Service. 1998. *Statistical Yearbook of the U.S. Immigration and Naturalization Service*. Washington, DC: Department of Justice.

U.S. Immigration and Naturalization Service (INS). 1999. *Statistical Yearbook of the Immigration and Naturalization Service*. Washington, DC: U.S. Government Printing Office.

U.S. Supreme Court, Roger Brooke Taney, John H Van Evrie, and Samuel A. Cartwright. The Dred Scott Decision: Opinion of Chief Justice Taney. New York: Van Evrie, Horton & Co., 1860, 1860. [PDF] https://www.loc.gov/item/17001543/.

Vickerman, Milton. 1994. "The Responses of West Indians to African-Americans: Distancing and Identification." In *Research in Race and Ethnic Relations*, vol. 7, edited by Dennis Routledge. Greenwich, CT: JAI Press.

———. 1999. *Crosscurrents: West Indian Immigrants and Race*. New York: Oxford University Press.

Waters, Mary. 1993. "West Indian Immigrants, African Americans, and Whites in the Workplace: Different Perspectives on American Race Relations." Unpublished paper, Harvard University.

———. 1994a. "Differing Perspectives of Racism: West Indians, African Americans, and Whites in the Workplace." Paper presented at the annual meetings of the American Sociological Association, Los Angeles, California.

———.. 1994b. "Ethnic and Racial Identities of Second-Generation Black Immigrants in New York City." *International Migration Review* 28: 795–820.

———. 1997. "The Impact of Racial Segregation on the Education and Work Outcomes of Second-Generation West Indians in New York City." Paper presented to Jerome Levy Institute Conference on the Second Generation. Bard College, October 25,1997.

———. 1999. *Black Identities: West Indian Immigrant Dreams and American Realities*. New York: Russell Sage Foundation.

Wilson, William J. 1980. *The Declining Significance of Race: Blacks and Changing American Institutions*. Chicago: University of Chicago Press.

———. 1989. "The Declining Significance of Race: Revisited but not Revised." In Caste, Class Controversy on Race and Poverty, edited by C. Willie, 22–36. Dix Hills, NY: General Hall, Inc.

Zaffiro, James. 1992. "Review of the Western Media and the Stereotyping of Africa." *Africa Today* 39: 81–82.

Zeleza, Paul. 2002. "Contemporary African Migration in a Global Context." *African Issues* 30 (1): 9–14.

Zhou, Min. 1997. "Segmented Assimilation: Issues, Controversies, and Recent Research on the New Second Generation." *International Migration Review* 31 (4): 955–1008.

Zinn, Baca M., and Thornton Dill. 1996. "Theorizing Difference from Multiracial Feminism." *Feminist Studies* 22 (2): 321–331.

Index

AFRICAN IMMIGRANTS

Algeria, 21, 25, 62, 68, 72, 88
appreciable increase, 23
Arab immigration, Africa, 4, 28, 34
Arab-speaking countries, 27–28, 64, 69–70, 75, 79–80
arrival cohorts, 123–124
asylee, 23, 24, 32, 34, 56–58, 65, 69–72, 90, 91, 149, 150, 151

Black Africans, 52, 63
Black African immigrants, xxiii, 1, 5, 8, 9, 41, 51, 65, 98, 104, 109, 111, 114, 116, 119, 121–122, 133, 136, 137, 139, 142, 154, 187
Black female immigrants, 10, 143
Black immigrants 1, 7, 8, 9, 38
Black African female, 10
Black men, 44, 72, 78, 105, 132
Black women, 72, 96, 105–106, 115–116, 120, 137
brain drain, 47

Cameroon, 22, 56, 57, 81, 82, 83, 85, 91, 151

Central Africa, 28, 74–75, 77–79, 147, 158
changing gender composition, xxiii, 26
changing racial/ethnic composition, 25
changing composition, foreign-born Black population, United States, xxii-xxiii, 1–4, 16–19, 44, 147
changing composition, U.S. Black population xxii, 1, 18–19, 32, 147, 158
changing gender composition, gender parity, xxiii 32, 148, 149
changing immigrant composition, xxiii, 16–20
changing racial/ethnic composition, xiii, 27, 29, 32, 147–148
concentrated presence, Long-Term Sending Countries, 22, 146
Congo (DRC), 34, 58, 68, 149
contemporary debates, 96
country-level comparisons, 80

Diaspora, 4, 8, 97
discrimination, 6–8, 32, 39, 40, 42, 48–52
demographic portrait, 11
diverse paths, legal permanent residency, 91, 149

diversity, xxiii, 20, 22, 146, 147, 148, 149, 155
diversity, racial/ethnic transformation, U.S. Society, xxii, 1, 148
diversity, socioeconomic profile, 59
diversity, Visa lottery, 19, 24, 57

East/eastern Africa, 4, 28, 62, 68, 73, 74, 76, 77, 78, 79, 147, 158
economic inequality, 46, 47
education, xx, 8–9, 13, 29–30, 32, 34–35, 37, 39, 43, 45, 72, 77, 92, 98–102, 110, 115, 120, 122, 125–129, 133, 143, 149–150
Egypt, 4, 21, 22, 28, 58, 80, 81, 82, 86, 88, 89, 151
employment, 7, 29–32, 49, 53, 57–58
employment-based preferences, 24, 47, 56, 57, 58, 149
entry status, 23, 25, 47, 56, 57
English-speaking countries, 26, 64, 65, 75, 124, 150, 152
Ethiopia, 21, 22, 56, 57, 80, 81, 82, 86, 88, 89

family-based preferences, 24, 47, 56, 57
foreign degrees, 72, 77

Gambia, xiii
gender differences, 47, 63, 64, 86
gender gap, 64
gender consistent, 80
gendered salience, race, 70, 75, 87, 106, 110
gender, status attainment, 9
Gendered Country-Level Disparities, 82
gendered variations, Labor Market Disparities, 66
general linear regression estimates, 67, 77, 113–15, 138, 140, 158
Ghana, 21, 22, 51, 56, 58, 81, 82, 86, 89, 90, 150, 151
Gini Coefficients, 88
Gini index, 88
growth, African immigrants, 1–2, 11

growth, Black immigrant population, 2, 28

higher-than-average refugee measure, 72
hourly earnings 30–31, 65, 66, 71, 76–80, 85, 87–89, 94, 106, 113–114, 140–142, 154

immediate relative of U.S. citizens, 24, 56, 57
Immigration Act of 1990, 19, 57
immigration, patterns, trends, 15–23
increasingly visible component, U.S. population, xxii, 1, 19
income inequality, 48, 88–89
intra-African, xxiii, 12
intra-African group hypotheses, 150
intra-group comparison, 52

Kenya, 21, 22, 51, 56, 80, 81, 82, 85, 86, 87, 88, 89, 91, 92, 152

labor force participation, 66–76, 106–112, 133–136
Labor Market Disparities, xxiv, 65–66, 86, 90, 106, 114, 119, 122, 152–153, 155
legal admission status, 57, 58
legal/lawful permanent residence (LPR) status, 1, 15–17, 157
Liberia, 21, 22, 56, 68, 80, 81, 82, 83, 85, 86, 88, 149
Libya, 21
linguistic heritage, 26, 51, 63, 64, 66–70, 124, 149
logistic regression estimates/models, 65–73, 106–112, 133–136, 158
long-term sending countries, 23, 147

Morocco, 21, 22, 56, 58, 80, 81, 82, 86, 90, 150, 151
multivariate regression, 65

new African Americans, 3, 55, 145
new Americans, 3, 55, 145

Nigeria, 21, 22, 51, 56, 58, 80, 81, 82, 87, 88, 89, 90, 150, 151
North/northern Africa, 4 27, 28, 62, 63, 69, 73, 74, 77, 78, 147, 158

occupational prestige, 59, 62, 64–65, 76–80, 82, 86–89, 102, 104–106, 114–116, 129, 131–132, 140–41, 143, 153, 155

race, immigration, xiii, xiv, xvi, xviii, xxii
racial earnings gap, 63
regional variations, 62, 69
refugees, 24, 56, 57, 58, 70–71, 149, 150, 151

self-employment, 59, 62–66, 69, 72–75, 82, 86–89, 94, 102, 104–106, 110–112, 117–118, 129, 131–133, 137, 142–143, 149
Senegal, xiii, 51
shifting composition, racial, gender, linguistic heritage, 25–28
shifting U.S. immigration policy, 22
shifting socioeconomic profiles, 29
"shithole countries," xxii, 4, 96
Sierra Leone, 21, 22, 56, 81, 82, 86, 88
sociodemographic characteristics, 25
Somalia, 21, 22, 23, 56, 58, 65, 80, 81, 82, 86, 90, 149, 150, 151
South Africa, 21, 22, 51, 56, 58, 65, 80, 82, 86, 88, 89, 92, 149, 152
Southern Africa, 62, 69, 76, 77, 78, 158
Sudan, 56, 58, 80, 81, 82, 86, 89, 90, 150, 151
successful immigrant incorporation, 146

Tanzania, 56, 58, 72, 149
Theoretical Analysis, 91
theoretically Relevant Country-Level Comparisons, 87
top sending African Immigrant Country Sources, 20, 55, 56, 57, 91, 147, 151

U.S. degrees, 72, 77, 160
unemployment, xx, 7, 29, 31, 46, 59, 62–63, 65–69, 70, 72–73, 74–76, 82, 86–89, 94, 102, 104–106, 110–112, 117–118, 129, 131–133, 137, 140, 142, 149, 155
Uganda, 21

variations, legal entry status, 23, 56
voluntary African immigration, xxii, xxiii, 1, 26, 28

Wald tests, 72–75, 87, 89, 90, 116–117, 140
West Africa, xiii, 69, 74, 75, 77, 78, 79, 158
white African immigrants 5, 9, 63, 64
white Africans, 63–64, 72–73, 103–104–107, 114–117, 124–126–132, 137, 139–141–142, 152–154
work-related measures, 102, 129

GENERAL TOPICS

1964 Civil Rights Act, 42
1965 Family Reunification and Refugee Act, 46

advantages of invisibility, xviii.
American Community Surveys, 5, 16, 17, 157

Black "n," xiv
"boy," xiv
Civil Rights Movement, 42
"cracker," xiv
color line, xv, xix, 40, 121

Donald Trump, xxii, 4, 96
Du Bois, xv, xix
Du Boisian, xv
double consciousness, xv, xix

earnings 31, 45, 46–47, 113, 140
East Carolina University, xix
economic inequality, 46, 47
educational attainment, 29
Emma Lazarus, xxi

Federal Judicial Center (FJC), xx

Gardner-Webb University/
    College, xvi, xvii
Genesis of book, xiii

hourly earnings, 76, 77, 141

income inequality 48, 88
Immigration Act of 1990, 19, 57
Indigenous population, Gambia, xiii
Integrated Public Use Microdata Series/
    samples (IPUMS), 5, 16, 17, 157
"invisible man," xvi
Inequality, xx

micro level-variable, xix
"N" word, xiii, xiv
neighborhood segregation, xix

Partus Sequitur Ventrem, legal
    doctrine, 96
Patrick Buchanan, xvii, xxii
pre-civil rights, 42
post-civil rights, 42

race, social construct, xiv
race, immigration, xiii, xiv, xvi,
    xviii, xxii
race, master status characteristic,
    xxi, 65, 119
race, micro-level processes, xx
race relations xviii, xix
racial discrimination 49
racial earnings gap, 63
racial identity, xiii
racial segregation, 42
racism, 49
Ralph Ellison, xvi

social inequality, xx
social inequality, confluence
    with race, xx
social construction of reality xvii
socioeconomic status, xxiii
sociological perspective xvi
status characteristic, xv

The New Colossus, xxi
theoretical analysis, 91
Trans-Atlantic Slave Trade, 2
triple consciousness, xix
triple heritage, xix
"Tubaab," xiii

U.S. Census, 4, 5, 9
U.S. Census Bureau, 157
U.S. Constitution, Article I,
    Section 2, 95
U.S. Constitution, Three-
    Fifths Clause 96
U.S. Immigration Law, 46
U.S. Supreme Court, Dred Scott
    Decision, 95–96
unemployment, 65–76, 106,
    112, 133–136
USC, xviii

Virginia House of Burgesses/General
    Assembly, 95, 96
veil, xv

W.E.B. Du Bois, xv, 121
Washington Post, xxii, 4, 96

Yearbook of Immigration Statistics, 1, 5,
    15–16, 55, 150, 157

IMMIGRATION THEORY AND RESEARCH

all Black society hypothesis, 40

Index

Anglophilia, 49, 51, 52, 92, 151

colonial immigrants, 50, 51
colonial/racial subjects, 50, 51
coloniality of power, 50, 52
comfort factor, 49, 52
context of reception, 6–7, 51, 97
context of reception hypothesis, 7
cultural argument, 37, 38, 42
cultural exchange, 87, 91, 151
cultural inferiority hypothesis, 38
cultural superiority hypothesis, 38

demand-side argument, 37
demographic argument, 40
developing countries, 46

early birds, 44, 48, 91, 151
economically motivated emigrants, 25, 43, 70, 91, 150, 151
economic migrants, 25
economic inequality, 46, 47
English-speaking world, 41, 92
enslaved, 39
ethnoracial, xxiii
extractive societies, 87, 88

foreign degree, 31, 73, 78
generation, 44
generational transfer, 44

historical context, 42
historical perspective, 38–39
human capital advantage, 48

immigrant adaptation, 4, 6, 97
immigrant adaptation, adjustment period, xxiv, 6, 97, 121
immigrant generation, 44
immigrant incorporation, Visa Type, 25, 48, 90
immigrant quality, declines, 97, 122
immigrant quality-income inequality proposition, 90, 152
incorporation processes, 4

Intersectionality, 10, 47, 51
intervening variables, 44
"invasion" immigration, xvii

migration costs, 44
migration theory, 97, 150
migration selectivity, 37, 40, 42, 43, 48

nativity, 6
negative selectivity, 46–48
non-European countries, xvii, 121, 146
non-settler colonies, 41, 42, 87
non-white migrants, 47

overtaking point, 6, 97, 121

pioneer immigrants, 44, 151
political migrants, 25
politically motivated emigrants, 25, 43, 70, 91, 150, 151
positive selectivity, 43, 44, 45, 48
predominant Black society, 41
primary movers, 44, 48
provision ground economy, 38, 40
pull factors, 22
push factors, 22, 47

Queuing Theory, 48–49

racial demographic composition, 38–39, 40
racial status, 97
residual method, 48

secondary movers, 44, 48
selectivity theory, 48, 91, 146, 151
settler colonies, 41, 42, 87, 91, 151
settler societies, 87, 88
slavery, 38–40
Segmented Assimilation, xxiii, 92, 121
Sociological research, immigrant adaptation, 6

Thomas Sowell, 38–39
tied movers, 44

U.S. degrees, 72, 77
U.S. Immigration Law, 46
U.S. Immigration Policy, 19
U.S. style slavery, 41
Uncontrolled flow, immigration, xvii
Undocumented immigrants, 3

Waning immigrant quality, recent immigrants, xxiv, 46, 97, 122
Western civilization, xvii
Western civilization, decline, xvii
White favoritism hypothesis, 49, 151

NATIVE GROUPS

Asian Americans, 29, 128–129, 130–131, 137–138, 140, 141

Domestic interstate migrants, 123

Educational Attainment, 125, 127, 128, 129
Educational differences, 125, 126

Gender distinction, 129

Internal migration, 124, 129, 132, 140, 154
Internal movers, 8, 123, 124, 129

Native Americans, 126, 130, 132
Native Asians, 126, 128, 130, 154
Native Black American, xv
Native Black movers, 123, 126, 127, 129, 140, 141
Native Black nonmovers, 124, 129, 140, 141
Native-Born Blacks, 38, 45, 49, 51, 127, 132
Native groups, 133, 141, 154
Natives, 125
Native non-White Hispanics, 127, 129, 130

Native Whites, 124, 126–127, 130, 138–141, 144, 154
Native White Hispanics, 126, 127, 130, 141
Non-Hispanic Whites, 131, 132, 154

Sociodemographic changes, 147

U.S.-born groups, 153

White wage premium, 125

OTHER IMMIGRANT GROUPS

Asians, 116, 117, 118
Asian immigrants, 7, 34, 98, 99, 104, 121
Australia and New Zealand, 100–101, 104–105, 116–118

Black-White Disparities, 106, 113

Canada, 97, 98, 110, 111, 115, 116, 122
Canadian immigrants, 98, 99, 104, 117
Canadians, 116
Caribbean, 37–40, 111, 112, 117, 118
Caribbean immigrants, 38, 40, 41, 45, 98, 99, 105, 116, 118, 158
Caribbean immigration, patterns, and trends, 15–19
Central America, 111, 117, 118
Central American immigrants, 98–99

English-speaking Caribbean, 45, 124
Europe, 97, 98, 110, 111, 117, 122
European immigrants, 99, 104, 111
Europeans, 116, 117, 118

Major immigrant sending areas, 98–100
Mexican immigrants, 98, 99, 117
Mexico, 111, 112, 116, 117, 118

Pacific Islands, 111, 112, 117, 118
Pacific Islanders, 118
Pacific Islander immigrants, 98, 99

Racial differences, 105, 132

Racial Disparities, 112

South America, 111, 112, 117, 118
South American immigrants, 98, 99, 117

About the Author

Mamadi Corra is professor of sociology at East Carolina University (ECU), where he is Graduate Program Director (and Chair of the Graduate Studies Committee) for sociology and is also affiliate faculty with the ECU African and African American Studies Program, and Research Associate with the ECU Center for Natural Hazards Research. Professor Corra is also an Associate Editor of Immigration and Society, a specialty section of *Frontiers in Sociology*, and was co-guest editor of the recent (2021) special issue of the *Journal of Economics, Race, and Policy* (JERP), "The Status of Black Sociologists in the 21st Century." Dr. Corra was the 2018–19 American Association for the Advancement of Science Judicial Branch Science and Technology Policy (Science and Law) Fellow-in-Residence (9/1/2018–8/31/2019) at the Federal Judicial Center in Washington, DC. He holds a Ph.D. in Sociology from the University of South Carolina at Columbia and an M.B.A and a B.S. (with double majors in Business Administration and Sociology) from Gardner-Webb University.

Dr. Cora's current research focuses on three related areas of interest in racial and ethnic stratification and inequality: sociological social psychology (focusing on power and status structures and processes), immigration and the racial/ethnic context within which it occurs, and, more generally, race, ethnic, gender and class inequalities (broadly defined), and the intersections of these. His research has been funded by grants from the National Science Foundation, and his more than three dozen refereed articles and chapters have been published in scholarly journals including *Ethnic and Migration Studies*, the *Journal of International Migration and Integration, Sociological Theory, Sociological Perspectives, Sociological Inquiry*, the *Canadian Journal of Sociology, Race and Social Problems*, and the *Western Journal of Black Studies*.

As part of his Science and Technology Policy Fellowship with the Federal Judicial Center, Dr. Corra conducted a year-long study on accessibility of various entities of the federal judiciary, including the judiciary's electronic case filing and processing systems, homepages of federal judiciary websites, and published Judicial Conference and Administrative Office policies on disability and access. The resulting report is accessible at the website of the Federal Judicial Center at https://www.fjc.gov/content/343147/disability-and-federal-courts-study-web-accessibility; or directly at https://www.fjc.gov/sites/default/files/materials/24/Disability%20and%20the%20Federal%20Courts.pdf.

www.ingramcontent.com/pod-product-compliance
Lightning Source LLC
Chambersburg PA
CBHW020119010526
44115CB00008B/888